WRITING
IN A MODERN TEMPER

ESSAYS ON FRENCH LITERATURE AND THOUGHT
IN HONOR OF HENRI PEYRE

STANFORD FRENCH AND ITALIAN STUDIES

volume XXXIII

ANMA LIBRI

WRITING IN A MODERN TEMPER

ESSAYS ON FRENCH LITERATURE AND THOUGHT IN HONOR OF HENRI PEYRE

EDITED BY

MARY ANN CAWS

1984

ANMA LIBRI

Stanford French and Italian Studies is a collection of scholarly publications devoted to the study of French and Italian literature and language, culture and civilization. Occasionally it will allow itself excursions into related Romance areas.

Stanford French and Italian Studies will publish books, monographs, and collections of articles centering around a common theme, and is open also to scholars associated with academic institutions other than Stanford.

The collection is published for the Department of French and Italian, Stanford University by Anma Libri.

Foreword

Some of the authors of the pieces which follow are former students of Henri Peyre. Others are former colleagues. Several are both. All are his friends, admirers, and well-wishers. And therein lies the most important value they all hold in common, and perhaps the best chance for this volume to achieve genuine unity. The twenty authors are as different from each other in their intellectual outlooks, tastes, and biases, as they are by virtue of the generations to which they belong, the topics on which they chose to write, or the addresses at which they reside. What binds them together more than anything else is their affection for a man and their awareness of their debt to him. Whenever they see each other, at the MLA, the BN, or anywhere else, they talk about him. They swap anecdotes. One may hope that, some time, one of them will collect and publish these in the form of a *Peyreana*, which would outsell all the Festschriften published in his honor put together, not excepting the present one.

This is as it should be. It is fitting that at the center of their preoccupations should be the man in the center of whose own preoccupations each of them at some time was. For, if we were to look for "constants" in this universal and protean man, surely his ever-present and ever-effective willingness to help students, colleagues and friends would come to mind first. Seldom have so many owed so much to a single individual.

No keynote could therefore be more appropriate than the accent placed on diversity, as it appears in the table of contents of this volume;

for the freedom to be different is, in the intellectual world which we inhabit, perhaps the most basic, and therefore the most threatened. Among the innumerable achievements which instill a feeling of wonder in Henri Peyre's admirers, the one which on reflection I find perhaps the most astounding, is that, in spite of the exceptional force of his personality and of his convictions, he should have so steadfastly resisted the temptation of forming disciples according to a preconceived scheme; that he should have succeeded in being an authentic and exceptionally effective teacher, and yet have refrained from founding an *école*: in short, that he should offer a model which one can hope to emulate only by not imitating it.

Having begun his professional career as a classicist, he then became an *agrégé d'anglais*, proceeded to a doctorate in comparative literature, spent most his life teaching French, and consequently always refused to list any specialization under his name — just as he also never admits to cultivating any hobby, other than "reading." As those who know him fully realize, it would even be inaccurate to label Henri Peyre a literary scholar or a humanist, since some of his most enduring intellectual curiosities lead him in the direction of art, political science, and economics.

When faced with a universal mind such as his, and especiallv when — as was the case with Picasso — genius is compounded with longevity, one is tempted, in an effort to probe and embrace it, to resort to the notion of "periods." But, in Henri Peyre's case, it is not possible to distinguish and label these periods by reference to the subjects of his preoccupations, in the manner of the textbooks of yore in their chapters on Montaigne, Chateaubriand or George Sand, for in each period one observes an equally dazzling variety of topics and outlooks. Taking our lead from historians of art, some of us, aspiring Peyrologists, are tempted rather to label these periods according to the color of the ink he uses in writing the vast number of letters which we have all, at some time, been privileged to receive from him. To this day, for example, Henri Peyre's great "purple period" swells with nostalgia the breasts of many of his friends and correspondents. I recall that it was both preceded and followed by a "blue period." Nowadays we observe a "black period," which, we trust, will be of short duration. Few of us, however, except members of the more ancient generations, realize that, at some point in the past, there also was a brief "green period." I am proud to say that, as evidence of it, I keep among my memorabilia, a penny postcard, dating back to the year 1945, on which the color of the ink used by Henri Peyre harmonizes with the emerald one-cent stamp imprinted on the card. *O saisons, ô châteaux!*

Regardless of the premium on diversity, however, one must concede that the adjective "modern" in the title of this volume is not amiss. One of Henri Peyre's first books — his fifth, I believe — *Hommes et oeuvres du vingtième siècle* (1938), bears a title symptomatic of an interest for the contemporary scene which has never waned, in spite of the wide variety of historical eras touched upon in his writings and his teaching. The editor of this book was, therefore, wise to choose this adjective, as she was to avoid the nouns "modernism" or "modernity," which seem to imply some sharp break with the past, whereas Henri Peyre's own outlook on modern works is based on a belief in the continuity of culture, and on a knowledge and appreciation of the traditions which lie behind them. This obviously has something to do with the fact that another focus of his love and curiosity has long been the literatures of classical antiquity, in particular that of ancient Greece, a focus which was accordingly chosen for the special issue which *Yale French Studies* published in his honor in 1967.

Were we to look for yet another focus, I believe we would have — perhaps unexpectedly — to think of religion. As I write these words I realize of course that he may not believe his eyes when he reads them, and will accuse me of teasing him. I cannot deny that there would be some justification for this accusation, as I submit there would also be for the alleged teasing. Henri Peyre has enjoyed teasing so many of us, so much and for so long, albeit also so affectionately, that it may seem only fair that we should take after him, as we gather symbolically in the pages of this book to pay him homage. Nor is this my only excuse: a little friendly teasing may alleviate the gravity and solemnity which I find it so hard to avoid completely in this, the most *ingrat* of genres, the foreword, realizing all along how much Henri Peyre loathes pomposity.

And yet, teasing notwithstanding, is it not remarkable to observe that so strong, eloquent and militant an unbeliever as Henri Peyre should so consistently have been attracted by the works of writers like Claudel, Renan or Pascal? No other observation — facetious or serious — can perhaps give better evidence of a rare and precious virtue which Henri Peyre possesses to a supreme degree: true open-mindedness. By this I mean much more than mere toleration for opinions different from his own, but a sustained willingness to make the effort to appreciate the reasons lying behind these differences of opinion, a true and sympathetic curiosity for the minds of others — which, incidentally, goes a long way toward accounting for his outstanding ability to interpret works of literature of all kinds. Such a gift is especially rare when, far from implying indifference or timidity, it combines with strong convictions, and healthy likes and dislikes, when it is based therefore on a genuine and generous interest in those who happen not to share them. So many of us, present or not in the pages of this book, could say of Henri Peyre what Jacques Rivière once said of Ramon Fernandez: "Une dispute — outre l'amitié — nous rapproche."

As far as I am concerned, I am happy to report that differences of opinion — let alone *disputes* — have been almost nonexistent in the course of a friendship which began nearly forty years ago. There is, however, a small disagreement which I shall yield to the temptation of bringing up, since the opportunity of writing these few lines may well provide me with a unique chance of having, for once — at least on paper — the last word I have long been surprised (and chagrined) that a man so full of force and energy (whose very initials stand for horsepower), a man so rich in vitality, *bien vivant* as well as *bon vivant*, should so persistently have declined to share my taste for the works of the great comic geniuses of French literature, like Rabelais, Molière or Voltaire. Not to mention lesser ones, like Labiche, Feydeau or Courteline, who are among his *bêtes noires*.

But he has not said his last word, and fortunately there is always room for wishful thinking. Let us place our hopes, therefore, in the future. Let us daydream and anticipate perhaps a "red period" or a "gold period" in the life and works of Henri Peyre, one in which, for a while, he may turn from Euripides to Aristophanes, from Racine to Molière, from Mallarmé to Jarry, and from Claudel to Ionesco, not to mention other pleasant surprises which he no doubt has in store for us. And let us especially look forward, as we pause and express gratitude for the past, to the continuation of his beneficial presence among us, and for a friendship which has been one of the most enriching and enjoyable privileges of my life, a feeling which, I am confident, is shared by all those who wrote the pages which follow, as well as by many who will read them.

GEORGES MAY

Preface

From meditations on epistemology and narrational devices to a general
consideration of rhetoric, humanism, and literary criticism, and from
individual poets (Dante, Hugo, Nerval, Baudelaire, Mallarmé, Rimbaud, Valéry, Reverdy, and Esteban) to individual practitioners of
other genres (Balzac, Delacroix, Proust, Mauriac, Breton, de Chazal,
Dali, Sartre, and Beckett), these twenty essays are concerned with
a rereading of authors and topics we have come—perhaps wrongly—to
take for granted. This collective presentation is meant as a reopen-
ing of various lines of thought in a mode sometimes combative and
sometimes rather more quiet.

The contributing authors, of whose homage Georges May has
spoken, were not given any reductive form to adhere to, and no collective party-line: the essays are not intended as linear presentations
in any sense, but rather as a gathering of some kinds of current
criticism, literary and philosophical around a specific group of titles
taken from the works of Henri Peyre. The essays join the detailed
to the general, the analysis of text to the overarching motifs of poetics
and narration and humanism. They are neither deconstructionist nor
strictly defined by century, being modernist in outlook, if those two
terms are taken in their broadest sense; they concern themselves with
presentation and moment, with power of description and portraiture,
of self and other, with modes and lives as with rhetoric and thematics.

Our view is meant as outlooking and as self-questioning, and would
opt to be at once singular and collective, enthusiastic and analytic,
non-linear and non-party-linear, in short to be open-ended and open-
minded.

MARY ANN CAWS

Our warm thanks to the Peyre Institute and to all the loyal and enthusiastic supporters with whose help this volume appears.

Contributions to the work of the Peyre Institute, which presents varied programs and publications in the area of the humanities, are gratefully received. Tax deductible donations may be sent to:

Mary Ann Caws
John W. Kneller
Co-Directors, Peyre Institute
Graduate Center of the City University of New York
33 W. 42nd Street
New York, NY 10036

Contents

Rhetoric, Reference, and Mode
Literature and Sincerity • *Jean-Paul Sartre*

Narration and Knowing

HISTORICAL AND CRITICAL ESSAYS ·
PROUST AND PAUL VALÉRY

Epistemology and Literary Theory

ROBERT GREER COHN

1. Introduction

The epistemology called "polypolarity" (which has antecedents in Kierkegaard and particularly Mallarmé, as well as Joyce) can illuminate literary theory, starting with linguistics and moving successively through general narration, novel, sub-genres of the novel, point of view in the novel, and modes of presentation of consciousness in the novel. I offer a schematic demonstration in the pages to follow, beginning with an outline of polypolarity.

A traditional bi-polar paradox — e.g., of Zeno, or of a Sartrean proposition like "a man is both free and not free" — can, upon deeper examination, be seen as a tetrapolar one, i.e., the initial paradox can be stated to be both true and not true, thus setting up "paradox squared," "to the third power," etc., with possibilities of (fallible) resolution at all levels, starting with the zero-infinite core (resolved as a concrete point), passing through the triadic synthesis to "quintessential" synthesis and so on through "polypolar" play.

This synchronic view is complemented by a temporal one: at the tetrapolar level which we will emphasize here, if we see Becoming in the "Hegelian" terms of thesis-antithesis-synthesis, there is a fourth term which radically negates traditional synthesis. I call this "anti-synthesis."[1]

[1] For a fuller development, see my *Modes of Art* (Saratoga, Calif.: Anma Libri, 1975). Note that the temporal aspect generates, in Mallarmé, the "seasonal equation" which is (an aspect of) the armature of the *Coup de dés*.

3

In this wide-open play, as in relativity theory, there are givens or absolutes, limitations[2] which make direction or meaning (*sens*) possible and are the source of the varying aforementioned resolutions. The irreversibility of time is basic in this *operational* sense. But as in Nietzsche's Eternal Return and current scientific theory (temporal regression of electron movement, for example, according to Feynman), there is a ghostly suggestion at least of "anti-synthetic" reversal even here.[3] Generally, however, in what follows, the irreversibility of time — engendering duality, distinction — is maintained as an archetypal "prevailing pattern": thus the important distinction between vertical (holistic, "metaphoric") and horizontal (fragmentary, "metonymic") is generated. But, again, the possibility of radical reversal or paradoxical interchange ("vibrancy") of these epistemological dimensions is of major importance to our thought-drama.[4]

From this summary base we move on to the core problems of linguistics.

2. A Sketch of Polypolar Linguistics

Philosophical linguistics is commonly assumed to be the origin — with Ferdinand de Saussure, in the early years of our century — of modern

---

[2] The total limitation on human manipulation (thought, etc.) I call "the kinetic excess" — surpassing life — noting its affinity with "faith" (and "impulse"); cf. Freud's *Unheimliche*.

[3] In terms of plot, a good example of anti-synthesis is the death of a child (who represents a synthesis of mother and father principles, etc.) as in the *Coup de dés* or *Doctor Faustus* or *The Plague*. Or Malvolio (Frye's "churl") in *Twelfth Night*, who is the reverse of the marrying priest (synthesis of male and female) — this is, of course, a comic example; Shylock is a more serious one. Shakespeare's awareness of the "whirligig of time" (or fortune wheel), the *circular* scheme of things — involving the ambiguities of multiple polarities — is expressed at the end of the play where we feel that Malvolio will have his *turn* in the sun ("I'll get even with the pack of you"). There is a further strong hint of these reversibilities and balancings in a sort of final reconciliation between Malvolio and the community. He is like the winter with potential of spring, in the procession of seasons à la Mallarmé. In the case of Shylock, this process is far subtler, hidden in passages of deep forgiveness.

[4] A prime example is when synthesis becomes a new thesis, in Hegel; this is clearly a dimensional switch, leap, "double-take," based on the underlying paradoxical sameness of the dimensions, before time as it were. Cf. the rift and exchange between cardinal and ordinal, between metaphor and metonymy in Lacan and Rosolato, between world and earth in Heidegger's *Origins of Art*, etc.

structuralist thought. But the true fountainhead of modern thought is epistemological — critically philosophical — rather than linguistic, though the two domains are obviously close. Mallarmé in his *Notes* was working toward a sophisticated general linguistic theory, but it is clearly grounded in an epistemology: "la fiction lui semble être le procédé même de l'esprit." "Vision" is a more incarnate and artistic version of epistemology (or pure theory), but the two are practically interchangeable, especially if we say "epistemological vision" or "theoretical vision." The two are dialectically related, and we could generate a whole series of such nuances, spirally all related to one another through polypolarity (including terms such as "syntax," midway between epistemology and grammar), but we will not go through that elaborate whirl here; instead, we will move on to a brief exploration of contemporary linguistics.

In linguistics as in other fields, modern thinkers have dared to go down into the "structures" of the very elusive field of humanistic thought, so elusive that only the deeply sacrificial, intuitive, relativist and probabilistic pattern which runs from Hegel through phenomenology to Derrida and involves the absurd, antinomies or paradoxes, can have a chance, just as is the case with the relativistic and contradictory sophistications of modern physics. In this sense the lineage runs from Hegel and Kierkegaard through Mallarmé and Nietzsche to Derrida rather than through Saussure who was insufficiently grounded philosophically and has had to be radically revised by Jakobson *et al.* Accordingly, Roland Barthes, who was the leading semiotician of our time, looked back to Mallarmé directly: "All we do is repeat Mallarmé" (*Interview with Stephen Heath*); the semiotician he most admired, Julia Kristeva, likewise bases herself largely on the symbolist poet-thinker.

In applying Mallarméan epistemology to linguistics, we note that a noun-verb relationship would be seen as a vertical-horizontal dialectic: a noun is relatively holistic, "metaphoric" (Jakobson), vertical, circular, both above — like the original Word, static, total, and overriding — and below — primitively rooted, solid, heavy with being, *en-soi*, and so on. The verb, usually expressing an action in time, is relatively "metonymic," linear, median. *But*, the two dimensions are also continuous and reversible, as in the verbal noun ("a going") or noun used as verb ("to clown it," etc.); there is a continuity of *flow* (flowing from *wholeness*) in the horizontal, it has its infinite. Verb both precedes, philosophically, and follows the noun, as in the infinite regress of the male-female dialectic and cognate philosophical patterns, e.g., the form-matter ("substance") whirl in Aristotle's *Metaphysics*, properly understood.

Language and linguistics evolve as follows:

1. A hypothetical prehuman "sleepy" condition is crossed by a creative awakening, a radical revolt of reflexive consciousness, as *language* (a vertical crosses a horizontal in our epistemological terms). Language ("half-art, half-instinct," Darwin) is "always already" dialectically both above and below the preceding horizontal norm: above, as a new level of abstraction and below, as an innate capacity being newly tapped (cf. Chomsky). Altogether, at this stage, language is a rich "new twist" or (spiral, same-different) *Aufhebung* of (human) being.[5]

2. The creative vertical becomes in time a horizontal again, in a new frame of reference: people babble away relaxedly (*parole*). This can become the "wilful individual act" implied in the *parole* of Saussure in creative or alert moments of speech (vertical). *Parole* thus can be either or both of these dimensions.

When *parole* is individual, the conventional aspect of language is called *langue* (horizontal, social, rational).

3. A linguist, Saussure, creating a synchronic language system, performs an act of reflexive revolt (vertical) on *parole*, now seen as

---

[5] Articulation, like simple stitching, is a series of "baptismal" loops (skinny spirals of plunging for rebirth and moving on), in which the consonants mark the arrest-plunge and the vowels the rise-moving on, relatively. But there is an overlap and, eventually, unity between vowels and consonants, which are obviously polar, dialectically related. Thus a consonant alone contains some rudimentary vowel impulse, and a vowel some consonantal element.

Take the simple speech act of the indefinite article "a" in English: one makes a glottal stop before the release of the vowel sound; the usual sound "uh" in "a man" is thus neutral, a sort of androgyne of language, neither vowel nor consonant, or hardly so.

It is interesting to note that in German *ein* tends, certainly in dialect, to this "androgyne" (which is neutral also in position on the scale between high and low pitch) and even French *un*, rapidly pronounced as in *un chien*, *un verre*, or southern Italian *uh pizza*. In modern French the "in" sound of *un* is also close to our "a" in lazy simplicity, which is like the bare bones of articulation itself, a sort of grunt of mere oral presence, renewed (looping) and going on.

a passive field of reality including the inherited system of *langue*. Insofar as it is rational science—including the dualism of synchronic and diachronic—as opposed to the more fully creative act of art, Saussure's system is also, ambiguously, horizontal, a (conscious, spirally *aufgehoben*) version of *langue*. But the main direction of Saussure's impulse and influence here is in *depth*: his emphasis on language as escaping the individual and even the social will while also involving "wilful" acts moves thus in a dialectical, ambiguous or vibrant, up and down direction characteristic of the *human* sciences, as Foucault shows in *The Order of Things* and Saussure before him in his *Course on Language*. "To say that language is a product of social forces does not suffice to show clearly that it is unfree... [We note] the existence in the total phenomenon of a bond between the two antithetical forces—arbitrary convention by virtue of which choice is free and time which causes choice to be fixed" (*Course*, p. 74).

Or again: "We can speak of both the immutability and the mutability of the sign" (p. 74).

Or: "language... is free and can be organized at will. Its social nature considered independently does not definitely rule out this viewpoint" (p. 78).

Derrida correctly observes in his *Grammatologie* that there are limits to Saussure's dialectical openness, in his bias for speech and "presence." For example, in the above quotation about the two forces, a suppler approach would show that both of these contain their opposite as well (in polypolar becoming).

Saussure's latterly-discovered work on anagrams (edited by Starobinski) moves in this ambiguous, poetic, metaphoric direction of modern linguistics. Jakobson will follow suit with his new emphasis on the metaphoric axis.

Note: Freud's dialectical relation of language and the unconscious; Lacan's emphasis, likewise, on the vertical crossing of the S/s bar ("De l'instance de la lettre"). Mallarmé preceded them with his "savants abîmes" (of the deep psyche) in *Hérodiade*.

4. In a higher synthetic moment, the two axes are seen as interrelated in a global reality by Jakobson. Likewise, the synchronic and diachronic antinomy is overcome in a new (provisional) synthesis.

In sum, language is both above, as creatively free new forms of expression (in Saussure's *parole* or Jakobson's modified poetics-linguistics) and below (as Chomsky's innate patterns, givens) the norm at any given moment of history, the world of relatively passive *ad hoc* communication, clichés, etc. In this view, Chomsky is too one-sided and unhumanistic.[6]

This above-below vibrancy crossing a past-future dimension of time (or the social norm) — which can be seen as paradoxically vibrant too in terms of spiral returns, etc. — constitutes one stage of the polypolar becoming of language, in a concatenation of frames of reference which cover the well-known aspects of linguistics.

The whole psychic-physiological realm of phonemes can be seen in this light. For example, the vibrant polarity of sound (or letter) vs. silence (or space) is crossed by the cognate consonant-vowel polarity giving a basic tetrapolarity at this level; dimensions such as front-back, high-low, acoustically, can be added in a "polypolar" cross.[7]

At the level of the word, in *Modes of Art* (1975) we saw it basically at a crossroads: vertically, the Greater and the Less of meaning in discourse is one polarity, and on this dimension the word is a Mean

---

[6] George Steiner's well-known critique of Chomsky is based on the pluralist position of Joseph Greenberg, seeking language universals inductively and hence with more variation or freedom along a pragmatic axis. But that is not the deeply rooted understanding that comes with Mallarméan philosophy (epistemology). And we note that Greenberg's vast project ends with an admission that the true basic universals of language have not been plumbed as yet and will not be for years. Other critiques suggest that the core of language is semantic, i.e., total meaning precedes linguistic forms in evolution. But precisely a chicken-and-egg whirl à la Derrida (trace vs. presence) is what semantics is immediately involved in, in other words the deep dialectic.

[7] Thus Being is to Nothing as (irreversible, fallen and linear) time-as-Becoming is to pure space-time (or pure space alone as we commonly conceive it: emptiness) and a trace is to sheer presence, speech to silence, writing to speech, etc. All of these entities are complexly related, reversible, as our series itself at points illustrates: from Nothing comes the purity that gives presence its concreteness (thing in itself) even as it is Nothing that dialectically makes abstract form possible; hence the very trace that violates its purity is its (Nothing's) paradoxical heir. Vowels and consonants are related too in this vibrant way to each other and all the other terms: vowels are closer to speech, consonants to the negating differentiae of trace or writing. Again, the abstraction of trace gives it one form of priority (purity) but its linearity makes it less pure than presence (speech, vowels), less "prior" theoretically. Accordingly, our best view is a polypolar diagram, noting both the restless play and the "prevailing patterns" of traditional practice and codification in grammars, the latter through the subtle bias of the diagram where certain favored entities are (provisionally) put up high (diagram E).

of meaning and has the quality of human presence, a fallible resolving synthesis, a compromise in the *aspiration* to grasp meaning, the glimpsed totality which could alone give real meaning. This fallen but nostalgic-for-the-whole status reflects microcosmically the original Word of the Bible which was "with God and... was God"; the closest to it is the fully symbolic word, as in Symbolist poetry. The vibrancy of epistemology itself (fiction) is in any word, but acceptedly so in metaphor or symbol. But any word, including the poetic symbol, is also, horizontally, on a dimension of the operational, the syntagmatic, the linear-sequential, the metonymic, the real in irreversible time. So it is at a crossroads of the metaphoric and the metonymic, as Jakobson, Guy Michaud, and others see it. The horizontal is also the dimension of the text as a line, going somewhere (as in narration). The epistemological reversibility of the two axes — as in Jakobson's definition of poetry as the invasion of the holistic vertical (the metaphoric and paradigmatic) into the horizontal (the syntagmatic and metonymic) — is always a possibility. The horizontal as textual timeline has (ultimately reversible) poles of past and future, and in this perspective the word is the now-focus (present). It has enough flexibility in number (as well as phonemic or alphabet variety) of sounds and shapes of letters to be adaptable to a humanly manageable (including temporally, i.e., within the human time-span, of breathing, rhythms of living such as attention-span, life-span itself) vast range of phenomena, extending far into the past and future of the text, yet enough limitation, e.g., in length, to be suitable for a simultaneous "now" experience of identity.

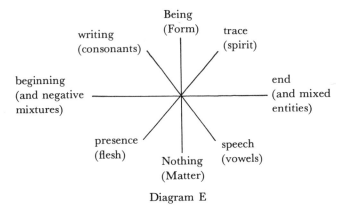

Diagram E

At this level, of the word, the nominal and verbal are cognates of the other vertical and horizontal phenomena, metaphoric-symbolic vs. metonymic-referential or realistic, etc. Again there is "vibrancy," reversibility: verbal nouns, nominal verbs.

In relation to the referent: the merest phoneme as in our silence-sound (or space-letter) polarity is in the same paradoxical situation as the symbolic word (or Word): *is and is not* the object or referent (note: our levels spiral too). This vibrancy, with Saussure, gave S/s in the sign. In *Modes of Art* I observed that this duplicity should be duplicated in the referent, to give a tetrapolarity. At the time I did not know, until belatedly, that Hjelmslev had proposed the same view.

This can be spelled out as follows:

Long before Saussure, Mallarmé spoke lucidly of the duplicity of the sign, for example in his famous: "Je dis: une fleur! et... musicalement se lève, idée même et sauve, l'absente de tous bouquets" ("Crise de vers"). The signifier (*fleur*), signified (*idée d'une fleur*), and referent (*fleur dans un bouquet*) are all already there.[8] Moreover, the *musicalement* and *suave* indicate that the flower thus evoked is the essential or *real* flower—the flowery flower, as it were—of art and experience.[9] In short, the two phases of the sign—arbitrary word and common or essential idea—have been joined by two phases of the referent: relatively random object and "real" object of art and life. Malraux later outlined this position in *La Condition humaine* when the painter Kama noted that the flower is a sign of the real flower in the same way a word is a sign of a flower. He also went over this ground in a television interview on Japanese art. (Ponge sees the same 4-polar situation in *La Fabrique du pré*.)

Our next level is the pronoun: it becomes through its various persons in the polypolar pattern of any word. At the hypothetical core

[8] The referent is reinforced, in the text, by "le souvenir de l'objet nommé." This brings out, as Wordsworth's daffodils do, that art gets at the real real of an object dialectically, through distance as in *souvenir* or *suggestion*.

[9] Not a Platonic idea: Sartre has rightly said, in his article on Mallarmé published by *Obliques* (nos. 18-19, pp. 169-94) that "only knaves or dupes" accuse Mallarmé of that; he sees him as "existential." I prefer "rounded"; he is a poet of full life. Accordingly, this *fleur* is artistically real, up and down, like the music which Mallarmé invokes, supremely sensual (consonant with *suave*) as well as transcendent, a *rooted* reality, closer to Aristotelian and Sartrean essence.

is the I (already not-I in a vibrant sense: me, thou, he, it, etc.). In terms of the phases of time (ek-stases) which evolve in a parallel pattern, this core corresponds to an eternal present, now.

Operationally, this splits into: vertically, a subjective I above paired with below, an objective me (as thou, i.e., reflexivity) and thou. On this holistic dimension the subject and object are co-subjects and there is (almost) full reciprocity as in love; the relation is a circular one, a field of force.

Horizontally, there is the I-he (or you as fully objective object) relation, metonymic, divisive; also he-you, he-her, etc.

As we implied already in our core image, the two dimensions are dialectically related (vibrant) and reversible ultimately. A loved self or "other self" becomes distant, a cold "you" or even "it" in the same text, e.g., of Racine.

In a spiral becoming, these persons can proliferate complexly through the four mentioned poles and further dimensions created by reflexivity of reflexivity (see section 4).

Likewise, the eternal present, which is the basic time of all narration and life, evolves through the split into past and future (horizontally; corresponding to the third person) and relates intimately to the spatial (vertical) polarity of high and low as it seems to speed up excitedly or stagnate.

In "Linguistics and Poetics," Jakobson's scheme of six poles of communication, corresponding to six functions, is demonstrably inadequate. A fuller view emphasizes not poles but relations, as in diagram A:

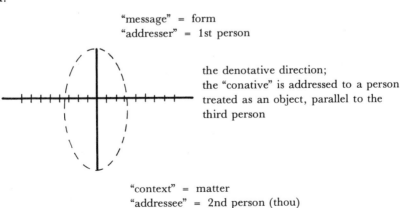

"message" = form
"addresser" = 1st person

the denotative direction;
the "conative" is addressed to a person
treated as an object, parallel to the
third person

"context" = matter
"addressee" = 2nd person (thou)

Diagram A

In this fuller view, the poetic function occurs in the fluid ambiguous, up and down holistic vertical *relation,*[10] not the pole ("message"). The denotative or "referential" is another kind of *relation* between form and matter: prosaic, fragmented, discursive, metonymic. The I-thou relation between persons is, on the other hand, parallel to the poetic dimension: it is integral (co-subjective) as in "I love you"; it is a circular field of force as opposed to the linear and divisive "conative": "You do this" (a command, imperative). The mind-body relation is co-subjective in the sense of Freud, Lacan ("instinct," "ça parle").

Jakobson's remaining two poles are "contact" and "code"; they too are relational: micro to macro. "Contact" is at or near the neutral zero point of origin, in our view, a mere germ or hint of life-presence as in "hello." "Code" is the synthetic (macrocosmic) entity of the whole language system.

One is aware of the "code" only through a dialectical relation to the (near) zero-point of the microcosmic "contact," i.e., when, as in procreation, one negates the whole system to renew it. This totally critical or reflexive relation may be scientific (linguistic) or artistic as in the revolutionary use of the whole language by Joyce.

Thus, we add to our diagram A the entities in diagram B.

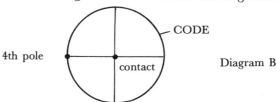

4th pole   CODE

contact   Diagram B

Note: The fourth pole on our diagram is merely negative, negation of communication (this can be termed "anti-synthesis," since it is symmetrically opposite the position of synthesis, the third term, or third pole, or third person position). It is operative only in extreme returns to silence, experienced as a suggestion of temporal reversion to an earlier state, as in "I take back all I said." Cf. the "eternal return" of Nietzsche, cyclic reversal of time.

All the other phenomena Jakobson discusses in "Linguistics and Poetics" are better seen as polypolar. The relation of speech rhythm to superimposed meter is clearly axial, two-dimensional. Syncopated rhythms add dimensions: he shows them in parallel lines, but the true

---

[10] And, more freely, in the relation of relations between the vertical and the horizontal (e.g., poems mean as well as are).

relation is, as in Lacan's amendments of Saussure (in "De l'instance de la lettre"), between a polarity of upper and lower rhythmic lines vertically and a time-past time-future polarity horizontally. Rhyme adds a dimension to this play as do all the other devices of raising ordinary speech through structure toward the "original" unity of all.[11]

3. Narration and Plot

Narrative plot, to put it mildly, has been much discussed in our time. Propp, Polti, Souriau, Shklovsky, Todorov, Frye, Gerald Prince are some of the better-known participants.[12] Although Propp settled for many variants of plot, the general aim is to cut down on the number and find, if possible, one generative pattern, often based on a linguistic (grammatical) model. That is too abstract, as we show in *Modes of Art*: "value... is the total ordering principle in the last analysis" (p. 121). I was speaking there of Frye's genre modes, but plot (which pertains particularly to certain genres) is equally under that law, despite frequent attempts like Frye's to dispense with value in the name of free openness, sophistication, scientific objectivity — which has limits, we now know, even in the realm of science. Mallarmé, as sophisticated as anyone, said, "You can't do without Eden." I tend to use the word "tone" for ultimate meaning in that sense without which there is no art or anything else worth staying around for.

Propp's thirty-one plots have been often commented upon and challenged; latterly, Todorov has reduced these to an equilibrium-disequilibrium-equilibrium scheme, echoed by Prince's "stative-active-stative." This "dumbbell" shape is what I call a "prevailing pattern" of universal epistemology;[13] it is at best an approximation to the truth, which is rather more complex.

As we demonstrated in *Modes of Art*, totality breaks down operationally into vertical and horizontal dimensions of reality such as fallen space and fallen (chronological) time, nouns and verbs, poetry (holistic) and prose (fragmented), etc. By abstracting prose away from its poetic

---

[11] These devices are studied in my *L'Oeuvre de Mallarmé* (Paris: Librairie Les Lettres, 1951), ch. 6.

[12] Jonathan Culler in his *Structural Poetics* gives useful outlines of the different approaches. An article by Janet Levarie Smarr in *Poetics*, no. 8 (1979): "Some Considerations on the Nature of Plot" shows flaws in their arguments, very plausibly. I am indebted to her in several ways

[13] See *Modes of Art*, p. 34 and *L'Oeuvre de Mallarmé, passim.*

"half," narration in chronological time arises as a mutilated perspective based on some very human operational "bad faith." Instead of one global reality, which we can visualize microcosmically as a single round point, we have *two* constructed points, a (fake) beginning and end. Thus Mallarmé commented: "Un livre ne commence ni ne finit; tout au plus fait-il semblant" (*Le Livre*, p. 181). These points always echo *the* archetype of a split unity in Western tradition: divine totality (Eden) lost and regained. There are equivalents in all other cultures, as far as I know.

The story or narration—plot is just the essential skeleton of this, involving a further reduction to the horizontal, irreversible, linear principle of fallen time—is between these two terminal entities which are, to repeat, fallen versions of globality. Hence there is an attempt in truly ambitious works to *boucler la boucle* and have the end rejoin the beginning (Dante, Mallarmé, Joyce, Proust). The fact that Eden is not quite paradise in Christian tradition reflects this problematic. Even when Eden is "fully redemptive" as it is in modern theology (Barth, Tillich), there is the epistemological problem. But in this realm which is religious, visionary, and *poetic* in a broad sense, narration disappears: it is swallowed up in the terminal globes (and even more the looping total unity) or in their degraded forms (short of paradise but mirroring it distinctly) of deep satisfaction and value, approximations to stasis, quality, "class," "tone."

As soon as the (roughly speaking) Adamic hero of any plot falls (vertically) from grace he is on his way (horizontally) out of Eden; fallen space and fallen time arise simultaneously, as do nouns and verbs, etc. (*Modes of Art*, p. 38). In this realm of becoming, all one has is a glimmering glimpse of the lost and future totality: underneath all our hopes and expectations, palimpsestically, there is the ghost of that final *Coup*, as in Kierkegaard's "repetition." Desire, in the fragmentary sense of Freud and Lacan, is this groping dialectical becoming: separation from an object vertically implies simultaneously separation from it in time; the object lies always somewhere ahead (cf. Derrida's tetrapolar *différance*). These two main axes of linearity or polarization (separation, alienation) in desire—the spatial and the temporal axes—are joined by all sorts of other (fallen) polarities which we can arrange in a polypolar cluster around the idea of fallen Eros, or desire[14] (i.e., desires, plural). (See diagrams C and D.)

---

[14] Note that desire can be mental or physical; the polarity here too arises from the operational fall, and there is an underlying yearning for reconciliation of mind and

Diagram C. *The Main Operational Axes.*

Vertical:
(STATIC SPACE: nouns, values or states, qualities, certain adjectives)

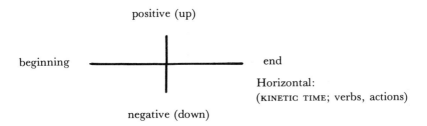

positive (up)

beginning   end

Horizontal:
(KINETIC TIME; verbs, actions)

negative (down)

Diagram D. *Some Other Important Polarities*

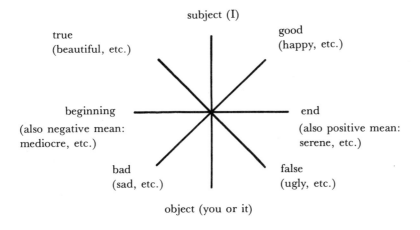

subject (I)

true
(beautiful, etc.)

good
(happy, etc.)

beginning

(also negative mean:
mediocre, etc.)

end

(also positive mean:
serene, etc.)

bad
(sad, etc.)

false
(ugly, etc.)

object (you or it)

body, supplied by superior artistic moments, "beacon" instants which may be found even along the way of narration, as in Proust. Note also that our polypolar cluster is altogether fallen in this way to some extent (and not just in the end-beginning duality), but that, again, in good plots as in fine art generally, the aspiration to globality or roundedness is patent in ambiguous relations between the polar terms.

The truer distinction is mind-body vs. mind *and* body.

True to the underlying paradoxical reversibilities of the non-fallen pure polypolarity (*Modes of Art*, pp. 24-27; 45), all of these poles except beginning and end—the *sine qua non* of linearity, direction, narration, echoing the irreversibility of fallen time—can, in a sort of distant yearning for the lost globality, restlessly jump around and change places in a familiar dance of phenomena (this includes movement to the *mean* position on our chart). These permutations give the various plots. And, as we said, their significance comes from the Adamic return to the zone where horizontal "takes off" and at least promises to rejoin the alienated poetic vertical in a refound globality, i.e., on the *threshold*, vibrantly or asymptotically, to Eden (in the "fully redemptive" sense) or whatever approximation to it—such as rounded maturity (in the *Bildungsroman*)[15]—in modern "secular" terms (which word "secular," as Mallarmé said, made no real sense).[16]

Examples: a sad beginning can lead to a happy end. An ugly frog can turn out to be a handsome prince. And the reverse, as in the tale of Mélusine. A boy can get (or not get) a girl ("you") or a kingdom ("it")—these may overlap, woman (Shekhina) and place. If he does get either, or both, it may be defeating in effect. Etc., etc. There is also a relic of totality at the microcosmic core of desire, the zero crossroads echoing the macrocosmic infinite, where ambivalence or neutrality can occur, e.g., "the lady or the tiger?" Usually they arise in true poems or poetic works clearly aiming *beyond* narration, as in the quotation by Mallarmé.

In those cases, cited for example by Shklovsky (as Smarr notes) where plot is made meaningful by a reference to nature in the background, the seasonal round, the cosmic scheme, narration is obviously "taking off" and "rounding out" poetically in this sense. In some sense it always more or less does, in its limited way.

---

[15] In the idea of rounded maturity there is dialectically involved the horizontal dimension (Adamic way of Time as linearity), and many narrations see the reconciliation of the vertical and the horizontal in this wise as It, the quasi-Edenic goal (Goethe's *Wilhelm Meister* illustrates this well). But a deep novelist like Alain-Fournier will both allude to this—François Seurel who is closest to him does reach a sort of maturity embracing both dimensions, at the end—and break it open through an anti-synthetic event, in this case the return of Meaulnes who takes the child away from him and spirally rebegins the dialectical *movement* of life, in essence (cf. our term "kinetic excess" in *Modes of Art*, implying that movement, life as on-going, prevails in *this* life and is the basis of *faith*).

[16] The globality of paradise as garden has concrete forms, for example, a divine womb, woman (mother) and thus vibrates between person and place (as well as the

Although plots are extremely various, generally they "go somewhere" both in the sense of irreversible time, horizontally, and in the complementary vertical dimension of approach to total meaning, salvation. Even when they end on a depressing note as in tragedy, the feeling is of a victory for truth (one of our charted poles), or art itself, "the play's the thing." As Gilbert Murray observed of the Greeks (see *Modes of Art*, p. 177), tragedies end often in a comforting theophany and at one time seem to have ended even in joy in that sense of truth, a divine order.

Sartre's "freedom" (in *Qu'est-ce que la littérature?*) is a modern move in this direction of "totalization" (his favorite word latterly). At the very least, meaning implies some fragmentary approach to this, such as the enhancement of experience, in moral or cautionary tales, even naughty or picaresque ones. But always behind a *satisfying* plot, partly at the moment of dénouement but more at that instant described by Frye in which a work appears to us in its simultaneity, the approach to totality, however humbly tentative, is evidenced by the overall gracious phenomenon of fulfilling, meaningful tone.

Narration is linked with our imperfect striving condition and is hence a part of all literature (or art) just as fragmenting reason, metonymy, the classic and normative dimension are. But to focus on it so obsessively and exclusively as many critics have done in our time is egregiously to err: to the extent that art is superior, it always aspires to the fuller condition which includes a powerful visionary and poetic

---

sexes) as in all those myriad images where woman emerges organically from a site (the woman-city of medieval literature treated by William Calin, Pissarro's peasant girls, Proust's dreamed-of girls in Roussainville or in his readings, Joyce's Dublin as mother...). Behind paradise or divine woman or man is Eros itself as site and psyche (God as world and/or person). The basic movement of narrative thus is from divine love lost through struggle to divine love (or Being, or "primary narcissism," cf. Freud's *On Narcissism: An Introduction*). A typical pattern, then, is: girl (mom) — lose girl and search for her — get her back, as mate, substitute. *Daphnis and Chloë* is an approximation to this, an archetypical plot.

In real life, this drama is finished *une bonne fois* with the consummation of first marriage; the child is the confirmation of the ideal union. All our childhood and adolescence through, men are secretly oriented by this goal of yearning. After? A kind of half-life with a vague sense of a pale repetition possible, in many cases. Some go through the cycle again more or less, remarry, etc. Some chase a Muse. Some die, or should... Sometimes the child dies in a drastic antisynthetic moment. All these are plotworthy. And merit sympathy.

axis: this, however obscurely put, is what Walter Pater meant by his "aspires to the condition of music." So that almost all the recent talk about narration is not only inadequate philosophically (or critically in that "meta" sense) but it is also reductive, flatly rationalistic, forcing lively organic entities into petty manipulative molds.

4. The Novel as a Genre

Theoretically, narration stems from the epistemological horizontal or Becoming, and thus has particular affinities with the *factual*, as we saw in our previous section, and poetry stems from the vertical or holistic epistemological dimension, which can also be called that of "fiction" (Mallarmé tended to use "fiction" in this way; Northrop Frye uses the term "hypothetical"). So it is slightly confusing — it illustrates the law of epistemological leaps or reversals of the dimensions in dialectical axial Becoming — when the narrative, whether novel, short story, or prose play, gets to be called "fiction" but so it is. Anyway, at times very clearly, the two dimensions are mixed together, and it is only our sense of order that is slighted: certainly to call a poetic novel "fiction" seems appropriate, and there is really always *some* poetry (or aspiration) in any novel or story. Conversely, there was always some narrative in almost any poetry, and one can call all literature "narrational" if one likes. But here we are emphasizing the generic *prosaic* aspect of narration.

Because of its generality, in our evolutionary series we put (in a previous section) narrative first: it includes various of the genres which will arise from this archetypal source — novel, short story, plays, even poetry or aspects of it. Then we look at the *novel*, arbitrarily singling it out and ignoring all sorts of other genres, for simplification; and we move on from there to sub-genres of the novel and their modes of presenting consciousness, along one line of becoming. This strand is supposed to illustrate the other strands which develop in parallel ways.

In discussing the novel as a genre and its main characteristics, the concatenation of "frames of reference" of axial distinctions ("polypolar" diagrams) is approximately as follows (noting that in each case the first term is vertical epistemologically, the second sloping, the third horizontal):

A. *Genres*
 1. Poetry: whole vision, metaphoric dimension, 1st person
 2. Theater: in-between, "sloping" entity, mixed 1st and 3rd persons (the 2nd person is co-subject, either the public or a beloved partner, self as "thou," body, etc.)
 3. Novel: narration and objective fragmentation (ta-ta-ta), metonymy, 3rd person(s)

An extended discussion of genre will be found in *Modes of Art*, chapter 6.

B. *Sub-genres of the Novel*
 1. "Lyric" novel (*récit*; Constant, Woolf, Giraudoux)
 2. Mixed (Tolstoy, Proust)
 3. Realistic, reportorial, etc. (Fielding, Michener)

C. *Point of View in the Novel* (varying between and within novels):
 1. Authorial ("I," omniscient, "telling")
 2. Mixed (an authorial protagonist among other characters)
 3. Figural (objectively described characters, "showing")

Like the other categories, *point of view* is parallel to our definition of the real (*Modes of Art*, ch. 9) and of the present. At the zero-infinite microcosmic core of a polypolarity is the eternal I, real, present. It moves to the peak of the subjective vertical and to its base (the I-thou relation on this circular dimension—cf. mind-body dialectic as in Freud, Lacan—is easily reversible, as in a communion of love). On the epistemological horizontal dimension, it becomes our objective past or future selves, he (or it) as we look at them, or an Other who comes to much the same thing authorially: a projected version of the I, a puppet self. That is, in good writing—Camus makes this point in *The Rebel*—the characters are all in some deep sense the author, I, as well as objectively observed: axially vibrant in this sense. In other words, the two dimensions are ultimately interchangeable. But operationally, on the way to that ultimate, there is a spiral Becoming, a proliferation of narrative viewpoints—parallel to our "retotalizations" of the real—generated by first person becoming third, i.e., every time the narrator I looks back at himself or looks back at the looker ("je me voyais me voir," Valéry). Thus Marcel Muller has found eleven versions of narrative selves of Proust in *A la recherche*. Sollers, Robbe-Grillet, and Barthes emphasize this fugitive mobility of the self (but Bellow, after Woolf, reminds us in his Nobel talk that there is the "true and simple" aspect of character, corresponding to Proust's *vraie vie*, and our concept of "tone": something persists). Butor's "you" (*La Modification*) is an attempt to mediate the two axes. "Yuh" could be another such attempt, or "One."

D. *Depiction of Consciousness*
    1. Subjective: "interior monologue," "stream of consciousness"
    2. Mixed entity, "style indirect libre"
    3. Objective narration of thoughts-feelings

Since all consciousness is axially vibrant ("I-he"), the second stage seems more adequate to the true paradoxical condition of *fiction*, but really the first and third stages are vibrant too. Thus Dorrit Cohn (in *Transparent Minds*, Princeton, 1978) reminds us that interior monologue is *quoted*. And the objective narration ("psycho-narration" in her terms) is of a subjectivity. The axes too are vibrant and reversible: the narrational axis which usually flattens a character into a type can dialectically rise above, or cut below, the interior subjective approach, as the author interjects stuff from the subconscious that an articulated monologue cannot well present. Professor Cohn is highly convincing on this as much else. I merely add that an axial—dimensional—approach to all this (with our leaps of interchange between the axes) can help to keep one's bearings in these subtle realms.

Dorrit Cohn, a fine theorist, needs correcting in one important respect, when she sees the unconscious as "radically devoid of language." This is to slight the persuasive views of Freud and Lacan ("*ça parle*"). Hence it is also wrong to see psycho-narration as the "unique" path to a character's deepest soul; poetically flexible processes such as those of Mallarmé and Joyce (*Finnegans Wake*) can do very well in this regard.

A Postscript on Semiotics

The principle of paradox as a base of all our knowing goes back far, to Zeno and Heraclitus at least, but it really gets going with the nineteenth-century absurdists. As Sartre points out in his preface to the *Poésies*, Mallarmé is the pivotal pioneer of our period in this respect, with his "fiction... le procédé même de l'esprit humain" (in his epistemological-linguistic *Notes*). But we ought to mention Hegel's deep dialectic, Kierkegaard's even deeper critique of it, Nietzsche's radical ironies and eternal return, the interplay of Dionysian and Apollonian, etc. Even Darwin gets into the act with his language as "half-art, half-instinct," and one reflects that the human sciences generally, since they represent knowing about (knowing) humans are a particular locus of the paradox-dialectic.[17]

---

[17] All reality is in the same boat in terms of original polypolar complexity, epistemologically, but, fallibly, we single out certain entities and see them as characteristically dialectical, for operational purposes. Thus the human sciences are typically seen (by Barthes, Foucault, Benveniste, myself) as vibrantly above-below a metonymic objective rational-real horizontal line of the (hypothetical) "exact" sciences. (Underneath, as I said, they are very problematic, too, and some modern scientists know that.) Thus we have dimensions of subjectivity (or co-subjectivity of mind and body; in Freud's and Lacan's view, as in Darwin's, subjectivity is not separated from body by a neat barrier but extends incalculably far down through instinct) and a handy objectivity.

As we proceed from mathematics and astronomy up through the standard hierarchy of sciences, each new one, beginning clearly with biology (half-way through, so to speak, in human biology, language arises) is in a *geometrical* relation to the preceding, as any two tones of music are. This is prolonged by even more holistic and vibrant fields of knowledge in the human sciences (including social ones and quasi-scientific criticism, linguistics, etc.) and further, the arts, each of its successive seminal masterpieces being a sort of field or universe of knowledge with a new "twist."

The exact sciences as a collective concept then neatly play the role of the old systems or codes of knowledge, morality and religion, as *limitations*—like incest prohibition and other "thou shalt nots"—which make sophisticated visions possible (partly by return to source, transgression in imagination, and an amoral wholeness as in Blake, Dostoevsky, and really all genius, cf. Bataille). All our metonymic knowledge and indeed all our imperfect knowledge—the whole syntactic tree of manipulatory knowing we got in Eden as an extension of the snake-line-barrier of the Fall (that tree can be seen as angelic, too, in glimpses of all we lost! by Mallarmé, Valéry, etc.)—plays this game of limited moves, and we need it to survive along our life-line. The concept of the irreversibility of time—that line defined Adamically by two points, birth and death—may be undercut by Einsteinian space-time, but even the latter's relativity needs absolutes of time and space, which are, truly, fallible new versions of Mallarmé's "omniprésente Ligne" (*La Musique et les lettres*).

Derrida's *trace* is a canny recognition of this old necessity. Though Plato and Rousseau thought of it (writing) as fallen, Derrida rightly sees it as just as "prior," and we need it all the way back and forward, in a chicken-and-egg whirl, like that of the two sexes. So, too, Becoming, with Hegel, and existence with Sartre, got a certain "precedence" in our time. Like Derrida, Sartre goes too far: essence is still

Since language arises in close cahoots with incest-prohibition, according to Amaury de Riencourt[18] and others, the sexual law's basic role in anthropology is obviously near to the root epistemological paradox. Lévi-Strauss observes that the event is undecidably natural and artificial.

Take the cry which is seen as the seed of language. It is a physical fact and yet not: it is already abstract in a sense, a sign, separate from the rest of reality, standing out and for, "getting a handle on" vast entities, at the cost of exile, as Adam did. It is already too, at times, a communication, a warning signal perhaps. So it is at a crossroads of the vertical and horizontal in what we call polypolar epistemology, cognates to Jakobson's metaphoric-metonymic dimensional pair.

From this it is patent that the idea of semiotics — a "general science" of signs, which is really a human science, i.e., problematic like language and anthropology, etc. — is rooted in the very seeds of language and indeed of all perception. Words (or images) and things are all bound up *ab ovo* and in our neo-primitive visionary view. A word is a thing, whether the physical phenomenon of the cry or writing or type on a page, as well as not, always. Our usual concept of its being apart *only* is a typical operative hypothesis of culture, particularly Enlightenment rationality.

Saussure taught us to see a duplicity in the sign: the plurality and arbitrariness of signifiers and the single idea they stand for. Along with Hjelmslev and Ponge (but independently of them) I noted in various theoretical texts that the same was true of the referent: a plurality of objects, say, all sorts of random chairs, *point to* a single essential "chairey" chair, the "realer than real" object of art (like Van Gogh's who has marvellously characterful chairs) or deep experience. The "whatness of allhorse," Joyce said of the problem, scholastically. But we add the corrective to idealism, the high-low problematic, the living full-range of art and existence.

there, all along, and can *precede* as well. But the emphasis on *trace* (and the recognition of the limitation of *clôture*, cf. Mallarmé's wise awareness, in *Le Pitre châtié*, of his mere humanity as artist, *ici-bas*, and tricks of the trade) had its uses, though again the sorcerer's apprentices get carried away.

Derrida is, to put it mildly, a familiar reference, but, of course, all his concepts are out of Mallarmé: *trace, pli, blanc,* bipolar *indécidable* and tetrapolar *différance,* all are first in the master and referred-to directly in our *Oeuvre de Mallarmé* (*trace*, p. 82; *pli*, p. 261; *blanc*, Appendix A; paradox, everywhere).

[18] Amaury de Riencourt, *Sex and Power in History* (New York: Bell, 1972).

That is the first semiotic moment, though from what we said above it is clear that words and objects are fundamentally in the same boat of signifying essentials. So semiotics can encompass all signifying (including human singling out of objects for signifying, like badges or emblems); conversely, "language" can mean all that, as in "body language" or the "language of the stars," or "the world's book..."

This unessential-essential *relation* is the first dimension of signifying, for both objects and words: when the unessential (or *less* essential) sign aims hard at essentiality (totality, divinity) as Adamic man often does, we get (metaphoric) symbols, verbal or objective. But again, we emphasize, it is a *vibrant* (high-low) *relation* (and not an abstract, merely upper pole, *ideal*) that is *en cause*. Both kinds, verbal and objective, in polypolar becoming, also relate metonymically (horizontally, contingently, partially) to all sorts of entities by association or repetition-conditioning, habit. A cloud can stand for rain, one word can make you think of another. But analogies of form (as in letter symbolism, phonostylistics) betoken rather the metaphoric dimension of art and wholeness, again.

Since our essentialities eventually go back to totality, the meaning of all reality, verbal or objective (or really both) is related to what we call "language sense"; everything depends on the whole "system" or show, however obliviously or remotely.

Ordinary meaning — operational, daily, practical — depends on the fall and forgetting, a sort of tunnel vision based on the vast all-too-human life-Line or Adamic way of existence; thus *sens* in French is both (ordinary) "meaning" and "direction." But both ultimately point to a deeper meaning, and *sens*, as in Chrétien de Troye's usage, can be the medieval (or modern) totality. To emphasize the vertical, metaphoric dimension of meaning in texts as Julia Kristeva and Roland Barthes do (after Jakobson) — from the brilliantly intellectually high straight down to the sensually deep realm of body, emotions, and things, slighting to some extent the ordinary syntagmatic-chain meanings — is to move in this "totalizing" direction, along with the poets and visionaries.

Narrative Time: The Musical Values of Commonplaces

HANNA CHARNEY

> Le temps s'en va, le temps s'en va, ma dame,
> Las! les temps non, mais nous, nous en allons...

Ronsard, in his variations on the commonplace of *tempus fugit*, reverses the initial proposition, and offers another commonplace instead: "nous, nous en allons." The meaning locks itself into place with a satisfying shock of recognition consecrated by the end of the line.

Of the commonplace, Sartre said in his brilliant preface to Nathalie Sarraute's *Portrait d'un inconnu*:

> Ce beau mot a plusieurs sens: il désigne sans doute les pensées les plus rebattues mais c'est que ces pensées sont devenues le lieu de rencontre de la communauté. Chacun s'y retrouve, y retrouve les autres. Le lieu commun est à tout le monde et il m'appartient.[1]

Sartre's metaphor of the meeting place recalls the playing space, or *platea* of medieval multiple staging, where the action is as ubiquitous as it is universal. There, also, angels and souls can fly—as on the "wings of song," meeting in mid-air a charming German expression meaning household word, or commonplace: *geflügeltes Wort,* 'winged word.' Valéry, speaking in "La Conquête de l'ubiquité," of the way in which music "nous tisse un temps de fausse vie en effleurant les touches de la vraie,"[2] suggests this magical animation of the world in what he describes as a "foreign theater":

---

[1] Nathalie Saurraute, *Portrait d'un inconnu* (Gallimard, 1956), pp. 8-9.
[2] Paul Valéry, *Pièces sur l'art, Oeuvres*, II (Pléiade, 1962), 1284-87.

24

Il me souvient ici d'une féerie que j'ai vue enfant dans un théâtre étranger. Ou que je crois d'avoir vue. Dans le palais de l'Enchanteur, les meubles parlaient, chantaient, prenaient à l'action une part poétique et narquoise. Une porte qui s'ouvrait sonnait une grêle ou pompeuse fanfare. On ne s'asseyait sur un pouf, que le pouf accablé ne gémît quelque politesse. Chaque chose effleurée exhalait une mélodie.

Another evocation of the ubiquity of music, another variation on the commonplace, "music is a universal language." As Michel Butor puts it: "Que la musique soit un langage, cela est, je crois, évident pour tous."[3] What also, according to Butor, should seem evident to all is that "Musique et roman s'éclairent mutuellement" (p. 42).

The meeting of music and the novel, like that of language and meaning, can take place in the "meeting place" that Sartre defined, where the ultimate argument of classical criticism, as in Boileau, presides over the exchange of values: *le bon sens*, common sense. This place can also be the stage where a general truth, an old expression, a hackneyed thought is transformed. Some of the most glorious successes of humorous verse spring from the substitution of the second proposition—which we expect to be derived from the first—by something else, preferably a complete *non sequitur*, as often in Ogden Nash:

> I think that I shall never see
> A billboard lovely as a tree.
> Indeed, unless the billboards fall
> I'll never see a tree at all.
>
> *(Song of the Open Road)*

The first movement—"I think that I shall never see"—like Ronsard's "Le temps s'en va, le temps s'en va, ma dame," leads us onto the stage, the common place; in the middle of it, substitution and exchange transfigure the meanings.

What happens in the middle is essentially the stuff of myth and mythology. A short time before his death, Roland Barthes was much preoccupied by the Dantesque irresolution of the middle of the road, where the form of the novel, as for Proust, might show the way out. Here again, Ogden Nash puts the matter succinctly: "Middle age is when you've met so many people that every new person you meet reminds you of someone else." "So many people" is the general, as

---

[3] Michel Butor, *Répertoire*, II (Minuit, 1964), 31.

in "le temps s'en va," or the overly familiar "I think that I shall never see"; but after that moment when the commonplace is, in Sartre's words, "everybody's," we stop. Then, the meaning becomes mine — "it belongs to me" — or yours, or his, or hers, or ours, or theirs. Pronouns change, as personal events and destinies insert themselves into the mythical statement: From "le temps s'en va," which can only be indefinitely repeated — "le temps s'en va" again — "Nous," *we* become engaged in the action. At the end, the pronoun is personalized, whether it is through the amorous "nous" of Ronsard or the defiant "moi" of Corneille's *Stances à la Marquise*:

> Pensez-y, belle Marquise:
> Quoiqu'un grison fasse effroi,
> Il vaut bien qu'on le courtise,
> Quand il est fait comme moi.

Now, in the novel, how is time transformed into narrative time? How, when, and where does the exchange take place? These questions, in various and differing formulations, have much preoccupied novelists and critics. Butor, in *La Modification*, offers a thorough illustration of the ways in which myths are exploded around the middle of the journey, so that the personal pronoun, *vous*, finds its place in the world, just as the train carrying you or Léon Delmont from Paris to Rome and back follows its own course in the scheduled departures and arrivals of trains.

I do not mean to exaggerate the importance of middles, tempting as this may be in view of the prevailing critical interest in beginnings and ends. But that is not the purpose here, except just to point out that the reader has to come some way into the narrative place before time becomes narrative time. Butor explains, in connection with song, words, and music:

> La structuration de l'espace musical dans lequel la parole va pouvoir intervenir peut prendre beaucoup plus de temps que l'émission proprement dite de celle-ci; telle mélodie peut exiger un immense prélude...
> (*Répertoire*, p. 34)

Similarly, in the novel, we have to be within the narrative time, the common place, where, as in a train, passengers from different points of origin and with different destinations are gathered together for the length of their journey. We can then say with Lady Bracknell in Oscar Wilde's *The Importance of Being Earnest*: "Until yesterday I had no idea that there were any families or persons whose origin was a Terminus."

Why, one might well ask, all these protestations? Basically, to reclaim a commonplace: a musical analogy for narrative time. This analogy was quite widely accepted from the 1920s to the 1940s—in E.M. Foster's *Aspects of the Novel*, for instance—although not fully enough pursued, perhaps, to resist new perspectives in criticism. Butor, in "La Musique, art réaliste," reasserts its need: "La musique est indispensable à notre vie, à la vie de tous, et jamais nous n'en avons eu autant besoin" (*Répertoire*, p. 41). Butor's plea, from the literary side, echoes the ideas of such music critics and musicologists as Victor Zuckerkandl on the necessity of music as a system of philosophical and physical explanation.

A renewal of musical analogizing would have great advantages for the novel now. The thirty years or so of "spatial form" theories seem to have run their course, leaving useful insights into the ways in which the novel (the modern novel particularly) tends toward what Joseph Kestner calls the "secondary illusions"[4] of painting, sculpture, and architecture. Despite what individual novelists, theorists, and critics might intend or practice, there are some general structures that inform "spatial" thought: a retrospective point of view—rereading being the characteristic tool of inquiry—and a denial of narrative time in its "naive" flow, directionality, or historicity. These structures (as well as others) are equally applicable to musical analysis—just as, reciprocally, rhythm, repetition, composition, and temporal experimentation have been emphasized in pictorial analyses—but the great difference is that they are not then overdetermined by the analogy itself. It is in part to counteract this overdetermination that a return to music would be welcome.

The power of a structuring image is at least as great in the novels themselves as it is in criticism. The *Nouveau Roman*, and Robbe-Grillet in particular, tend to deal with *cliché* in its connotations of photographic reproduction and its likeness to the still (as in *Instantanés*) rather than with Sartre's "lieu commun." The *cliché* is not, like the commonplace, a place to come to, to meet in, to depart from, to return to; it is a momentary image fixed in time to which all returns and about which all probings become ironically fruitless. Time relations which derive from it only multiply its inherent ironies, repeating, reproducing, endlessly perpetrating the same units of clock time. These units can

[4] "Secondary Illusion: The Novel and the Spatial Arts," *Spatial Form in Narrative*, ed. Jeffrey R. Smitten and Ann Daghistany (London; Ithaca, N.Y.: Cornell University Press, 1981).

be exchanged, translated, or converted, but they remain untransformed and undeveloped except by the textual fabric which signals them.

In *Le Voyeur*, for example, time is expanded, shrunk, spread, accelerated, and decelerated; it is translated into: distance, speed, selling watches (Mathias is a traveling salesman), talk, silence, bicycle riding, and any number of other activities, including a possible murder committed during some of those same times. Whether or not any watches are actually sold ceases to matter; whether or not the bicycle with its broken chain moves also becomes unimportant. Distorted or not—"à la base du verre bombé, il vit l'ongle long et pointu de son doigt. Naturellement ce n'est pas de cette façon-là que le voyageur les taillait"[5]—time takes over with all its numerical ironies.

> Mathias se mit en devoir de récapituler ses arrêts et déplacements depuis son départ du café-tabac-garage. Il était à ce moment-là onze heures dix ou onze heures un quart... Les arrêts, ensuite, avaient été rares et très brefs—deux ou trois minutes au total. Les deux kilomètres accomplis sur la grand-route, entre le bourg et le tournant, à grande vitesse et sans le moindre détour, ne comptaient guère pour plus de cinq minutes. Cinq et trois, huit; et quinze, vingt-trois... (*Le Voyeur*, p. 202)

These time units function essentially like a currency. As 4 francs may equal \$1, 6 visits × 2 minutes = 12 minutes = 6 watches sold, or *not sold*; things said, or not said; things done, or not done. But the narrative time units are the same as those of real time, and are the same whatever the purpose to which they are put.

It is the underlying set of analogies which is characteristic here. Gérard Genette, quoting Christian Metz (in *Essais sur la signification du cinéma*), spells out the monetary analogy at the beginning of his discussion of the time of the "récit"; the duality of the temporal sequence, Metz says, invites us "à constater que l'une des fonctions du récit est de monnayer un temps dans un autre temps."[6] This way of speaking both asserts and denies mimetic conversions: "un temps," presumably mimetic time, is taken as a unit (unproblematically so); "un autre temps" is taken to be a corresponding unit in another medium, with the passage from one to the other executed by an easy analogy.

[5] Alain Robbe-Grillet, *Le Voyeur* (Minuit, 1955), p. 202.
[6] Christian Metz, *Essais sur la signification du cinéma* (Klincksieck, 1968), p. 28; Gérard Genette, *Figures III* (Seuil, 1972), p. 77.

Music makes it clear that the notion of temporal exchange is an impasse: Measure and musical time are radically different. The exchange value of the measure is its irrelevant function; the only relevant functions are the nonexchangeable ones. In the film *The Go-Between* by Pinter and Losey, the first sentences, spoken by the narrator, state: "The past is a foreign country. They do things differently there." The statement is itself a sort of intertextual commonplace, echoing Hemingway's story *In Another Country* and many other allusions to Marlowe's *Jew of Malta*: "But that was in another country: and besides, the wench is dead."[7] The past is a foreign country, with another currency; even if the coins remain, their value may have totally changed. Similarly, the time used by music is simply time—physical time, philosophical time, clock time, anybody's time. But, as Victor Zuckerkandl explains in *The Sense of Music*, its value is entirely relative.

This may be one of the reasons why Zuckerkandl, in *Man the Musician*, can proclaim the utterly personal character of musical time: The composer's time is inalterably his own, and no man can compose on another one's time. We might also say that the time of a composition, analogous to narrative time, becomes irreplaceable and unique. From the common good, the common place of time, which is "everybody's," the work moves into a time which belongs to the author, and also, in Sartre's words, "belongs to me." This appropriation is produced by the movements which take us from the common beginnings in our common language to the meeting place of themes, characters, reader, author, and text, all individuated "there," leaving us not with time, which, at any rate, the work cannot give us, but with the forms that narrative time has brought forth.

Proust seems to point to the same conclusion at the end of *Le Temps retrouvé*, when, in an extraordinary image of giants "plongés dans les années,"[8] he reclaims for men a place in time, "à côté de celle si restreinte qui leur est réservée dans l'espace, une place au contraire prolongée sans mesure." The measure of narrative does not mete out units of time; like music, it measures "without measure."

[7] Christopher Marlowe, *The Jew of Malta* (Lincoln: Regents Renaissance Drama, University of Nebraska Press, 1964), Act IV, Scene i.
[8] Marcel Proust, *A la recherche du temps perdu*, III (Pléiade, 1970), 1048.

The Literary Enthusiasms of Valéry*

† JEAN HYTIER

1. *A rebours*

At the conclusion of a study entitled "Five Literary Dislikes of Valéry," I said that it would be interesting to weigh against these dislikes the passionate adhesion Valéry showed for certain other works, and after having listed a few titles, I suggested that Huysmans' *A rebours* would have to be included among them.[1]

Huysmans represents Des Esseintes for us as "saturated" by Baudelaire and three masters whom he names as Flaubert, the Goncourts, and Zola. There is no need to elaborate on the fact that both Goncourts are telescoped into one: that was already the joke of all the parodists. Des Esseintes felt no strong attraction to poets, except for Verlaine, Corbière, Théodore Hannon, and Stéphane Mallarmé, to whom six pages are devoted.[2]

Mallarmé might perhaps have been flattered to be placed in the same category with Verlaine who, before Huysmans, had spoken of him among his *Poètes maudits*, but we might wonder if the same was

---

* Translated by Mary Ann Caws. The French version of this article (*French Studies*, 26, no. 4 [October 1982]) includes an extra part, on *Restif de la Bretonne and Pigault Lebrun* (tr. and ed. note).

[1] *French Studies*, 25, no. 2 (April 1981), 153-69. I have found a twelfth dislike, reduced to one epithet: "Wells stupid," in a letter to Gide of July 12, 1899 (*Correspondence*, p. 350). In the *Mercure de France* in May, Valéry had preceded his chronicle, "Methods" on "Time" by these suggestive words: "The Time Machine. The novel we have read here, thanks to our Davray — precipitates its reader in the absurd, then the arbitrary is explored. It is not my role to judge this work. I am leaving the fable, I shall think about Time."

[2] J.K. Huysmans, *A rebours* (Fasquelle edition, 1970), pp. 228-29, 232-33, 240-45.

true of Hannon, doubtless better known then than today, but quickly forgotten nevertheless. Théodore Hannon (1854-1916), hardly mentioned in 1903, with no passages quoted at all, in the excellent Anthology prepared by Fonsegrive and Van Dooren, published a weekly paper, *The Artist*, in which Céard, Zola, and others collaborated, and where *Knapsack on My Back* had appeared in 1877.[3] René Dumesnil affirms that "in order to acquit the debt of gratitude he had contracted towards Théodore Hannon, Huysmans prefaced *The Rhymes of Joy* by his friend, a book published with illustrations by Rops, at Gay and Douci in 1881."[4]

We might think that the inclusion of Hannon between Corbière and Mallarmé was also a lack of friendship, more than a little condescending. When he was preparing *A rebours*, Huysmans announced to Hannon that his novel would contain "the exhausted refinement of everything having to do with literature, art, flora, perfumes, furnishings, gems, and so on."[5] Nothing better shows the systematic and artificial allure of Huysmans' composition.

He adds to the mixture an ineradicable prejudice, assuring us that "a literature's decadence, irreparably tainted in its weakened organism... worn out... was incarnate in Mallarmé in the most consummate and the most exquisite way... this was... the quintessence of Baudelaire and Poe" (p. 245) and he declares this style "faisandé." Today this adjective seems ridiculous to us. Did that imply recognizing the originality of Mallarmé, and were we meant to take it as a global condemnation of some inevitable waning? On this point, we have Mallarmé's word-for-word denial in a letter to Léo d'Orfer and a rectification, both subtle and veiled, in his "Prose for Des Esseintes." In September of 1886 he writes to d'Orfer: "Decadence, what an abominable title, and it is time to turn our backs on everything of that sort."[6]

Lloyd Austin, in "Mallarmé, Huysmans, and 'La Prose pour Des Esseintes,'" makes clear all the subtle nuances of this friendship and

---

[3] August 16; September 9, 13; October 7, 21.

[4] *La Publication des soirées de Médan* (Malfère, 1935), p. 81. André Salmon, *Souvenirs sans fin, Première Époque (1903-1908)* (Gallimard, 1955), p. 233, mentions Hannon: "Mysterious character, who is said to have let himself be called the son of Baudelaire, probably as true as that Apollinaire was the son of an archbishop."

[5] Quoted by R. Baldick, *The Life of J. K. Huysmans* (London: Clarendon, 1955), p. 109; translated and published at Denoël in 1958.

[6] Stéphane Mallarmé, *Oeuvres complètes* (Pléiade, 1945), p. 1442. Hereafter cited as *OC*.

its restraints, pointing out that in the poem Mallarmé suggests another sort of paradise than a sensual one, that of the mind, the loveliest flowers being Ideas; Huysmans seems not to have understood, writing to Zola that "this absolute antipode of my preferences permitted me to express a few genuinely sick ideas and to glorify Mallarmé, which seemed to me an agreeable joke."[7] This joke is bothersome today, to say the least. Austin is quite right when, in a note to Mallarmé's *Correspondence*, he qualifies the "praise of Mallarmé" in *A rebours* as "more or less sincere."[8]

Huysmans' reaction to the "Prose" is found in his brief letter of January 14, 1885: "Let me send you a warm handshake for this delicious and artificial voyage which is lacking in *A rebours*, but which you have wonderfully checkered in *La Revue Indépéndante*, for Des Esseintes."[9] It has to be admitted that this praise is a bit weak, even taking into account the specific use of the patterning technique of "checkering," fortunate for the lover of art. He must have noticed it in Boissier's *Analogical Dictionary*, whose rubrics he poured into his luxurious descriptions, just as he used the *Dictionnaire des communes* to find the names of his characters, or catalogues to transform specialized terms into images.

As for Valéry, did he remain the admirer of a book which had been his Bible at eighteen, which he had probably first read when he was sixteen?[10] Mondor says that later he was to "analyse again this style superb in its strength or disconcerting in its bad taste and its blatant luxury" and its stylistic excesses (*OC* I, 229). In 1931, Frédéric Lefèvre will pick up on the instructive comments of Valéry on Huysmans' influence: "He prepared without realizing it the transmutation of naturalism into symbolism, a fatal consequence of a style pushed to the extreme, of a sort of systematic increase of expression… It is not

---

[7] *Revue de l'Histoire Littéraire de la France* (June 1954), pp. 145-89, esp. pp. 180-82.
[8] *Correspondance de Mallarmé*, II, ed. Austin (Gallimard, 1960), 233-34, n. 2.
[9] *Ibid.*, pp. 262-63, n. 2.
[10] The sonnet "Solitude," of 1887, bears witness at once to the influence of *A rebours* and to Valéry's idiosyncrasy:

> Loin du monde, je vis tout seul comme un ermite
>
> ......
>
> Et je jouis sans fin de mon propre cerveau.

Discovered by Octave Nadal, it was communicated by him to Henri Mondor, and both published it several times. See the note in *OC* I, 1587-89.

so far from this kind of writing to that of Mallarmé,"[11] which could be argued or should at least be amended. If the style of Mallarmé conquers the reader who has grasped its nuances, the excesses of Huysmans, after having amused him, end up by irritating him. The exasperated style becomes exasperating.

I think a partial originality is enough to influence us and the faults of a book, suited to a particular climate of sensitivity, do more than its good qualities for its immediate success: take *L'Astrée*, for example, or *La Nouvelle Héloïse*! Huysmans wanted to rival the real in making it stronger. He should have said to himself, like Valéry: "For a poet, it is not a matter of saying that he was appreciated—but a matter... of creating his place."[12] Doubtless, and La Bruyère knew it perfectly well, but all the poet can do is to bring down a rain of words, stubbornly, and the deluge can be more destructive than fecund.

2. *The Red Badge of Courage*

The subtitle of this volume, "An Episode of the American Civil War," is often forgotten.

In the *Gazette du Mercure de France* of February 1953, Maurice Saillet reminds us of Valéry's intention to translate this work of Stephen Crane.[13] He quotes a letter of 1897 to Vielé-Griffin, which had just been published in the *Letters to Some People* (March 31, 1952), where Valéry says he has begun "to work on the *Badge*; I warn you right away that I plan to omit everything that would be hard for me to translate—American slang or ellipses, idioms, etc."

But the proposed project of translating it together is not realized: "only thirteen years later does the French version appear, and without his signature..." Saillet wonders why in 1897 Valéry was so enthusiastic about translating it, and thinks the reasons might have been that the hero of this "'flight forward' evokes Monsieur Teste in more than one way," finding this confirmed towards the end of the book, when the hero, in a conclusion "worthy of M. Teste... finds himself able to con-

---

[11] Frédéric Lefèvre, *Entretiens sur Huysmans* (Horizon de France, 1931), pp. 39-41.

[12] Paul Valéry, *Cahiers* XVI (Centre National de la Recherche Scientifique, 1933), p. 24. What did Valéry think of the "Prose for Des Esseintes?" The only mention I have been able to find to it is at once a diatribe against "professional analyses": "The humor of genetic explications of the 'Prose for Des Esseintes'!" *Cahiers*, XXIII (1944), 1721.

[13] "Paul Valéry and *La Conquête du Courage*."

template with the gaze of a judge the tawdry and shabby ideas he used to hold to, and his joy was great to find he despised them."

If Maurice Saillet had waited for the publication by Robert Mallet in 1955 of the *Correspondence* between Gide and Valéry, he would have found a letter prior to the letter to Vielé-Griffin, sent on February 7, 1896, and proving that before he thought of a translation, Valéry had planned an article "on a recent English or rather, American novel; by a young man, about war. It is the impression of a battle, the deflowering of a young man with respect to war, and very strong, extremely strong, especially if you take into account that the author is twenty-three. I am condemned to talk about other authors, and it is necessary..." To earn his living, without the job he had hoped for in a ministry, "one must be a public writer." Valéry will not produce this article any more than the translation.[14] But at least we know his taste for a tale in which a young man, in another field entirely, learns his own nature, his gifts, his strengths.

Valéry's admiration had its share of illusion. Posterity has consecrated the book as the proof of its author's talent; it has often been reedited, often translated, but historians have not failed to point out that this tale, which gives every impression of having been lived, was totally imaginary. Now this could only have pleased the author of M. Teste, and would not be the first time that life has brought an artist the confirmation of a dream. But, in this case, alas, the authenticity of his foretelling was to be paid with his early death, on June 5, 1900.

3. A Cavalry Officer: *The Memoirs of General L'Hotte*

Judith Robinson has shown how this book that Valéry placed at the head of a list of his "good books" in 1938 has to stimulate him. L'Hotte furnishes the material to establish a parallel between two lives, that of the celebrated horseman Baucher and of Valéry himself, then a second parallel between two trainings, that of the human mind and that of the horse, from which there came the idea of a treatise never composed, the "Gladiator," of which Judith Robinson found several of the elements in the *Cahiers* and which she was to put in chronological order in 1973 in the *Pléiade* edition.

---

[14] The translation of the book was to appear in 1912 with the *Mercure de France*, translated by Vielé-Griffin and Davray.

From his reflections, taken from the *Cahiers*, her article of 1966[15] retains two passages on the lightness and the purity in the management of strength which Valéry had underlined in pencil in his copy of the book of L'Hotte. She could have added this passage in a letter to Coste of 1915 where Valéry says that his "ideal would be to construct the scale and the system of relations of which thought would be the music," and where he exclaims "what a beautiful thing... a race horse trained every morning, pushed to his limit, held back in time, weighed, and fed intelligently..."[16]

After the overall view where d'Aure and Baucher are quoted by L'Hotte, we might wonder what L'Hotte himself thought of the training of the horse. I don't think Valéry read his *Equestrian Questions* (1901) or his contribution to the Cavalry Regulation of 1876, "The School of the Cavalier," any more than the Comte d'Aure's *Treatise on Equitation* (1834) or his *Course in Equitation* (1855), or any of Baucher's works of which the most widely-read had appeared in 1842: *A Method of Equitation Based on New Principles*. What L'Hotte said of it was enough for him and it is from L'Hotte that he takes everything he knows of these famous horsemen.

But L'Hotte does not say much about his own ideas, except to approve what his teachers say. The few readers of his *Mémoires* will easily perceive the reason for such discretion: the book is unfinished and the tale is interrupted in the middle of his youth. Baucher and the Count d'Aure appear in it as two leaders whose favorite pupil L'Hotte had the good fortune to be. After a sketch of the history of equitation and an overall glance at the equestrian centers of the eighteenth and nineteenth centuries, the *Mémoires* stop abruptly when L'Hotte is twenty-five.

To the passages about Baucher, I would add this generalization which seems to me like Valéry in mood: "He liked to establish relations between horsemanship and different life situations. Thus, in a conversation with M. Thiers, he applied to politics one of his great principles: 'Equilibrium must be set up without changing the motion, and, on the other hand, motion must not disturb equilibrium in any way.'"

---

[15] Judith Robinson, "Valéry's concept of training the mind," *French Studies* (1966), pp. 227-35.

[16] *Lettres à quelques-uns*, LII, 108. The sentence on music is found at the same epoch in the *Cahiers* (V, 777; *OC* I, 334), followed by the notations: "This is a Gladiator himself."

In *About Corot*, Valéry had reminded us how old Baucher was when he dazzled his favorite pupil by traversing the riding-ring at a dead slow pace: "a perfect centaur... 'There,' said the master, 'I am not showing off. I am at the summit of my art. To walk without one mistake...'" What advice to give to any poet, to any prose-writer, to any artist, to any professor...

I wonder if Valéry ever looked at the very popular lectures of Ernest Legouvé. In *The Art of Reading* (1873), we are amused today to see the art of Baucher and of the Comte d'Aure taken as examples, and their possible application to the art of verse. Baucher is "the riding-school horseman par excellence," and d'Aure, "the open-air rider. Baucher's horse is always powerful, although a captive, M. d'Aure's is always docile, although independent." Whence this risky but suggestive comparison: "M. Baucher's horse is the Alexandrian or the stanzaic verse, and M. d'Aure's horse is free verse."[17]

Did Valéry go that far in his revelatory comparisons?[18]

4. *The Spiritual Songs of Saint John of the Cross*[19]

Valéry, who was not a "great reader of mystical works," declared in 1941 that he had discovered, thirty years before, the *Spiritual Works of Saint John of the Cross* in an old in-quarto dated 1641. He does not tell us how he found it "to hand." It would be a quite imprudent hypothesis to attribute this meeting to a friend, a well-known translator, Davray, responsible to the *Mercure de France* for English literature and with whom he had planned in 1897 to translate *The Red Badge of Courage*, but I was moved, in his translation in 1904 of *Spanish Literature* by Jean Fitz-Maurice Kelly, to read that John of the Cross "is a poet who knows how to express in angelical tones the ardors of a spiritual love. His only fault is that he remains in a fog in which music takes the place of reason, where words are only vague

[17] It is, of course, a matter of the traditional or classic free verse, that of La Fontaine, for example. I take the liberty of referring the reader to pages 164 and 166 of my *Questions de littérature: Etudes valéryennes et autres* (New York: Columbia University Press, 1967; Geneva: Droz, 1967), and a lecture at the a.i.e.f., July 26, 1964: "Autour d'une analyse valéryenne."
[18] All Valéry specialists who have studied his thought have necessarily given a place to the training of the mind: I shall only mention J. Duchesne-Guillemin, Ion Cheorge, Edison, and Daniel Moutote.
[19] Verse translation by le R.P. Cyprien, o.c.d. *Oeuvres*, I, 445-57.

symbols of inexpressible thoughts, unspeakable ecstasies."[20] Transform this retrained observation into a compliment and you will be very near pure poetry.

Leafing through the old book, Valéry found by chance some French verses across from a facing Spanish text: "I saw, I read, I murmured to myself on the spot: 'At the dawn of a dark night...' Oh! I said to myself, but this sings by itself. There is no other certainty about poetry." This is being caught in the act! And we are astonished that the reverend father possessed, to perfection,

> this charm, in which the greatest simplicity and the most exquisite sense of distinctions were united in admirable proportions.
> I thought: How can it be that this monk has acquired such a lightness of stroke, of the formal phrasing, and seized instantly the thread of the melody of his words? (p. 259)

When I studied *The Poetics of Valéry*[21] I had, in concluding, to insist upon the importance of the sacrifice of effects and to give as a theoretical proof of these declarations, so strange on his part:

> It seems to me that the soul alone with itself and which speaks to itself from time to time, between two absolute silences, never uses anything more than a small number of words, and no extraordinary ones. It is by that that we know there is a soul, in that moment... (p. 296)

I indicated that the tone of this passage was exceptional, for in itself the word "soul" resounds in a fashion as little Valérian as possible.[22] Perhaps Valéry, I suggested, "thought he should accommodate his courtesy to the piety of his heros," concluding:

> This is what the ambitious project of reducing poetry to a scientific maneuver of sensitivity leads to: "the soul alone with itself and which speaks from time to time," this naked simplicity of the conscience listening to its song, with no heed given to the effect — did Valéry ever come nearer than in this rare moment of perfect humility to the secret of poetic creation? (p. 299)

---

[20] Jean Fitz-Maurice Kelly, *Spanish Literature* (1898, English edition; rpt. Colin, 1922), p. 259. Quotation is from the Colin edition.

[21] Jean Hytier, *La Poétique de Valéry* (Colin, 1953), pp. 296-99.

[22] The *Cahiers* had not yet appeared. About the personal exigencies of Valéry concerning the vocabulary to use in his daily research, I note this formal exclusion: "The word soul ruled out," *Cahiers* (1928), XIII, 107.

What caused Valéry to abound in praise? That the centenary of the translation of the *Spiritual Work* was approaching? He is right to claim the honor of the "discovery": "I propose... considering from now on one of the most perfect poets of France, the Holy Father Cyprien... until now almost unknown... for his first edition, in 1917, by Catholic Art, which was rapidly sold out, could not have reached more than a very few... ," and he notices his absence from all the anthologies. He is astonished that even the Abbé Bremond, a great poetry lover, in his *Literary History of Religious Feeling in France*, speaks of him only in passing, in a few lines, about other works and never mentions the Songs.[23]

Valéry devoted his course of January 6, 1940, at the Collège de France, to Father Cyprien. On May 15, *La Revue des Deux Mondes* published the article: "An Unknown Poet: Father Cyprien," which became the preface to the edition of the Songs published by Rouart in 1941 and was reprinted in 1944 in *Variété V*.

In these verses where the purity of the sound meets the purity of meaning, or more exactly of feeling, an authentic poetry is revealed, which had not had much echo before Valéry rang the alarm. No one had thought before this of quoting passages from it in any anthology or of mentioning it in a history of poetry.[24] After Valéry had resurrected the translations, things began to change. In 1944, René Caillois, in Buenos Aires, published in his collection at the Lettres Françaises, "Strait Is the Gate," Valéry's text, under the title "An Unknown Poet." In 1961, Jean Rousset in his *Anthology of French Baroque Poetry* gives eleven stanzas of the Spiritual Songs.[25] Raymond Picard, in 1904, in *French Poetics from 1640 to 1680*, where he gives a great deal of room to "Religious Poetry," was not able to keep Father Cyprien because

---

[23] Abbé Bremond, *Literary History of Religious Feeling in France*, V, 387-90, as the author of the *Recueil des vertus et écrits de Mme la Baronne de Neuvillette, décédée depuis peu dans la ville de Paris* (1666).

[24] Of course it was not the custom to include translations, and yet there were some remarkable ones which might well have been included, for example an imitation of "Gray's Elegy in a Country Churchyard" by M*** de Saint-Malo (i.e., Châteaubriand), or Virgil's *Bucolics* in blank verse by Valéry (see note in *OC* I, 1718).

[25] Jean Rousset, *Anthology of French Baroque Poetry*, II (Colin, 1961), 206-08. Commentary of Valéry quoted in the note, pp. 312-13.

he had to exclude all the works composed, if not published, before 1640, but in his foreword he reminds us of Valéry's "discovery."[26]

5. *The Little Chronicle of Anna Magdalena Bach*

I shall not dwell on the last discoveries of Valéry for, because of their lateness, he was not able to go back over them as he liked to do for the older ones. Here is what we find in 1938: "I read in the train the *Little Chronicle of Anna Magdalena Bach* given me by Marguerite Fournier in Marseilles. Few works have seized me so strongly. Few give a stronger desire to work—'for what?'—and to the greater glory of God, with all due reserve for God but certainly for someone other than oneself" (*Cahiers* xxi, 370).

In spite of the brevity of this statement, we recognize it in what Valéry prized above all else in a reading: its value for stimulation, for arousing the ambition of accomplishing some work which would go past the vain satisfaction but also the uncertainty of the goal: "for what?"—this undetermined feeling which was the secret wound of a ferocious quest.

I suppose that the gift of Miss Marguerite Fournier, whom he had already seen in Cassis before meeting her again in Marseilles (*Cahiers* xxi, 375), was a copy of *The Little Chronicle of Anna Magdalena Bach*, in a translation by Marguerite and Edmond Buchet. The original had appeared in London in 1925, with an engraving of Bach from J.E. Rosenthal's portrait, and, on page 183, these words: "Those familiar with the known and authenticated facts of Bach's life will realize that certain episodes in this book are imaginary." It is in the German edition that the pronoun Anna will enter in the title: "Die Kleine Cronik der Anna Magdalena Bach," and that the name of the author of the work is indirectly revealed as being Esther Meynell.

I don't think that Valéry was worried about the origin of this charming biography, which revived in him his admiration for Bach, as well as for Wagner, to which his *Cahiers* bear witness. It could perhaps also, but he says nothing of this, have inspired in him a certain form of reverie. A reader fond of sentimental previews could wonder if the

---

[26] *Poètes français d'aujourd'hui: Panorama critique* (Seghers, 1955), p. 187, and the revised and enlarged edition: *Les Nouveaux Poètes français: Panorama critique* (Seghers, 1959), p. 214.

prodigious renewal of inspiration Johann Sebastian found in the fervent love of Anna Magdalena was the prelude to the idyll of the old Faust and his young secretary Lust in his unfinished "My Faust."

6. Itard and *The Wild Boy of Aveyron*

A remarkable book *The Wild Boy of Aveyron* by Doctor Itard

> No progress other than verbal in psychiatry since that time. But a quantity of words and — naturally — the use or the experiments at random on the sick people of all the new means of physics or chemistry. Nothing else to do. Itard uses shock procedures, which he invents.

Lost in the left corner of the bottom of a page of the *Cahiers* (xxv, 876), these lines have not been quoted by any of the best exegetes of Valéry's thought, even those who had brought to light the myth of the Gladiator or the one of Robinson as an Intellectual, nor, of course, by the most recent biographers the wild child taken captive on January 9, 1800, at Saint-Cernin and turned over on August 6 to the Institute of the Deaf and Dumb in Paris.

It was only quite late that Valéry read the two reports of Itard (Jean-Marc Gaspard, 1775-1838), both addressed to the Ministry of the Interior (in 1801 and 1806), probably in the reedition of 1894: *Reports and Memoirs of the Wild Boy of Aveyron.* Valéry was then seventy years old and lived, as he often did during the occupation, with his friend Robert de Billy, in the château of Montrozier, not far from Rodez, where Valéry had given a lecture in May, and where the child who was to be called Victor was kept from February 4 to July 20, 1800. It is not surprising that in the course of his sojourn in the Rouergue, Valéry had the occasion to read the precise observations of Itard about this child of the forest who inspired such curiosity in everyone.[27]

The brief reflections of Valéry are to be added to his profession of scepticism about psychiatry, condemned to verbalism, to impotence and to illusory remedies. All the more lively in his admiration for Itard who drew up an efficacious technique, the "shock treatment." They will be found in Itard's analyses. I imagine that Valéry, like every reader, must have been struck by the immense joy felt by Itard when Victor bit his hand furiously for having been punished for his good conduct — the proof which had been hoped for of his capacity to tell the difference between what is just and what is unjust, and whose emotional impact has not yet been diminished by the ebb of time itself.

[27] See Rober Shattuck's study of Truffaut's film on the subject and of the source: *The Forbidden Experiment: The Story of the Wild Boy of Aveyron* (New York: Farrar, Strauss, and Giroux, 1980).

Description and Perception: Valéry and Proust

MICHELINE TISON-BRAUN

Laden with years and glory, the man lay dying in a vast Spanish bed with carved bedposts. It takes no effort to imagine a lordly balcony, facing west, a few steps away, and, further down, the sight of marble and laurels and a garden whose stone steps are duplicated in a rectangle of water. A woman has placed a yellow rose in a vase. The man murmurs the inevitable verses which — to tell the truth — have begun to weary him a little:

Blood of the garden, pomp of the walk,
gem of spring, April's eye...

Then came the revelation. Marino *saw* the rose as Adam might have seen it in Paradise. And he sensed that it existed in its eternity and not in his words, and that we may make mention or allusion of a thing but never express it at all; and that the tall proud tomes that cast a golden penumbra in an angle of the drawing room were not — as he had dreamed in his vanity — a mirror of the world, but simply one more thing added to the universe.

This illumination came to Marino on the eve of his death, and, perhaps, it had come to Homer and Dante too.[1]

It is commonly believed that description depicts objects. It does nothing of the kind: it proposes meanings. What we shall try to determine

---

[1] J.L. Borges, "A Yellow Rose," in *A Personal Anthology* (Grove Press, 1967), p. 83.

is, first, how the relationship is established between the describer and the object described and, second, how, from meanings which are proposed to him, the reader reconstitutes objects which he has never seen.

1. What Description Describes

> Une scie à eau se compose d'un hangar au bord d'un ruisseau. Le toit est soutenu par une charpente qui porte sur quatre gros piliers en bois. A huit ou dix pieds d'élévation, au milieu du hangar, on voit une scie qui monte et descend, tandis qu'un mécanisme fort simple pousse contre cette scie une pièce de bois. C'est une roue mise en mouvement par le ruisseau qui fait aller ce double mécanisme; celui de la scie qui monte et descend, et celui qui pousse doucement la pièce de bois vers la scie, qui la débite en planches.[2]

This text is unquestionably a description in the most conventional sense of the term: it transposes in words the exterior aspect of a group of objects observed by the author and restores it exactly as it is to the reader. It is even an exemplary description: nothing is lacking, nothing is superfluous. Everything can be represented in it. We could construct a working wood model of it; it could have been designed for the *Journal de Trévoux* or an illustration of the *Encyclopédie*, intended for people who have never seen a saw-mill. The author is definitely Henri Beyle, an engineering graduate of the Grenoble Polytechnic School. No one would think of attributing any poetic quality to this text. In itself it describes a utilitary apparatus. Within the economy of a novel it has no other role than that of making the danger incurred by Julien clearly understood — Julien who is the victim of the paternal slap — and of presenting two characters in a typical situation. The description is indispensable to the episode, but does not go past it. It is not a test of profusion, or of luxury at the source; it provokes no meditation, does not lend itself to dreaming, offering nothing either picturesque or piquant. It is a pure functional report, functionally inserted into the tale. It poses no problem. It does not put the world into question.

On the contrary, the texts which we are now going to read are all problematic in their own way. Their meaning goes past the objects described, so that the latter is only the support, perhaps just the pretext

---

[2] Stendhal, *Le Rouge et le noir* (Pléiade, 1963), I, 231.

of a meditation on life and art, finally including even the creative act in its accomplishment.

The Fountain of the Prince of Guermantes

Dans une clairière réservée par de beaux arbres dont plusieurs étaient aussi anciens que lui, planté à l'écart, on le voyait de loin, svelte, immobile, durci, ne laissant agiter par la brise que la retombée plus légère de son panache pâle et frémissant. Le 18e siècle avait épuré l'élégance de ses lignes, mais, fixant le style du jet semblait en avoir arrêté la vie, à cette distance on avait l'impression de l'art plutôt que la sensation de l'eau. Le nuage humide lui-même qui s'amoncelait perpétuellement à son faîte gardait le caractère de l'époque comme ceux qui dans le ciel s'assemblent autour des palais de Versailles. Mais de près on se rendait compte que tout en respectant, comme les pierres d'un palais antique, le dessin préalablement tracé, c'était des eaux toujours nouvelles, qui, s'élançant et voulant obéir aux ordres anciens de l'architecte, ne les accomplissaient exactement qu'en paraissant les violer, leurs mille bonds épars pouvant seuls donner à distance l'impression d'un unique élan. Celui-ci était en réalité aussi souvent interrompu que l'éparpillement de la chute alors que de loin, il m'avait paru infléchissable, dense, d'une continuité sans lacune. D'un peu près, on voyait que cette continuité, en apparence toute linéaire était assurée, à tous les points de l'ascension du jet, partout où il aurait dû se briser, par l'entrée en ligne, par la reprise latérale d'un jet parallèle qui montait plus haut que le premier, et était lui-même, à une plus grande hauteur, mais déjà fatigante pour lui, relevé par un troisième. De près, des gouttes sans force retombaient de la colonne d'eau en croisant au passage leurs soeurs montantes et, parfois, déchirées, saisies dans un remous de l'air troublé par ce jaillissement sans trève, flottaient avant d'être chavirées dans le bassin. Elles contrariaient de leurs hésitations, de leur trajet en sens inverse et estompaient de leur molle vapeur la rectitude et la tension de cette tige, portant au-dessus de soi un nuage oblong fait de mille gouttelettes, mais en apparence peint en brun doré et immuable, qui montait, infrangible, immobile, élancé et rapide, s'ajouter aux nuages du ciel. Malheureusement un coup de vent suffisait à l'envoyer obliquement sur la terre; parfois même un simple jet désobéissant divergeait, et si elle ne s'était pas tenue à une distance respectueuse, aurait mouillé jusqu'aux moelles la foule imprudente et contemplative.[3]

The fountain has in common with the sawmill its functional character. But it is in no way useful. Its ingeniousness, its gratuity,

---

[3] Marcel Proust, *A la recherche du temps perdu* (Pléiade, 1954), II, 656-57.

and the pleasure which it provides make it a sort of surrealist object, source of a lively astonishment, inexplicable, perhaps childish, like all spectacles of water and reflection, but irresistible. Think of the fountain of Héron, in *Les Confessions*, which is just a hydraulic tourniquet. No temptation, however, in Proust to evoke *"les grands jets d'eau sveltes parmi les marbres,"* nor the Baudelairian rainbow, nor the *Cité des eaux*. For the fantasy which it stimulates is of another nature entirely. The fountain of the Prince of Guermantes is originally only a physical phenomenon, observed more closely than is ordinary, described with a magnifying glass by an author who forbids himself any indulgence in the dream, the better to concentrate his attention on a technique of illusion.

There are two movements in this description: two chains of opposite sensations mingle without being completely fused in this ambiguous object, the fountain, whose nature is revealed as it is inversed, whether it is seen from near or far. From a distance it forms part of a whole, included in an architecture of waters, marbles, and vegetation, created in this golden age of parks where landscapes of stones could be moved and waters could be immobilized, where the vegetal thrusts could be controlled, and even the clouds sculpted — clouds of that epoch, floating above the palaces — and where the columns of water could be softened into panache shapes evoking leaf, feather, cloud, and rainbow. This baroque phantasmagoria mixed domains, imposing upon each a mimetic necessity which, going against its nature, forced it to display itself in a series of endless substitutions. Enclosed in its trees as in a halo, *réservé* in its space, preserved in time also — an old-fashioned one — the fountain of the Prince of Guermantes remains like a pure idea of "the architect."

Close-up, the illusion is dispelled, but reveals another source of wonder: "life" arrested and as it were frozen by "style," frees itself so that "the impression of art" makes way for "the feeling of water." Here, description becomes technique and follows the *périple* of the drops themselves, in a style consciously labored. At the same time, a slight drama of an interrupted fall finds precise and pathetic personifications. Submissive "to the age-old commands of the architect," each drop rushes forward, its place taken by others towards some unknown first unchanging mover, then separated from its "sisters," knowing that only the whole of the work will be saved, falls once more, "chavirée," and consenting to sacrifice like an artist dead at his task. This exhausted good-will of the material, is it the other side of creation, the price it must pay in order to remain living? There is no great art, in fact, which does not strain in order to tear itself away from some ground or from some nature. That is perhaps the way the equilibrium is established between these two opposed principles, this counterpoint of flight and of matter, of soaring and density, which differentiates between artists and styles. Between the distant apparition of the fountain, where life takes refuge in the "pale and trembling plume," and the analysis too close-at-hand, entailing the loss of all form, Proust varies the distance: like a magician who, after having shown how a trick works, nimbly repeats it, he withdraws again, comes back, retreats, and finally establishes himself exactly at the point of ambiguity where the illusion vanishes and reappears ceaselessly in the motionless coming and going which is the existential mode proper to imaginary objects. Master of his subject and his art, the describer has disdained the banal magic of the ripple and surge of waters, and has then recreated and enriched it: the reader feels from now on the illusion as it is eroded by knowledge and brought back to life by desire.

This tiny *ars poetica* finishes with a pirouette: the object, in revolt, splatters symbolically over the creator, the spectators, and the readers.

The Tiger

> *L'énorme fauve est couché tout contre les barres de sa cage. Son immobilité* me fixe. *Sa beauté* me cristallise. Je tombe en rêverie devant cette personne animale impénétrable. Je compose dans mon esprit les forces et les formes de *ce magnifique seigneur qu'une robe si noble et si souple enveloppe. Il porte sur ce qu'il voit un regard incurieux*. Je cherche ingénument à lire des attributs humains sur son mufle admirable. Je m'attache à *l'expression de supériorité fermée, de puissance et d'absence*, que je trouve à *cette face de maître absolu, étrangement voilée, ou ornée d'une dentelle très déliée d'arabesques noires très élégantes, comme peintes sur le masque de poil doré.*
>
> Point de férocité: quelque chose plus formidable, —je ne sais quelle certitude d'être fatal.
>
> Quelle plénitude, quel égotisme sans défaut, quel isolement souverain! l'imminence de tout ce qu'il vaut est avec lui. Cet être me fait songer vaguement à un grand empire.
>
> Il n'est pas possible d'être plus soi-même, plus exactement armé, doué, chargé, instruit de tout ce qu'il faut pour être parfaitement tigre. Il ne peut lui venir d'appétit ni de tentation qui ne trouvent en lui leurs moyens les plus prompts.
>
> Je lui donne cette devise: SANS PHRASES![4]

[4] Paul Valéry, *Oeuvres* (Pléiade, 1957), I, 294-95. Only expressions in italics in Valéry's text are descriptive (italics mine).

A human creation, the fountain is as simple as a theorem. It poses no problem to the mind which the mind cannot resolve; it offers an aesthetic pleasure indefinitely recreated. The odd and almost monstrous aspect which the innumerable dissemination of the drops of water provides him is absorbed once more in the unchangeability of an element which is always identical to itself. The spectator, knowing that to take one step back would be enough to reestablish the order of things, is more intrigued than troubled by his discovery of the infinitely small.

The fountain, like a theorem, is assimilated by the mind. But a tiger? Nothing less plausible, less motivated than the very existence of such a being. It does not, therefore, ordinarily appear in art and folklore unless it is laden with mythology. The mere thought of these usual accretions is enough to appreciate the radical pruning which Valéry has undertaken. How many clichés must have been plucked, like so many fleas, out of this coat of hair invaded by cultural prehistory: Racinian rhetoric ("Tiger, thirsty for blood..."); Romantic imagery like the sketch of Delacroix; historical knowledge, ever since Nineveh has provided us with the bas-relief carving of the wounded lioness; even some childhood memories, for Captain Corvett's hunts have imprinted on all tigers born in all zoos the creepers of their ancestral jungle and the colors of arid lands. Valéry has also disposed with tragic symbols, particularly moral ones, which cling to the caged beast: useless power, *Vae Victis*, Vercingétorix at Caesar's triumph Vigny's *The Death of the Wolf*, stoic pride... All this hodgepodge is rejected with its colorful background of the Assyrian hunts. Valéry's tiger has no fictitious depth, no secret. It is, it just is. But that is not simple either, for each perception, bearing in itself an inexhaustible detail, is then inserted into all the neighboring perceptions. Weighed down besides with everyone's memories and desires, it runs the risk of being dissipated in a thousand confused dreamings, in the midst of the "forests of symbols." Thus, the describer who is trying to escape the labyrinth of this thought by hanging on to "reality" is lost in an inexhaustible gaze, where the possible detail is limitless. Here, for example, is the tiger's "golden mane": now Memling has pictured a fur collar whose hairs are painted *one by one*. We must immediately interrupt this picturing, refusing this hopeless rivalry with nature.

We have italicized in Valéry's text the notations which are properly said to be descriptive. They take up about eight lines out of twenty-five, say a third: the rest is the author's reflection. Still, descriptive words are more often than not abstract and stripped of the picturesque. (immobility, beauty, nobility, etc.). There remains at the very beginning the sketch of the animal, and later, the delayed and quite surprising discovery of the lace mask. This text is then above all a meditation for which the concrete object serves as illustration. However, it offers a marvellous illusion of perception. Perhaps this *trompe l'oeil* is due only to the simple detail of the painted mask, so precise as to awaken, here and there in the text, certain modest notations (the dress, the form). The obedient reader reconstructs the animal without noticing that it is only offered to him in an enigmatic light which casts on everything the intangibility of a mirage. For in Valéry, enemy of nostalgias and of the vague, the image does not arise in the depths of instinct, but rather from sensation as it is thought out, often even from the words themselves; his precision helps to create the illusion of something perceived, all the while further from reality.

Once every trace of the picturesque is abolished, the tiger is only raw presence. "The enormous beast was lying right up against the bars of its cage." Each word carries a charge in this sentence which begins with the word *"énorme"* and ends by the illusory security of the "cage." "Right up against the bars"—at the very limits of the possible—the animal exists in the mind of the reader with its mane in a brush, its excessive body and almost with its odor. And the first effect is to fascinate. The reader is "pierced," "crystallized," and his reverie (in the sense of Descartes, not of Lamartine) takes the form of a metaphysical interrogation: who is "this impenetrable animal person?" The Other has risen up in front of us; all the more other, irreducible, in that he belongs to the same biological realm as we do, subject as we are to fear, to hunger, to rage—a will at once restless and dangerous—but absent from himself and protected against adversity by the formidable rampart of the unthinking. The spectator tries "ingenuously" to chip into this invulnerability, that is to say to propitiate the object by bringing it back to the touching human incompletion. Repulsed by "the uncurious look" which nevertheless "sees" him, he tries once more to bring it back forcefully into his universe, lending it other attributes, oriented by an unconscious metaphysics which summons the Nietzschean cliché: lord of the sands. Scarcely is it presented before it makes way for the cliché of the veiled man of the desert. A new reminder of raw presence stops this romantic flight. What grows back now is not absence but rather an absurd and charming presence, even frivolous, of the mask, evoking the perfectly unjustifiable character, taken on often by aesthetic experience.

Even ferocity is ill-suited to the enigmatic beast. "No ferocity: something more formidable, — I do not know what certainty of being lethal." Power and absence, serenity by detachment from everything, even from oneself: such are attributes which have always been reserved for the gods. Not for the bird-gods, not for the jackal-gods, those fetishes whose gaze is only implacable, but to the great divinities of natural forces whose power has transmitted itself to their sacred animals — lions and tigers, bulls — in whom we find perhaps once more, magnified, our dreams of omnipotence, but which remain forever ir-reducible to any human meaning. Now we have understood; this tiger is an "in-itself." It escapes us not only because it is of another species while being of the same biological realm, but because it is the object of our perception. The strange relationship which unites it to us physiologically accentuates the breaking-apart of being into subject and object. Here there arise memories of Valéry: the bite of the *Jeune Parque*, the silent slipping away of the snake, the irrefutable worm of the *Cimetière marin*, the "fault in the purity of non-being." This tiger is an "in-itself." Its true attributes are fullness, coincidence with itself and its nature, as well as inaccessibility to human consciousness. Regardless of his attention and his reflection, Valéry, having turned the object around in all directions, admits himself vanquished. The object dominates.

This text is not only an admirable literary piece, drawing from a spectacle its full metaphysical significance: it is a complete represen-tation of a drama of perception with the double movement of con-sciousness, movement towards the object, search for presence un-adorned, effort to find a meaning: first human, fraternal, and then any meaning whatsoever, which might be able to integrate the object into an intelligible universe. Repulsed, sent back to its own solitude, the mind gives up. A series of notations, briefer and briefer, leads to the final abdication: "WITHOUT SENTENCES."

2. The Purpose of Description

Why should we describe? Is it to remember or to share with others the emotion of the spectacle? But then why should we have recourse to words at all, when painting or drawing or even photography would suit the purpose? How should we translate in words a visual reality which is heterogeneous to language? We are forced to concede that the author of descriptions is not giving in to the simple need to preserve a memory. On the subject of his real vocation, Proust's work is revealing. If Proust of the last years tries to bring back memories, those stick to the young narrator, almost without a past, who in front of certain spectacles, becomes conscious of a summons present and pressing. Things call to him—a hawthorn-bush, a little stretch of sunny wall. It is a tender invitation but imperious all the same, quite like a maternal smile. What these privileged sensations demand of him, he does not know, he feels only this poignant, bitter-sweetness before Sleeping Beauty and the regret of not being able to wake her.

All these veiled appeals are marked with the same signs: 1. The spectacle hides more than it shows. *There is something behind it*; 2. The secret is impenetrable both to the senses and to the mind; 3. There is, however, an absolute obligation to try to penetrate it, and the young man withdrawing in front of his task carries about with him the bad consciousness of an enthusiasm deceived and of an unaccomplished mission. He suffers from his treason, but he has no time to deepen his provoked sensations, for he spends all his power of reflection in seeking—uselessly—a subject worthy of his future work. All the while he accumulates images of flowers, of churches, and of reflections and leaves them to dry "*dans son herbier mental.*" How to reply to the smile of things? How to find the key of their crystal palace? A first approximation of an answer can be found in Proust's description of hawthorns, suggesting as it does the pure visual magic of the object. The hawthorns of Combray which are beauty only, which inspire desire only, carry nevertheless at the tip of their stamens a painful mark of insufficiency and exile and the torment of erotic mystery. Literally, this famous description describes nothing at all. Under its flowery scattering of metaphors, it hides only the desolate affirmation of the impotence of words to render the impression produced by the flower and its perfume.

Hawthorns and Wheatfield

Je le trouvai tout bourdonnant de l'odeur des aubépines. La haie formait comme une suite de chapelles qui disparaissaient sous la jonchée de leurs fleurs amoncelées en reposoir; au-dessous d'elles, le soleil posait à terre un quadrillage de clarté, comme s'il venait de traverser une verrière; leur parfum s'étendait aussi onctueux, aussi délimité en sa forme que si j'eusse été devant l'áutel de la Vierge, et les fleurs, aussi parées, tenaient chacune d'un air distrait son étincelant bouquet d'étamines, fines et rayonnantes nervures de style flamboyant comme celles qui à

l'église ajouraient la rampe du jubé ou les meneaux du vitrail et qui
s'épanouissaient en blanche chair de fleur de fraisier...

Mais j'avais beau rester devant les aubépines à respirer, à porter devant ma pensée qui ne savait ce qu'elle devait en faire, à perdre, à
retrouver leur invisible et fixe odeur, à m'unir au rythme qui jetait leurs
fleurs ici et là avec une allégresse juvénile et à des intervalles inatten-
dus comme certains intervalles musicaux, elles m'offraient indéfiniment
le même charme avec une profusion inépuisable, mais sans me le laisser
approfondir davantage, comme ces mélodies qu'on rejoue cent fois de
suite sans descendre plus avant dans leur secret.[5]

This is then another description which describes nothing. The only
visual detail, that of the stamens, is absorbed into the vast chain of
metaphors constituting the text, transforming the hedge into series
of chapels, altars, the wayside shrines placed under the sign of the
Virgin and in the month of Mary. What is then the meaning of these
religious images? It has been a Romantic ritual and a determining
tradition from the time of Rousseau, Chateaubriand, and Lamartine to rise from nature to the creator and to finish each description
of a beautiful place by a hymn to the divine source of all purity and
all harmony. Proust does nothing of the kind. He does not believe
in God. If he tries to go past what is immediate to the senses, it is
not towards a creative and protective power. It is in himself and in
the senses that he seeks for that which is beyond the sensible object;
and in things by deepening the sensations with which they provide
him. The ecstasy which he feels before the hawthorns in their tangibili-
ty takes on a religious garb only through the association of ideas, by
a natural transfer from the hawthorns to the month of Mary, whose
celebration they perfume and, from there, to medieval pieties. The
religious images which he evokes have nothing pure, in the ascetic
sense of the term. Quite the contrary. The sensual charm of the flower,
of its perfume, with its "*blanche chair de fleur de fraisier*" introduces the
religious theme into description. The path "humming with the smell
of hawthorns" is narrow and hidden like the entrance of some church.
The narrator comes from without, where he was engaged in the quite
profane occupation of looking, through the hedge, for the possible
appearance of a little girl who interests him. Two steps further on,
he is assailed by the odor, odor of the incense, odor of the flower;

[5] Proust, I, 138.

something overwhelming is buzzing within his head. Of Gilberte, the little girl he desires, he has retained only the giddy essence. Desire has changed itself into a perfume. A sumptuously sensual adoration, born of a profound acquaintance with incarnation, has concentrated the diffuse hum, distilled the magic of springtimes, exorcised as does every great art the imprecise dispersion of desire into a real being — the perfume — "*aussi délimité dans sa forme que l'autel de la Vierge.*" Proust's feeling is not Christian, nor pietist, but sumptuously, almost insolently pagan, and Catholic also, insofar as, baroque or flamboyant, it exalts the desire for everything in order to channel it towards the impossible, before the Virgin's altar. Following the perfume and, as it were, drawn by it, images of luxury, of profusion — "*jonchées de fleurs amoncelées*" — are concentrated towards this altar and rise from there, higher still towards who knows what mystery of mediation. All the other descriptive elements are organized around this piling-up of beauty: the light, diffused like that of a stained-glass window, the branches in ogival form and the stamens like the ribs of a rood-screen and the mullions, down to the dancing motion of the great coquettes and of the bouquets. In vain does the author proclaim his incapacity to describe, for the reader, seduced, carried along, follows the current of the dominant metaphors. It is a mute symphony, an unmoving rhythm where the initial carnal sensation is found once more at the end, sublimated into "*chair de fleur de fraisier.*" like Gilberte's skin, white with rose-colored freckles. A brief transition to chase away from the sanctuary the wild roses, those naive and timid country-girls, "*au corsage rougissant qu'un souffle défait.*" Unsuited to scholarly sublimations, they are completely inappropriate here, but their incongruous entrance marks nevertheless the subsiding of mystic and sensual ecstasy which was induced by the "*bourdonnement*" of the perfume: "*J'avais beau... j'avais beau...*"

And now the implacable disillusion. Once the capricious grace of ecstasy has subsided, everything slips away. The other faculties are stricken with impotence before "*l'invisible et fixe odeur.*" It does not come from them: neither from thought "*qui ne savait qu'en faire,*" nor from sensation which can only repeat itself infinitely, nor from the motions sketched out in an imitative rhythm, nor from musical transposition. Thought declares itself incompetent; all the attempts at instinctive identification only end in an infinite repetition. Nothing will ever penetrate the *secret* of an irremediable separation.

Obsession threatens. The narrator pulls himself out of it and runs up the slope leading towards the fields. There, everything changes utterly. A new impetus raises him above the embankment, the horizon opens upon the immensity of the wheats.

> Quelques coquelicots perdus, quelques bleuets restés paresseusement en arrière, qui le décoraient çà et là de leurs fleurs comme la bordure d'une tapisserie où apparaît clairsemé le motif agreste qui triomphera sur le panneau; rares encore, espacés comme les maisons isolées qui annoncent déjà l'approche d'un village, ils m'annonçaient l'immense étendue où déferlent les blés, où moutonnent les nuages, et la vue d'un seul coquelicot hissant au bout de son cordage et faisant cingler au vent sa flamme rouge, au-dessus de sa bouée graisseuse et moire, me faisait battre le coeur, comme au voyageur qui aperçoit sur une terre basse une première barque échouée que répare un calfat et s'écrie, avant de l'avoir encore vue: "La Mer!"[6]

A magnificent vision, whose respiratory rhythm appears to annul the failure in front of the hawthorns. Such a perfect transfiguration had no need of a royally perfumed flower. No chapel here, no religious emotion. Nothing but the plain, the wheat, the sky with clouds of white fleece and soon, the sea. The sparse blooms of the slope form a border of *"mille-fleurs."* A complete medieval tapestry is drawn here. Only a few flowers are real; the rest is imaginative vision. One meager poppy with its heart of tar, its fibrous stem and the "flames" of its petals, brings forth a ship, waves, and the cry of salvation: "La Mer!"—identical for the sightseer sensing its presence and for the Ten-Thousands or the Crusaders lost in the Anatolian desert.

Is it quite the same ecstasy here as in front of the hawthorns? We have seen already that it is not religious; infinitely horizontal but not ascending; infinitely extended and no longer concentrated. An ecstasy totally pagan, coenesthesiac. But there is more to it. We have only to read the two passages in succession for common sense, which is never more than half-asleep, to make its prosaic tinkle heard. Hawthorns, it observes, flower in May. At this moment the unripe wheat forms just a light down upon the brown earth. There is no wheat field and Proust never said there was one. He only announced *"l'immense étendue où déferlent les blés, où moutonnent les nuages,"* and the sea, both sensed and found once more in the depths of cultural memory.

---

[6] *Ibid.*

Now if we bring together these two *tableaux* with opposed effects, the feeling of failure in front of the real flower and the enthusiastic evocation of the wheat field, where there is in reality only empty space, should we not conclude that opacity is not in us but in things themselves? Where there is nothing, imagination dialoguing with itself evokes a world; the only limits to its metamorphoses are those which a still classic taste imposes upon the author; however, the description of the real hawthorns describes nothing and proclaims the impossibility of description. The uneasiness of the artist in front of the real is quite expressly opposed to the sovereign imaginary freedom for which just the suggestion of a few banal flowers scattered here and there is quite enough. The barest indication unleashes what the profusion of the real held back. Such is the paradox of description in Proust. The splendor of the real world stifles, paralizes the artist instead of inspiring him: "*De l'éternel azur la sereine ironie / Accable, belle indolemment comme des fleurs...*" (these flowers which present their bouquets "*d'un air distrait*"). However, "*chaque fleur s'étalait plus belle*" in the imaginary gardens.

But Proust did not follow Mallarmé's suggestion. He described very few imaginary wheat fields and anguished his whole life long in front of the hawthorns before snatching from them their "secret." This secret does not lie, as is often believed, in interior life; nor does it lie in things nor in the relationship of man with a world which he has not made and which imposes itself upon him without his thought, his perceptions or the rhythm of his being joining this *other* creation. The remainder of the passage confirms this: once he has gone back to his hawthorns the narrator has learned nothing by his flight into the imaginary. "*Le sentiment qu'elles éveillaient en moi restait obscur et vague cherchant en vain à se dégager, à venir adhérer à leurs fleurs.*" Strangely enough, the hawthorns are compared to a "*chef-d'oeuvre*," whereas the imaginary wheat field and the sky above it and the sea beyond it, so powerfully natural in their unreality, seem to the author an undeserved gift from the Muse, a sort of diversion to his obtuse will to decipher the "masterpiece" of no creator. These inversed conceptions of art and nature lead us to suppose that facility is on the side of the imaginary, whose visions coincide so perfectly with the desire which has given rise to them, where perception leaves always a residue of imperfection like a misconnected current, an impossible contact. The artist, as we might predict, will wear himself out in order to "*adhérer à leurs fleurs.*"

The last part of this drama of creation is brief, almost a caricature. The narrator is drawn out of his contemplation by his father's voice pointing out to him a rose-colored thorn, whose exceptional color should give rise once more to his ecstasy, while aggravating his despair. But just the contrary happens. As if he had worn out his capacity for amazement, or as if he had grown out of strength in front of this new splendor, the rose color evokes in him only childish and banal, comestible images: pink biscuits, pink candles, pink Sunday dresses — almost vulgar images of expensive objects of a false luxury. They spin about, taking up once more in a frenetic mode the movement of the metaphors in the first text. They are marked with a descending sign (to speak like Breton). They spin about, but in country-clogs, going from the minuet to the *bourrée.* To be sure the narrator still talks of wonder, but he must fight against the contrary feeling, first brushed away in lengthy praeteritions ("*Et certes, j'avais tout de suite senti,*" etc....), and finally erupting with the blasphemous notion that Nature might have displayed the same naive taste as a village shopkeeper decorating a site for a religious celebration, "*surchargeant l'arbuste de ces rosettes d'un ton trop tendre et d'un pompadour provincial.*" This thorn, whose flowers seem to be smallish rosebushes in pots, "*cachés par un papier de dentelle,*" whose buds reveal the particular and irresistible essence of the thorn which "*partout où elle bourgeonnait, où elle allait fleurir, ne le pouvait qu'en rose*" — this thorn itself is without mystery. Unlike the first ones, closed as they were on their secret of profusion, the essence of this one is monochromatic. "*Elle ne pouvait être qu'en rose*" (in pink, and not pink). Dressed up in pink, in the Sunday outfit for the month of Mary, reduced to a "petit bourgeois" level, with flower-pots surrounded in paper lace, this shrub is "catholic" like all of Combray, and "*délicieux*" like pink candy; such "wonder," too fussed over, hides Proust's disappointment before this meagerness.

One can describe a natural object exactly, provided that it is right in front of one as an object, unequivocally. The description of the object thus perceived can moreover be accompanied by impressions and even dreams; it can make a place for mystery, as is shown by the astonishment in front of the raindrops as they leap about. But this mystery is not painful — only a bit curious, because the object has been posed as such, and has remained that way, because no attempt at communion has come to spoil the limpid perception. At the other extreme of human faculties, one can create an imaginary landscape from scratch, bringing before the convinced reader a sky and a wheat field, drawing out from a poppy which has already become the hull of a ship, all the expanse of the sea. Yet one cannot express, even in the most poetic language, the intimacy of the real. The text of the hawthorns suggests only the impossibility of contact. Of the hawthorns, one can say but two things: that they are there and that they are not ourselves. An unsurmountable presence-absence. Now it is precisely this secret, this suffering, which Proust would like to exorcise by art. There are scarcely any wheat fields in his work, and very few fountains; whereas when he creates (or paints) people, his imagination seems to touch the real quite without effort, his impressions of nature are neither objectively realistic nor frankly imaginary. We know the anecdote, told by Reynaldo Hahn, of Proust's ecstasy before the roses in a flowerbed. Proust himself said nothing of it. Probably no metaphor can manage to express what he feels, and which can nevertheless be expressed only by a metaphor, with the feeling of incompletion, of an impossible contact. *"Quelque chose en moi s'efforçait vainement d'adhérer à ces fleurs."*

If we were to chance an explanation, we might say that the imaginary wheat fields lead to nothing because they do not force us to go beyond ourselves. In spite of creative joy and interior well-being, the images as they surge forth do not give us the contact with the *other*, which is the dream of every descriptive author.

Styles of Naming in Honoré de Balzac and Marcel Proust[*]

JEANINE P. PLOTTEL

In everyday life connections between a name and a substance, our own name and ourselves for example, seem fortuitous, indifferent, and incidental:

> ...that which we call a rose
> By any other name would smell as sweet.

Hardly anyone takes seriously Gertrude Stein's portrait of Braque as: "Brack, Brack is the one who put up the hooks and held the things up and ate his dinner." We smile at her suggestion in *Portraits and Prayers* that Guillaume Apollinaire was: "Give known or pin ware." Yet such constructions are not completely absurd. Within a given language the link between sound and sense is unavoidable. Even supposedly unintelligible nonsense language reflects a connection between *signifiant* 'signifier' and *signifié* 'signified.' A speaker of English can detect the affectionate tone of Edward Lear's letter to his friend Evelyn Baring:

> Thrippy Pilliwinx - Inkly tinksy
> pobblebookle abblesquabs? Flosky? Beebul trimble
> flosky! Okul scratchabibblebongibo, fiddle squibble

[*] This essay was written while the author was a National Endowment Fellow, and was read in a somewhat different form at the 34th Annual Kentucky Foreign Language Conference, April 23-25, 1981.

tog/a/tog, ferrymoyassity amsky flamsky ramsky
damsky crocklefether squiggs.
Flinkywisty pomm
Slushypipp.[1]

A speaker of French can likewise experience the violence of Henri
Michaux's poem:

Il l'emparouille et l'endosque contre terre;
Il le rague et le roupète jusqu'à son drâle;
Il le pratèle et le libucque et lui barufle les ouillais;
Il le tocarde et le marmine,
Le manage rape, à ri et ripe à ra.
Enfin il l'écorcobalisse.[2]

In these texts, words are like magic incantations that create their
own references. There is no such thing in the real world as a 'pilliwinx,'
a 'flosky,' a 'crocklefether' or a 'squiggs.' In French, 'emparouille,' 'endosque,' 'rague,' 'roupète,' 'pratèle,' 'libucque,' and 'barufle' do not refer
to any actual gestures, movements, or actions. But in the language
world, these words shape whatever things, deeds, and emotions they
suggest. A pilliwinx and a 'pilliwinx' are identical. There is nothing
in emparouille that goes beyond 'emparouille.' Of course, the verbal
artefacts that result delight and charm the reader, and it is unnecessary
to postulate a serious purpose or a hidden level of meaning.

For the theorist of literature, however, the merging of nouns and
objects in these examples suggests a mechanism at the heart of naming of characters in fiction. Just as in the above examples, words and
things coincide, so in fiction or in drama, the name is identified with
the bearer of the name. An analogy can be made with the way so-
called primitive societies consider names. According to Freud, they
"do not,like us, regard names as something indifferent and conventional, but as significant and essential. A man's name is a principal
component of his personality, perhaps even a portion of his soul."[3]

At an archaic level of mental activity, name and being enter into
a metaphorical or metonymical relationship. Examples abound in the

---

[1] Quoted by John Lehmann, *Edward Lear and His World* (New York: Scribner's Sons, 1977), p. 34.
[2] Henri Michaux, "Le Grand Combat," *Qui je fus*.
[3] Sigmund Freud, *Totem and Taboo: Standard Edition of the Complete Psychological Works...* *13, 1953* (London: Hogarth Press, 1971), p. 112.

psychoanalytical literature of course, but we should not overlook the fact that writers are also keenly aware that names represent the persons themselves. Victor Hugo actually thought that names were portraits, as it were, and that names depicted persons the way words painted things. "Robespierre was a lawyer," he wrote. "His clothing and his heart are in his name."[4] It may seem far-fetched to take seriously the notion that a name is destiny, but those who change their names believe just that. Balzac, for example, was convinced that a name sealed the fate of its bearer:

> I can say that if my name were Manchot or Mangot—[in French the word means armless] and if I didn't like it or if it lacked euphony or was difficult to pronounce—all other illustrious names are easily spoken—then I should follow the examples of Guers, Voltaire, Molière and a host of other clever men. When Arouet called himself Voltaire, he planned to dominate his century...[5]

He himself experienced strongly the predestination of names. Is it a coincidence, for example, that 'Laure' was the first name of his mother, his sister, and two of his mistresses, Laure de Berny and Laure Permon, duchess of Abrantès? Of course, he was perfectly aware that 'Laure' was a sort of charm or talisman that captivated his very being:

> For me Laure is a cherished name. Up to now it has given itself up to me as a name bringing together all that is graceful, charming, friendly, brotherly and virtuous within the smallest possible space. It contains the idea of beauty, not perfect beauty—always cold and inanimate—but a beauty made more powerful by moral qualities and naive smiles of the soul. It holds the idea of unlimited confidence and of easy-going things, of openness, and of love. I appear before Laure the way I really am...
>
> From now on, the name will give me all that, but with something even sweeter and more enchanting, something or other that I cannot name.[6]

---

[4] Victor Hugo, *Pierres* (*Vers et Prose*), ed. Henri Guillemin (Geneva: Editions du Milieu du Monde, 1951), p. 189: "Il y a des noms qui sont des façons de portrait.

Etrange hasard (est-ce un hasard?) qui fait que les noms représentent quelquefois les hommes comme les mots peignent les choses. Robespierre avait été avocat. Son habit et son coeur sont dans son nom." Unless indicated to the contrary, all translations are mine.

[5] Honoré de Balzac, "Préface," *Le Lys dans la vallée*, in *La Comédie humaine et Contes Drolatiques*, II (Pléiade, Gallimard, 1959), 291.

[6] Honoré de Balzac, *Correspondance*, I, ed. Roger Pierrot (Garnier Frères, 1960), 153. Hereafter cited as *Corr.*

A few months later, on October 4, 1822, he wrote Laure de Berny: "It is in your name that I shall accomplish everything that will allow me to rise above other men. I want no other slogan than your cherished name..." (*Corr.* I, 208).

Was Balzac sincere, or was he merely engaging in a playful flirtation with words? 'Laure' or 'Laura' was also the subject of Petrarch's love lyrics in his *Canzoniere,* and a writer could be expected to exploit the overtones of courtly passion the name itself must necessarily have conveyed. But the author's fixation on the name was not merely a rhetoric exercise and reflected an actual emotion that was linked to 'Laure.' His use of the word 'devise,' 'slogan,' in connection with the name of his mother, his sister, and his two mistresses suggests that writing was an allegorical or metaphorical mode by which the first Laure, that is to say, the mother, could be put into words. The relationship he had with his own name confirms this further.

In a youthful letter to the Laure who was his sister, Honoré confessed that he often dreamt about making the name Balzac famous: "...think about my happiness if I were to make the name Balzac illustrious!" In French the sentence reads: "Songe à mon bonheur si j'illustrais le nom *Balzac*" (*Corr.* I, 36). His use of the word 'illustrer' may seem quite offhand and casual. Yet, 'illustrer' has the polyvalent meaning of illuminating, conferring distinction upon, enlightening, and elucidating. Furthermore, if we substitute the word 'books,' or 'writings' for the subject *je* in the phrase we have quoted, the phrase would read: "si mes livres/écrits/*Comédie humaine* illustraient le nom Balzac." The consequence is a metonymy in which the effect, 'books,' 'writings,' '*La Comédie humaine*' become a substitute for the self and its name. Let us also note that Honoré and Laure both contain the sound of 'l'or' 'gold,' 'money,' i.e., the commodity that obsessed Balzac If we adopt surrealist thinking for now, we can reason that since both names share *or* in common, then 'Laure' is enclosed in 'Honoré,' and that the names contain suggestions of personal title to gold and to the high honor, glory, renown, and fame it confers upon those who possess it.

In the light of recent emphasis in France on the significance of the name of the father and the body of mother for the development of the specular ego of the writer—Lacan, Derrida, Barthes, and Leclaire come to mind—I should like to suggest that for Balzac, the matronym 'Laure' represents a condensed metaphor of the imaginary function, but that the metonymical and symbolic developments of narrative are attributes of the patronym. What I mean is that the first name stands for the financial rewards and the social position that come about through writing. That, according to lacanian analysis, would probably belong to the realm of the imaginary, the reflection that is projected upon the world according to what is seen in the mirror: 'Honoré' reflects 'Laure,' the mother and her desire for wealth. 'Balzac,' on the other hand, the father's name, mediates the fictional material that will bring 'Laure,' 'or,' that is to say 'gold' to the son. The author's decision to adorn Balzac with a 'de' — an ever so slight improvement — reflects this semiosis of reality as it were.

Should this analysis seem preposterous, consider if you will Lucien de Rumbempré, who gave up his apothecary father's mortifying name, Chardon 'Thistle' and took instead his noble mother's maiden name, Rubempré, with its connotations of ribbon, field, and street. Lucien will live a double identity: one linked to the name of the mother, and the other to the name of the father. The fact that he will be loved by both men and women, by Vautrin and Esther Gobseck for example, sustains this anamorphic motif of the dual image of a 'he/she.' The change from Chardon, patronym, to Rubempré, matronym, is echoed further in the story of Lucien himself. His life reflects the well-known proverb quoted by Littré in his *Dictionnaire de la langue française*: "C'est un vrai chardon, qui s'y frotte s'y pique." Lucien's contact with high society, his rub against it, and his experience with corruption and crime will cause him to sting himself sharply, and he will end his days as if he had pricked himself on a thistle: he will hang himself in his room, a testimony to the unsuccessful metamorphosis of a Chardon into a Rubempré.

Balzac himself believed that names have occult powers and that they actually influence destiny because there are secret and unexplained concordances between life's events and people's names.[7] Indeed, most of us recognize the importance of names. Had we had the misfortune of being called Hitler or Hittler in the thirties, we would probably have proceeded exactly like the twenty-two families listed in the Manhattan telephone directory: we would have changed our name to Hilton.[8] The famous exchange between Alice and Humpty Dumpty comes to mind:

[7] *Z. Marcas* in *La Comédie humaine*, VII, 736.
[8] Robert M. Rennick, "Hitler and Others Who Changed Their Names and a Few Who Did Not," *Names*, 17, no. 3 (September 1969), 199-207.

"Must a name mean something?" Alice asked doubtfully.

"Of course it must," Humpty Dumpty said. "My name means the shape I am... With a name like yours, you might be any shape, almost.[9]

Another example from Balzac illustrates the belief in the power of names that explain why in our own generation Fred Austerlitz became Fred Astaire, Michel Igor Pechkowsky turned into Mike Nichols, Roy Scherer Fitzgerald is known as Rock Hudson, Lucy Johnson stars as Ava Gardner, and Myrtle Swayer is known to you as Nancy Walker.[10]

The name *Z. Marcas*, the title of the Balzac novella I have chosen, is an effigy of the character it designates. The hero's destiny is mapped out in advance by the very name Z. Marcas. Marcas means of course that he is a marked man, and the zigzag of the letter *Z*, the last letter of the alphabet, is a letter that stands for the sinister sharp turns and twists of his fortune, insinuating something fatal:

> Z. Marcas: the man's entire life is in the fantastic assemblage of these seven letters. Seven! The most significant cabbalistic number. The man was to die at the age of thirty-five. His life was made up of seven lustrums. Marcas. Don't you get a feeling of something precious that falls and breaks with or without any noise?[11]

While such occult beliefs are logically erroneous, psychoanalysis may confirm that their interpretation is psychologically accurate. In French, the initials Z.M. read 'Z aime,' that is to say, 'Z loves.' In the tale in question, *Z* is the first letter of Zéphirin, a name that reminds one of 'zéphir,' the poetic name for the wind and also a metaphor of love. The sound 'in' also suggests the word 'un,' 'one.' Zéphirin implies love of one, love of the self, and a love that is like the wind. The manifest story plot is like a zigzag because it depicts the rise and fall of the protagonist, erstwhile advisor to a powerful politician and the friend of two young men who live in the same pension. Furthermore, it is lined with a latent text, a coded story of inversion and perversion: the name itself is the key to the code because the Z. Marcas bears the mark of sexual deviance. The transgression inscribed in his name

[9] Lewis Carroll, *Through the Looking Glass* in *The Annotated Alice*, with an introduction and notes by Martin Gardner (New York: Clarkson Potter, 1960).
[10] David Wallechinsky, Irving Wallace, and Amy Wallace, *The Book of Lists* (New York: Morrow, 1977).
[11] *Z. Marcas* in *La Comédie humaine*, VII, 737.

is a displacement and a repression of desire. His last name begins with the last letter of the alphabet because he is the last of his lineage.

Roland Barthes's *S/Z*, a study that confirms the importance of onomastics in the case of Balzac, explained the significance of the metamorphosis of the letter *S* into the letter *Z* for a writer whose father changed 'Balssa' into 'Balzac.' He might also have pointed out that in many eighteenth-century French novels, including those of the Marquis de Sade for instance, men's names ending with the sound [-ac] were often used for professional seducers: Flourvac, Versac, and Bressac.[12] The link between the sound [-ac] and the seducer stock type seems further strengthened when we discover that Balzac gave the name Rastignac to a character he had first called 'Massiac.' It is also possible to couple the [-ac] sound with the toponymy of southern France. The model biography for Rastignac that Balzac drew up in the preface of *Une Fille d'Eve* specifies that he was born in Rastignac, in the Charente region. Of course, in French narratives, men from the Pays d'Oc are stereotyped as seducers rather more often than northern gentlemen.

The phonic elements of Balzac's names — alliteration, consonance, assonance, rhyme — could also be considered. It is doubtful whether any French novels of that period successfully reproduce Dickens' techniques of giving insignificant characters names with suddenly stopped initial or final consonants: Pott, Tiggs, Noggs, Bodds, Raddle, Wardle, Hubble, Guppy, Podsap, Tippins, Lillywick. But 'Gobseck' rhymes with 'obsèque', and 'Vautrin' suggests 'vaurien.' Onomastic games can be played with many other names in *La Comédie humaine*: Bauséant, Godefroid, Goulard, Goupil, Grancour, Grandet, Grandlieu, Grandville, Lecocq, Lemprun. Although such fictional seem to carry more meaning than "real" names, it is doubtful whether there is really a fundamental difference between these two types of names.

In *The Savage Mind*, Claude Lévi-Strauss describes the cycle of naming that exists in our culture. Plants and humans sometimes share the same name. The names Rose and Violet were borrowed from ordinary language and retain certain metaphorical connotations: fair as a rose, pink as a rose, healthy as a rose, shy, modest, or fastidious as a violet, a shrinking or a blushing violet. Such names may return

---

[12] Laurent Versini, "De quelques noms de personnages dans le roman du 18e siècle," *Revue d'Histoire Littéraire de la France*.

to ordinary language when they are joined with a so-called sacred name, that is to say, the name of an aristocrat or a celebrity. A Princess Margaret Rose is the name that was given to a certain variety of rose. The path goes from "ordinary language to proper name, from proper name to the 'sacred' language, to return finally to ordinary language."[13]

This is symmetrical to the mechanism whereby characters in literature have come to embody some psychological or social trait in our culture. A shylock is someone who lends money at high rates of interest. A romeo is not only a man given to love making, but is also a sort of man's slipper or shoe. In French a 'tartufe' is a hypocrite and an imposter. The road goes from the proper name to the "sacred" language — if we consider that the language in a literary work is indeed sacred language — to ordinary language.

Lévi-Strauss goes on to consider the naming of birds, cattle, dogs, and race horses. Of all these species, birds are the most likely to be given human christian names. The reason is that birds are perceived as forming an independent society that is analogous to human society. Yet this society is so far removed from our own society — biologically birds are so different from us that the implied resemblance of their society and ours does not constitute any threat to us:

> ...birds love freedom; they build themselves homes in which they live a family life and nurture their young; they often engage in social relations with other members of their species; and they communicate with them by acoustic means recalling articulated language. (*The Savage Mind*, p. 204)

When a man calls his pet parrot 'Pierrot,' 'Margot,' or 'Jacquot,' the relation with human society is a metonymic relation. The name of something, a person, has been used for something else, a parrot, and the two are connected insofar as they share the same names.

Now, writes Lévi-Strauss, in the case of dogs, the position is exactly the reverse. Dogs do not form an independent society, but as the very name 'domestic animal' indicates, they are a part of human society. Because their rank in this society is so low, a special series of names is reserved for them: Amor, Médor, Sultan, Fido. Cattle occupy an intermediary position. The French generally give their cattle descriptive terms, referring to the color of their coats, their bearing,

[13] Claude Lévi-Strauss, *The Savage Mind* (Chicago: University of Chicago Press, 1968), p. 212.

or their temperament: Rustaud, Rousset, Blanchette, Douce. All the dog names are like stage names, deriving from language, while the cattle names derive from speech. But both are metaphorical names, and the series they form is parallel to the names of people in ordinary life.

> Consequently when the relation between (human and animal) species is socially conceived as metaphorical, the relation between the respective systems of naming takes on a metonymical character; and when the relation between species is conceived as metonymical, the system of naming assumes a metaphorical character. (*The Savage Mind*, p. 205)

Names given race horses, not ordinary horses, but those that belong to high society's racing circles, are chosen by obeying certain special rules. The words that are used come from a language derived from learned literature and the names rarely, if ever, describe the horses themselves: Océan, Azimuth, Opéra, Belle-de-Nuit, Télégraphe, Luciole, Orvietan, Weekend, Lapis-Lazuli.

These principles are echoed in the names novelists and dramatists give their characters. Gobseck, Chardon, Chargeboeuf, Fontaine, Lupin, Maréchal, Marguerite, Minoret, Nourrisson, Portenduère, Rouget are names of *La Comédie humaine* that resemble names given dogs and cattle, insofar as they are probably meant to mark a distinctive quality of the person they designate. Names of commoners are especially descriptive and often refer to an occupation or a trade: Taillefer, Tanneur, Couturier, Crémière, Chapelier, Boucher, Chargeboeuf are other examples taken from Balzac. In these cases, relations between names and occupations are metonymical, and the names seem metaphorical. Another analogy with the naming of dogs and cattle can be shown in names that reflect physical characteristics. Proust's Beausergent and Legrandin come to mind, Balzac's Blondent and Bougrand, and Zola's Blond, La Rouquette, Mignon, and Rougon, for example.

A symmetrical relationship exists for aristocratic names. Here, the naming mechanism is like the one Lévi-Strauss describes in the case of birds. The principle is that many aristocratic French names usually have more than two syllables, and are metonymic extensions of the name of a region, a town, or a domain linked with the life of an ancestor or with the history of the family in question. Balzac, and also Proust, name their noble characters accordingly: Cadignan, Rastignac, Soulanges, Tillet, Guermantes, Villeparsis, and Agrigente are both place names and persons' names. Land and gentry have a metaphorical relationship, and names take on a metonymical cast.

Lévi-Strauss's description of the naming cycle was anticipated by Proust, who was especially fascinated with names associated with botany. Many of the pages of *A la recherche du temps perdu* reveal a great interest in the etymology of names:

> We have only to consider how often, even in the names of people, a tree is preserved, like a fern in a piece of Coal. One of our Conscript Fathers is called M. de Saulces de Freycinet, which means if I be not mistaken, a spot planted with willows and ashes, *salix et fraxinetum*; his nephew, M. de Selves combines more trees still, since he is named de Selves, *de sylvis*.[14]

Now, in the context of the novel, Brichot may seem a bore socially, but his etymologies suggest that the author selected the names of his book very carefully. Another example will confirm knowledge of onomastic mechanisms. Brichot continues a few pages later:

> One of the Forty is named Houssaye, or a place planted with hollies: in the name of a brilliant diplomat, d'Ormesson, you will find the elm, the *ulmus* beloved of Virgil, which has given its name to the town of Ulm; in the names of his colleagues, M. de la Boulaye, the birch (*bouleau*); M. d'Aunay, the alder (*aune*), M. de Buissière, the box (*buis*), M. Albaret, the sapwood (*aubier*), (I made a mental note that I must tell this to Céleste), M. de Cholet, the cabbage (*chou*), and the apple-tree (*pommier*) in the name of M. de la Pommeraye. (*SG* II, 931; *Cities* II, 107)

These examples indicate that Proustian characters may be given names that are chosen according to the same rules that determine the names of horses. What I mean is that the names of the characters may reflect mechanisms of the linguistic imagination rather than the manifestations of psychological insight.

Take the name Cambremer. It is a Norman name for Proust, and a near anagram of Camembert(t). Balzac, however, used it for a family whose origins were in Bourg-de-Batz, near Nantes in Brittany. Pierre Cambremer is the eldest of the Cambremer who are sailors from father

[14] Marcel Proust, *Sodome et Gomorrhe* in *A la recherche du temps perdu*, II, 931. Translation taken from *Cities of the Plains*, tr. C.K. Scott Moncrieff (New York: Albert and Charles Boni, 1927), II, 104. Hereafter cited as *SG* and *Cities* within the text.

to son: "Their name says it, the sea has always bent beneath them."[15] Of his own M. de Cambremer, Proust writes:

> At best one might have said of M. de Cambremer's plebeian ugliness that it was redolent of the soil and preserved a very ancient local tradition; one was reminded, on examining his faulty feature, which one would have liked to correct, of those names of little Norman towns as to the etymology of which my friend the curé was mistaken because the peasants, mispronouncing the names, or having misunderstood the Latin or Norman words that underlay them, have finally fixed in a barbarism to be found already in the cartularies, as Brichot would have said, a wrong meaning and a fault of pronunciation. (*SG* II, 913; *Cities* II, 82-83)

If, then, Proust's *Cambremer* is a mispronounced *camembert* ("un camembert mal articulé"), the name is a spoonerism, and the displacement of the sound coincides with the physical faults of both the character and the region he hails from. In a sense Proust operates as if he had internalized the antisemitic habit of identifying Jews by correlating Jewishness with physical traits, for example, the size of the nose and the color of the hair. He has turned this process to the names of the aristocracy. It is also apparent in the description of M. de Cambremer's wife, Madame de Cambremer. The camembert cheese also seems hidden here. The allusion is to a delectable and dissolving thing, a "chose fondante et savoureuse." However, this thing has been turned into a "galette normande," a Normandy cookie. We will give both the French and the English translations because the allusion cannot be caught in the English version:

> ...je regardais Mme de Cambremer. Et j'eus peine à reconnaître la chose fondante et savoureuse que j'avais eue l'autre jour auprès de moi à l'heure du goûter, sur la terrasse de Balbec, dans la galette normande que je voyais, dure comme un galet, où les fidèles eussent en vain essayé de mettre la dent. (*SG* II, 915)

> ...I was looking at Mme de Cambremer. And I had difficulty in recognizing the melting savoury morsel which I had had beside me the other afternoon at tea-time, on the terrace at Balbec, in the Norman rock-cake that I now saw, hard as a rock, in which the faithful would in vain have tried to set their teeth. (*Cities* II, 84-85)

---

[15] Balzac, *Drame au bord de la mer* in *La Comédie humaine*, IX, 888.

The "galette," the "rock-cake," may be an involuntary recollection of the Balzacian *Cambremer* and its associations with the ocean and the seaside. Furthermore, the faulty features linked to the faulty etymologies may be a coded comment to the effect that Balzac was wrong in placing a character with the name Cambremer in Bourg-de-Batz. Does the 'plebeian ugliness' of the countryside reflect Normandy or Brittany? An intertextual reading reveals that the ghost of Balzac may have determined many of the names of *A la recherche*. Most of Proust's names lend themselves to this type of analysis. They are hieroglyphic representations of their semantic and acoustic suggestions, condensations of fragmented associations that have come to be identified with the linguistic sign. Although they always seem real, perhaps even more real than actual reality, their system of reference is a linguistic system beyond empirical existence. That this is so for all of us may be reflected in the fact that proper names and proper names alone cannot be translated from one language to another.

The Literary Generations

VICTOR HUGO · WHAT IS ROMANTICISM? ·
WHAT IS SYMBOLISM? · MODERN MASTERS

Hugo, Shakespeare, the Promontory*

VICTOR BROMBERT

> Ce sera le manifeste littéraire du 19e siècle.

During his exile on the English Channel island of Guernsey, in between two visionary dialogues with the sea, Victor Hugo noticed, atop a promontory, a column commemorating a general by the name of Doyle. But who was this Doyle? The promontory and the column struck him as symbolic. England honored an obscure man of war, instead of its national poet. Hugo was scandalized. Where indeed was the column for Shakespeare?

General Doyle's column looms in Hugo's most celebratory text, *William Shakespeare*. He had agreed to write a preface for his son's translation of the complete works of the poet. But the "preface" grew so exceedingly in size and scope, it became such a dithyramb in honor of genius (his own included), that Hugo published it separately, in 1864, the year of the three hundredth anniversary of Shakespeare's birth.

The text reaches indeed far beyond its original purpose, far beyond a discussion of Shakespeare's art. Shakespeare became a pretext for

* This essay first appeared in substantially the same form with the title: "Hugo's *William Shakespeare*: The Promontory and the Infinite," in *The Hudson Review*, 34, no. 2 (Summer 1981), 249-57. © 1981 by Victor Brombert. It was read at the conference in honor of Henri Peyre, February 1981, at the Graduate School of the City University of New York.

71

dealing with what Hugo himself defined as the "mission of art" (153).[1]
This is not to deny that these heady pages provide striking observations on Shakespeare's fantasy, thematic coherence, power of vision.
He beautifully evokes the dreamlike haze, the complicity of sobs and
laughter, the carnavalesque effects of Shakespeare's theater, the plumb-
ing of the imagination, the baffling joy—"gaîté inintelligible" (236)—of
a poetic world where virgins coexist with monsters, where man sub-
consciously fears what he most desires and desires what he most fears.
Shakespeare exuberantly challenges all repressive laws, including those
of rhetoric. "Il enjambe les convenances, il culbute Aristote…" (240).
Mighty contrasts and parallels are established between the works of
Shakespeare and Aeschylus, between the figures of Hamlet and Prometheus. Hugo is an "intertextual" critic *avant la lettre*.

But the chief concern of *William Shakespeare* is not with a single
literary achievement or even a single genre. Hugo's broader ambition in having the "poet of France" (his own words!)[2] face the "poet
of England" was to provide the definitive manifesto of nineteenth-
century literature—an overwhelming assessment of the responsibility of the writer, as well as of the nature and function of genius. The
oceanic exile, as he approached his mid-sixties, meant to confront
the *hommes océans*, the unfathomable, inexhaustible creative spirits of
all time. The confrontation was of course also to be an exercise in
self-assessment.

The image of the promontory sets up the opposition of warrior and
poet. That Hugo's own father had been a general only invests column and promontory with added significance. *William Shakespeare* proclaims the demise of the warrior-hero, the entrance of the real giants
on the scene of action, the victory of the pen over the sword—in a
sense the victory of the son over the father. In the final section, the
men of violence, whose names fill history books, are seen in eclipse;
the human butchers, the "sublimes égorgeurs d'hommes" (312) who
have for so long usurped the rightful place of the thinkers, are fated
to vanish in the general twilight of the traditional hero. But this hoped-
for twilight of the "hommes de force," this liberation from hero-worship,
have their own sad grandeur. Not only is there nostalgia for the

---

[1] All numbers in parentheses refer to the Jean Massin edition of Victor Hugo's *Oeuvres
complètes*, XII (Le Club Français du Livre, 1967-1970).
[2] See the "Prospectus" for *William Shakespeare* prepared by his Belgian publishers,
Lacroix and Verboeckhoven, with important changes made by Hugo (*OC* XII, 358).

glorious old exploits, but irreverent rejoicing would be out of order. The hero deserves a worthy funeral. "N'insultons pas ce qui a été grand. Les huées seraient malséantes devant l'ensevelissement des héros" (323). Yes, jeers would be unseemly. Nonetheless, the death warrant of the warrior has been signed.

The fading away of the traditional epic virtues is seen, however, not as an end, but a beginning. It signals the emergence of a new symbolic epic. In his self-chosen political exile, Hugo develops a revolutionary ideology all of his own. The saga and aspirations of the French Revolution are read into the lines of a new providential text that sings the adventure of the human spirit and the prowess of the creative mind. Not only does genius take precedence over the hero, but the inkstand (*l'écritoire*) is destined to become the emblem of the era of ideology. "The supreme epic is being enacted" (323), announces Hugo as he glorifies *l'écritoire* and specifically relates the civilizing mission of the nineteenth century to the institution of literature. "Thought is power" (285), he declares in a spirit quite unlike that of Foucault, who, a century later, equated *savoir* and *pouvoir* in order to denounce traditional humanism. The power of Hugo's new "conquerors," of the poet-prophets who will crush the heroes, serves spiritual values. But these values, contrary to first assumptions, are not easily compatible with a historical notion of progress.

A curious anachronism, affecting Hugo's utopian vision, sets up indeed a basic contradiction. For the dynasty of men of genius, whose recognized superiority means the advent of a new era, remains totally unaffected by the notion of progress. Shakespeare is not inferior or superior to Aeschylus, Dante is not inferior or superior to Homer. The dynasty is made up of minds responsible, as it were, for their own origin and originality. "Supreme art" integrates the artist in the "region of Equals." There is no primacy among masterpieces, no hierarchy to be established between genius and genius. Each superior artist takes his place in a timeless collegium, participates in what Hugo calls the "famille dans l'infini" (242). Needless to say, this glorification of a communion in the absolute of art is altogether different from Baudelaire's or Flaubert's idealization of the free-masonry of artists which Sartre diagnosed as an escape into the realm of the posthumous. But there is no doubt that Hugo also stresses, though in a far more complex manner, the artist's ontological presence-in-death, hinting at the implicit desire to see himself, while still alive, as posthumously communing with an atemporal elite. "To be dead is to be all-powerful,"

he writes in the chapter entitled "Après la mort." This cryptic statement is clarified a few paragraphs later: "The poets being dead, their
thought reigns. Having been, they are" (295). The living man of genius
is thus a statue about to enter into the future that is already the past
(350). But this statue comes to new life. There can be no greater
glorification of the institution of literature than this apotheosis in death.
"Les poètes sont morts, leur pensée règne" (295).

   When Hugo asserts that art is more lasting than any given religion
(202), this is not to undercut the religious impulse, but to affirm more
strongly the sacerdotal function of the artist. The poet, according to
Hugo's definition is *Sacerdos magnus*. The poem "Les Mages" had already
established the vatic poet as the true spiritual leader. *William Shakespeare*
echoes this poem emphatically: "Il y a ici-bas un pontife, c'est le génie"
(170). Sharing the Symbolists' visionary and esoteric concerns, Hugo
sees the Book as a spiritual instrument, and poetry as a second creation. Interestingly, the Symbolists rarely attacked Hugo; Mallarmé
in fact reprimanded Claudel for speaking ill of him.[3] What
distinguishes Hugo from the Symbolists' as well as from Flaubert's
glorification of literature as an absolute — what separates him from
the Chevalerie du Néant as defined by Sartre — is that Hugo's notion
of "création seconde" never leads to the cult of negativity. God remains present to the mystery of art. "Dieu crée l'art par l'homme"
(170). The artist collaborates, substitutes, competes — he is never alone.
To suggest this association, Hugo invokes honored symbols and
metaphors: Socrates' demon, the bush of Moses, Numa's nymph, the
spirit of Plotinus, Mahomet's dove — above all the image of the summit (*la cime*), point of encounter between God and genius (172). Equali-
ty reigns not only between the Equals. Hugo speaks of the poet's apparent "égalité avec Dieu" (243).

   The theory of Equals leads Hugo into interesting difficulties. In
an oxymoronic juxtaposition of images, the "immovable" giants of
the human mind are defined as a "dynasty" (189). This word, referring to a succession of rulers, implies a sense of temporal continuity.
But art, Hugo insists, is precisely not successive or cumulative. The
originality of masterpieces rests in their own origin: they are always
other. Poetry is "immanent," he explains, stressing thereby the immediate and irreplaceable plenitude achieved by genuine master-

---

[3] See Henri Peyre, *Qu'est-ce que le symbolisme?* (Presses Universitaires de France, 1974),
pp. 10, 117.

pieces.[4] For art is not perfectible, not susceptible to improvement. It is governed by the absolute, exists in an eternal time, and constitutes the one exception to the law of displacement and replacement. The ideal does not budge, it knows no shifting horizons. The master poets do not outshine each other, do not climb on each other, do not use each other as a stepping stone. Each masterpiece is its own world: the result of a control that leaves no room to chance. "Il n'y a point de hasard dans la création de l'*Orestie* ou du *Paradis perdu.*" Each creation is the offspring of will. "Un chef-d'oeuvre est voulu" (198).

But how compatible is this notion of atemporal plenitude with the belief in historical process and progress to which Hugo is so strongly committed? Hugo comes out rather categorically: "L'art n'est pas susceptible de progrès intrinsèque" (197)—a statement which leads him to make an important distinction between art and science. If one looks for progress, he maintains, one must turn to scientific achievements. Gutenberg's invention of the printing press, for instance, holds out promise of perpetual movement and uninterruptible progress. It can happen, of course, that the distinction between science and art is illustrated by one and the same figure. "Pascal savant est dépassé; Pascal écrivain ne l'est pas" (201). For in the realm of science, contrary to that of art, all is relative and subject to the principle of replacement. There all is subject to linear time and chance; discoveries are the result of endless gropings and productive errors. Each successive scientist casts previous achievements into relative oblivion. Science goes on ceaselessly erasing itself, but these are fruitful erasures—"ratures fécondes" (198).

The contrast between the linear time of science and progress, and the timeless space of art, leads to another major difficulty that nettles Hugo during his exile years, as he tries to reconcile his beliefs in the autonomy of art with a deepening interest in the cause of Revolution. Having assumed, after 1851, a prophetic political role, Hugo felt increasingly the need to neutralize the charge that he had been one of the earliest proponents of art for art's sake. Of course, Hugo continued to believe in the primacy of form. As late as 1864, in a piece called "Les Traducteurs," he asserts that each and every stylistic detail has metaphysical implication (375). But that section of *William*

---

[4] On the theological echoes of the word "immanent" in Hugo's vocabulary, see Yves Gohin, *Sur l'emploi des mots immanent et immanence chez Victor Hugo* (Archives des Lettres Modernes, 1968), no. 94.

Shakespeare entitled "Le Beau serviteur du Vrai" is clearly designed to dispel the persistent image of its author as an advocate of the self-serving function of art.

The coining of the expression *l'art pour l'art* was indeed often attributed to Hugo. After all, he could not deny that, some thirty-five years earlier, in the first preface to *Les Orientales*, he had proclaimed that there are neither good nor bad subjects, that the poet is free and has no accounts to give, that a so-called "useless" book of "pure poetry" needed no justifying. But much as he liked to have been the first in anything, he hated to be trapped by his own formulas. And so, in *William Shakespeare*, the formula *l'art pour le progrès* is proposed as a loftier one. The mission of men of genius, we are told, is the forward march of humanity.

An even more paradoxical development on the usefulness of the Beautiful was finally not included in *William Shakespeare*. In pages entitled "Utilité du Beau" Hugo tried to adapt the aesthetic views he held in the eighteen thirties to his more recent political and metaphysical concerns—a somewhat acrobatic task. By means of curiously modern-sounding remarks on the hidden intentionality of the text, as well as Victor Cousin-inspired ideas concerning the identity of the Beautiful and the Ideal, Hugo boldly sketched a theory about the utility of the useless,[5] which foreshadows the rich developments, to be found in *Les Travailleurs de la mer*, on the mysterious ways God makes himself manifest in the apparently destructive toiling of the sea.

Hugo in fact goes far beyond establishing a relation between aesthetic pleasure and virtue. He places all of nineteenth-century art squarely in the service of Revolution. Hence, the baffling association of genius with progress. First we were asked to see men of genius in a timeless scheme (though Hugo cautiously uses the expression "intrinsic progress"). We are now told that God continues to add to the great roster of exceptional poets "when the needs of progress require it," that the function of genius quite specifically is to espouse and promote the Revolution. The benefit is supposedly mutual. The cause of the Revolution in turn serves the cause of art—and, beyond art, the spiritual needs of man. "Never have the faculties of the human

[5] The difficult relationship between aesthetic and political theory in this text have been intelligently discussed by Jacques Seebacher, in "Esthétique et politique chez Victor Hugo: L'Utilité du Beau," *CAIEF*, March 19, 1967, pp. 233-46.

soul, deepened and enriched by the meaningful ploughing of revolutions, been profounder and loftier" (194). The nineteenth century, which in this optimistic view marks the coming of age of humanity, also confers a new role on the writer. The political apocalypse signifies a new beginning, imposes new obligations, provides new opportunities. What Hugo is really saying is that political commitment defines the modern writer's originality.

The association of modern genius and Revolution is thus spelled out in apparent contradiction to art's supposed freedom from the laws of historical progress. In a preliminary note, Hugo went so far as to write: "Poets, above all, are devoured by the idea of progress" (345). The nineteenth century, according to Hugo, is without precedent. It is the offspring of an idea. And that idea—the Revolution—is the grand climacteric of humanity, the turning point in a providential plan in which good can take the form of the hydra, and every thinker carries in him something of the *monstre sublime*. Hence Hugo's fascination with the figure of Marat. But the monstrosity of Revolutionary violence (for that is what above all obsesses Hugo) also explains the dream of transcending revolution, of seeking higher harmony through an exit from history, through the negation of the destructive principle associated with any linear historical scheme. This dream of an exit from sequential and violence-ridden history is of course Enjolras' message, or rather sermon, from atop the barricade at the end of *Les Misérables*, as it will be the subject of Gauvain's visionary meditation at the end of the historical novel *Quatrevingt-Treize*.

What then is this notion of genius—at once committed to change and permanence, free from the laws of temporality, yet serving God's mysterious will-in-history? Hugo appears to reject any system. His theory of literature pretends to be thoroughly untheoretical. (Shakespeare is a genius, not a system" [268].) Yet the underlying pattern is clear. It is that of self-cancelling contradiction. Great art brings into fruitful and self-effacing clash will and predestination; it is based on what Hugo called "double reflection," the faculty of seeing the two sides of things simultaneously. Shakespeare is *totus in antithesi*, mirroring the ubiquity of opposites (236-37). The connivance between genius and the supernatural is the corollary of this insight into the "universal antithesis." The suggestion is that genius is more than human: a universal spirit, an "âme cosmique" (226).

Recurrent sea images convey the sense of power and of mystery, the sea changes that are part of the games of infinity, the fecund interplay of anger and of peace. The *hommes océans*, the creative and revelatory poets who hear and understand what the mouth of darkness has to say, they know the "intoxication of the high sea." Reflecting the divine principle, they are "All in One" in their inexhaustibly varied monotony" (159). The sea metaphor projects a double axis: "The horizontal expanse (analogue of the desert image associated with the voice of the prophet and a transfiguring fall); the depth to be plumbed, inversion of the image of an elating ascent. Each genius, according to Hugo, is an abyss as well as a summit. Hence, the symbol of the promontory, specifically associated with the apocalyptic vision of Patmos — the frightening "promontoire de la pensée," from which the visionary artist perceives the shadow (224). Revealingly, Hugo's list of the world's fourteen great men (the fifteenth remains modestly unnamed) includes at least five prophets or biblical figures: Job, who achieved greatness at the bottom of his spiritual pit; Isaiah, the "mouthpiece of the desert"; Ezekiel, the fierce "demagogue" of the Bible; Saint John, the man of Patmos, who faced revelatory violence with the tongue of fire and the "profound smile of madness"; Saint Paul, who, on the road to Damascus, fell into truth (173-83). And it is telling that the last two words of *William Shakespeare* should be the name of Jesus Christ.[6]

Three elements remain constant in Hugo's portrayal of genius: symbolic power, religious awe, and *démesure* or excess. The potential for symbolization appears boundless. It is as though all of human experience could be contained in a single brain. Elsewhere, Hugo wrote that a poet is a "world" locked up in a human skull. "Un poète est un monde enfermé dans un homme." Some of the chief tenets of symbolism are affirmed in *William Shakespeare*: the poet's intuition of the occult sense of existence, the heroic quality of poetic vision, the gospel of correspondences, the belief that the world is a text that speaks to us but needs to be deciphered, semiotic links between the realms of the visible and the invisible binding infinite manifestations to a single principle. The Symbolist poets, though often made uneasy by his overpowering voice, were perfectly aware of Hugo's contribution. Baudelaire had earlier praised Hugo's ability to decipher the great dictionary of nature, and to dig into the inexhaustible treasure of the *universal analogy*.[7]

---

[6] The association of Jesus and the artist-genius is part of the Romantic tradition. See Balzac's "Des Artistes," first published in *La Silhouette* in 1830 (*OC*, Conard, 38, pp. 351-60).

[7] Charles Baudelaire, *Oeuvres complètes* (Pléiade, 1963), p. 705.

The relation between this pervasive symbolization and a yearning for the *sacred* is obvious. Hugo stresses the poet's sense of religious terror. "He shudders at his own depth" (242). The *vates* or prophetic voice surrenders to an all-consuming "religious meditation." Even in the great poet's lighter moments, one can detect the pressures of the unknown, the all-powerful *horreur sacrée* of art. Their vision hurts our minds' eyes, much as Bishop Myriel's goodness in *Les Misérables* hurts and saves Valjean's conscience.[8] The breath of genius, the "souffle du génie," is defined as the "respiration of God through man" (302). Appropriately, the section that concludes with the metaphor of the promontory ("Un génie est un promontoire dans l'infini") evokes the elation of gazing at a beclouded headland jutting out into the sea, eerily inviting one to perambulate among the winds.

This image of the promontory takes on a special meaning if one recalls that one of Hugo's grandest animistic metaphors is that of "Le pâtre promontoire au chapeau de nuées," that the prophet's revelatory activity is repeatedly modelled on Moses' ascent of the mountain, and that shepherd and promontory are indeed featured in the important poem "Magnitudo parvi."[9] But more significant still is the title of Hugo's striking text on the relation of genius to dreams, *Promontorium somnii*. This symbolic promontory of dreams — the name evokes a lunar summit Hugo glimpsed through Arago's telescope at the observatoire — proposes itself as a mental topography of visionary extravagance ("allez au-delà extravaguez"), of *fureur sacrée*, of poetic madness. In *Promontorium somnii*, Hugo in fact inverts the old adage: "*Quos vult AUGERE Juppiter dementat*" — God makes mad those he wants to elevate (464).

These themes of extravagance and madness bring us closer to Hugo's definition of the nature of genius. For the most important characteristic of genius, from an aesthetic point of view, is what Hugo calls *démesure* — mad excess, overabundance, boundless prodigality. Shakespeare recognizes no limits, Aeschylus makes of sea and mountains the colossal protagonists of his drama. Genius simply cannot be measured by the restrictive norms of that "good taste" against which Hugo had inveighed ever since the preface to *Cromwell* and the

---

[8] The image is explicit. Hugo writes in *William Shakespeare*: "Votre intelligence, ils la dépassent, votre imagination, il lui font mal aux yeux" (262).

[9] See "Pasteurs et troupeaux" and "Magnitudo Parvi" in *Les Contemplations* (*OC* IX, 287, 196-214).

polemical pages of *Notre-Dame de Paris*. Impossible exhaustion is the corollary of impossible sobriety. Great art is orgiastic, it has profound affinities with the carnival, the Mardi Gras (216). Sacerdotal obscenity is at the heart of Aristophanes. The mysterious ferocious laughter of art is a manifestation of an excess of sap.[10]

The sexual connotations of *démesure* are aggressively obvious — especially when related to the sterility of criticism. Genius offends the academician as the stallion offends the mule (214). Chastity is the eunuch's pride; the seraglio displeases the impotent visitor. For genius is a condition of "orgiastic omnipotence" (241), a steady intercourse between "lewdness and thought," a movable orgy with the "bacchant" called inspiration (215, 239).

In rhetorical terms, the praise of *démesure* calls for a defense of hyperbolae, declamation, amplification. Hugo challenges the castrating prescriptions of rhetoric. Aeschylus' metaphors, Hugo claims, are outsized; his tragic effects are like blows struck at the spectators (215). What value then is there in textbook wisdom, what value in classifications and prescriptions, when deeper wisdom lies in such extravagance? Ever since his early pages on Mirabeau's eloquence, Hugo has been aware of the protean metamorphoses of his own images.[11] But this theory and praxis of metaphorical profusion serve a deeper fusion.

The praise of excess has indeed political implications. *Bon goût* is denounced not merely as a form of gastritis (241), but as submissiveness to Law and Order. Dethroned "good taste" is treated as a *ci-devant* form of divine right. Hugo equates the question of Taste with the question of Power. Ironizing on sobriety as nothing but a servant's qualification, Hugo sees a certain type of criticism as a literary police force faithfully serving the establishment, the "grand parti de l'Ordre" (260). But there are philosophical implications as well. Hugo's stance could, by anticipation, be called anti-structuralist. Hostile to all reductive schemes, he proclaims the irreducible uniqueness of genius. Just as divinity for Hugo is the "moi de l'infini," so genius is a "personnalité absolue." Hugo's cult of the singular voice means that, even though entire periods can be summed up by one figure

[10] Baudelaire, it is interesting to note, thought that excess was Hugo's natural domain: "L'excessif, l'immense, sont le domaine naturel de Victor Hugo; il s'y meut comme dans son atmosphère natale" (*OC*, p. 709).

[11] See Jean Gaudon, "Vers une rhétorique de la démesure: *William Shakespeare*," *Romantisme*, 3 (1972), 78-85. Hugo's text "Sur Mirabeau" (1934) appears in *OC* V, 192-221.

(320), the true identity of a great work is with itself. There can be only one Homer. Hence, the inappropriateness of all poetics. How applicable, Hugo asks, are the poetics of the *Odyssey* to Milton's *Paradise Lost?* Awe is the beginning of all sound criticism. It is as though poetics had to be reinvented to account for each great text. No matter what the laws of a given genre may be, a superior work of art is always a transgression, and this transgression instills fear in the author himself: "Il a horreur de sa profondeur" (242).

This fear of transgression is the obverse of the *pro-domo* defense of orgiastic creativity. The prohibition against haunting the "tavern of the sublime" (238) is very much perceived in terms of a self-glorification, which ends up by converting God himself into Supreme Poet. The motto *totus in antithesi* — the characteristic of Hugo's own art — applies first of all to divine creation (236-37). It is the perpetual yes *and* no which allows the man of genius not only to fill and fulfill an entire century, but to participate in the tragic delight "volupté tragique" (of all of nature). Hugo's own apotheosis is inscribed in the tribute to Shakespeare, as he sees him(-self) bending and weeping over human suffering, and achieving his transfiguration as he stands up, tender and terrible, above the *misérables* of this world (271).

Genius is ultimately associated with sacred lasciviousness, the "rut universel" of perpetual becoming (215). And this exuberance of all creation, this terrifying hilarity which is the tragic laughter of art as well as the ominous laughter from below ("Le mot pour rire sort de l'abîme" [216]), perhaps provides the deepest link between genius and the prophecies of history. For Hugo, the hour of laughter is indeed the hour of Revolution. And Revolution is that reading of the text of history which most clearly establishes God as preexistent, co-existent, and immanent author-genius mirrored or postulated (mimesis and poiesis) in the literary text.

Baudelaire and Delacroix:
The Celebration of a Mystery

BETTINA KNAPP

For Charles Baudelaire, to peer deeply into one of Eugène Delacroix's canvases was the celebration of a mystery; it was to witness a dramatic unfolding lived in a space/time continuum. What Baudelaire absorbed as his eye encompassed a picture's surface and depth, wandered about in form, color, and melody — longingly, lovingly, reverently, or rebelliously and hatefully — was a mirror image of his own pure yet tainted soul.

Baudelaire's critical appraisals of Delacroix's paintings, which appeared in his *Salon de 1845, Salon de 1846, L'Exposition universelle de 1855, Salon de 1859,* and *L'Oeuvre et la vie de Delacroix,* are not mere evaluations, although they fulfill this goal. They are in themselves creative acts, distillations of a spiritual adventure — Baudelaire's adventure. Like catalysts, Delacroix's paintings triggered Baudelaire's vision, prolonged, enriched, and expanded it. Form became a means of unifying the abrading conflicts which otherwise tore at him; color activitated an emotional climate veering from ecstasy to horror, shearing his quietude or impressing harmony upon his soul; tones, vibrations exuding from the figures, rhythms, and hues, seemed to send mellifluous or strident sounds into the atmosphere, flaying or comforting his psyche.

Delacroix's paintings with their *dramatis personae* and their scenarios sparked electric currents in Baudelaire, bringing viewer and canvas, subject and object, into close proximity.[1] The isomorphic relation-

---

[1] Charles Baudelaire, *Oeuvres complètes* (Pléiade, 1961). All quotations are from this edition; page numbers indicated within parentheses in the text.

ship that ignited as a result, between animate and inanimate worlds, activated an entire mnemonic sphere in Baudelaire, fusing "drama and reverie" as well as space and time (p. 970). That Baudelaire should have used the word "drama" so frequently in connection with Delacroix's paintings is not surprising. As a young boy he had dreamed of the stage and being an actor; as a young man he had even written plays, *Idéolus* and *The Drunkard*. In time, however, he wholly yielded to the power of the directly written word with its clusters of images, colorations, tonalities, complexes of vibrations, hieratic or serpentine gestures that worked more powerfully upon his soma and psyche than did the more removed world of the theater. Still, the drama and its conventions were never entirely abandoned; they remained at the heart of his work and particularly of his art criticism. Dialogue therefore was a potent factor between poet and painter: Delacroix's canvases spoke to Baudelaire, and he identified with their protagonists — Dante and Virgil, Mary Magdalene, Ovid, Sardanapalus, the Crusaders. When his eye immersed itself in a painting, it rested within its visible and invisible spheres, bringing mysterious forces to work upon his creative venture.

Baudelaire's art criticism sprang from subjective experiences: forays into a private world, distillations and articulations of affinities that existed inchoate within him (p. 882). When Baudelaire approached a Delacroix painting, it was as a *mystai* of old, with reverance and awe, and with the hope of transcending the dualities consuming his flesh. Well versed in the writings of Heraclitus, Pythagoras, Meister Eckhart, Jacob Boehme, Swedenborg, and the alchemists, Baudelaire searched for harmony and balance, that primordial Oneness that existed prior to the Creation, when division and conflict were unknown. This longed-for condition may be psychologically viewed as a *regressus ad uterum*: a desire to step back into a Paradisical childlike period when there were no polarities (man/woman, good/evil, solid/liquid, hot/cold) to destroy an all-embracing sense of belonging, when self-consciousness had not yet been born nor the limitations of individual life been realized.

Considered from the mystic's point of view, Delacroix's canvases afforded Baudelaire an ideal condition, absolving him of the sordid world of contingencies which he detested, since it brought him *ennui* and *spleen*, enabling him to ascend to celestial spheres. Rising to heavenly heights in this world, however, always entails descent, and with each return to earth, Baudelaire's pain and torment were also renewed. What might otherwise be described as a highly negative condition, also held its fascination for Baudelaire, who wrote of the excitement involved in flagellation, whipping, expiation. Contraries inflamed him; their friction caused heat and passion. Departure and return, death and transfiguration — opposites in general — took on an altogether different cast: they were part of a mystical adventure that enriched his visionary world as poet and critic. Delacroix's thick pigments, his broad, quick, and sometimes frenetic brush strokes, as well as his more subdued and tender ones, enhanced Baudelaire's sensate world, endowing it with rapture and pathos — paving the way for the *surnaturel* which he defined in *Fusées* as "the general color and accent, that is, intensity, sonority, limpidity, vibrativity, depth and resonance in time and space" (p. 1256). The *surnaturel* for Baudelaire did not imply hyperemotionalism or undisciplined inspiration, conditions so prevalent among the Romantics. Rather, it meant a blending of fire and water — of passion with detachment, flamboyance mitigated by order and symmetry. Both vision and technical excellence were needed to create the work of art, not one without the other.

The *surnaturel* and all it implied for Baudelaire were operational in Delacroix's canvases: giving rise to a synesthetic reaction. Synesthesia is a literary technique, but it is also a device that aids the mystic to experience higher spheres of consciousness. It implies a correspondence between the senses: the visual may be heard, smelled, touched, and tasted, or the tasted may be heard, seen smelled, and felt, and so on. Baudelaire experienced synesthesia as a giant awakening, a psychic happening, a rising of forces within his unconscious which affected his sensory system, soothing or shattering it. It also enabled him to experience simultaneity of sense impressions in a timeless dimension: he could, therefore, perceive the work of art at its inception, as it came into being, and in so doing relive a preformal experience, contacting and palping a panoply of signs, species, forgotten or nonexistent languages. Interestingly enough, it was in his *Salon de 1846* that Baudelaire first mentioned his theory of *correspondances*, an amplification of the synesthetic experience in a quotation of E.T.A. Hoffmann's *Kreisleriana*.

> It is not only in dreams, or in that mild derlirium which precedes sleep, but it is even awakened when I hear music — that perception of an analogy and an intimate connection between colours, sounds, and perfumes. It seems to me that all these things were created by one and the same ray of light, and that their combination must result in a

wonderful concert of harmony. The smell of red and brown marigolds above all produce a magical effect on my being. It makes me fall into a deep reverie, in which I seem to hear the solemn, deep tones of the oboe in the distance. (p. 884)[2]

Form, color, and music inhabit Baudelaire's world of *correspondances* and infinite analogies linearly and in a fourth dimension. Form, reproduced on the picture plane, is visible as an image — or images — and perceived as an idea. The intellect, a part of both soma and psyche, works on the emotions, awakening still another dimension of being. Color may also be said to take the same route: when incorporated in form, it too inhabits a spatial zone. Its emotional level, however, is frequently more highly charged than that of lines, cubes, circles, or whatever the compositional structure: the vibrations being ejected from the colors in unequal rhythmic patterns electrifying the viewer's psyche at multiple rates. Whether defined by Newton or Goethe, colors have their emotional equivalents and this was particularly important to Baudelaire. Reds, blues, greens, violets, blacks, yellows, ushered in specific emotional responses: serenity, passion, melancholia, moribidity, and the like. Music, for the mystic, inhabits the world of contingencies and the fourth dimension. Invisible to the naked eye, its harmonious or discordant tones exist in waves, subatomic particles, as mathematical sequences inhabiting both an outer and inner space/time dimension. Sonorities may be apprehended by an individual as a prolongation of a psychic state, or as detached and cerebral modulations. Baudelaire frequently wrote of the musicality Delacroix's paintings inspired in him and of their effect on his "ultra-sensitive nerves" (p. 974), flaying or relaxing them. The musicality of color and form helped him experience the sculptured three-dimensional structures he observed in Delacroix's canvases, intuit the historical scenes depicted in abstract and visceral dimensions.

Visual form, archetypal images, signs and symbols of every kind, had impressed themselves upon Baudelaire's mind's eye since earliest childhood. Perhaps this aspect of his personality had developed so powerfully because both his father and his mother had painted and sketched; and he had become accustomed as he grew older to spending long hours haunting museums and painters' studios — intoxicated,

---

[2] *The Mirror or Art: Critical Studies by Baudelaire*, tr. Jonathan Mayne (New York: Anchor Books, 1956). Most of the translations come from this volume; some were quoted directly and others in a slightly altered form.

he wrote, by the effect that the rendition of three-dimensional form and color had upon him: "The entire universe is nothing but a storehouse of images and signs to which imagination will give a relative place and value" (p. 1122). Interestingly enough, Baudelaire's art criticisms were among his earliest publications (the *Salon de 1845* and his poem "A une Créole") and were more extensive than his literary evaluations.

Archetypal images are endowed with powerful energy charges. As primordial visualizations, which amorphously exist in the collective unconscious, they frequently surface with such violence that their impact disorients the individual, affording him "luxury, calm, and sensuous pleasure" as well as excoriating sequences. Baudelaire's inner eye seized the archetypal images depicted in Delacroix's canvases, apprehended them, aggressively sometimes, piercing through form, color, and tonality, and, in so doing, created his own vision, his own dream.

Baudelaire's sense of sight functioned potently intensely: the eye of the seer or visionary takes from the cosmos at large what it needs to nurture an interior dimension. As an instrument of the intellect, it possesses its own soul and in this respect is comparable to what mystics allude to as Siva's Third or Cosmic Eye. It can leap into solar and lunar expanses, float along watery climes, embed itself in color and form, penetrate temporal and atemporal dimensions. Similarly, Baudelaire's eye could both indwell and outdwell, work continuously in shifting patterns and zones, absorbing, ejecting, distilling tangential and cyclical matter, transmuting a nonverbal world into the word — a feat of magic, to be sure, which led Baudelaire to continue his courageous and harrowing exploration into sacred and infernal domains.

Delacroix might be termed Baudelaire's "mystical brother." At the outset of his career he had wanted to be a poet and dramatist and had even written some tragedies. In time, however, the world of art strongly beckoned to him. Orphaned while still young, he first enrolled at Pierre Guérin's studio (1815), then for financial reasons transferred to the less costly Ecole des Beaux-Arts. Like Baudelaire, Delacroix refused to rely solely on the fire of inspiration; although at times he painted frenziedly, in bursts of "fury," method, order, discipline, were always his. He spent long hours studying and copying the old masters (Rubens, Michelangelo, Veronese, the Venetian School, and many others), doing research in relative color values, their historical use and chemical components.[3] Before he started to paint, he always saw to it that his brushes were clean and his colors laid out beforehand; studies prior to the inception of a canvas were always made. But passion and fire were also in him. When, for example, his friend Théodore Géricault invited him to see the still-unfinished *Raft of the Medusa* (exhibited in 1819), Delacroix's reaction was explosive: "So violent was the impression that it made upon me on leaving his studio I began running like a madman and ran through the streets the whole way."[4]

Like Baudelaire, Delacroix had an extraordinary visual sense. In 1825 when he went to England he was captivated by the canvases of Constable. Upon his return to Paris he seemingly repainted large chunks of his *Massacre at Chios* and *The Death of Sardanapalus* (1826), adding touches of flamboyant and violent color that enraptured him but enraged the conventional French art critics. A trip to Morocco (1832) further enriched his already powerful imagination, endowing his future canvases with lustrous semitropical and tropical colors as well as with the veiled forms of women whose concealment only seemed to increase their sensuality and desirability — *Women of Algiers* (1834), *The Jewish Wedding* (1839). A trip to Belgium and Holland (1838) impressed Rubens' fleshy and massive forms upon his consciousness and provided him with even more strikingly outrageous — so the critics suggested — coloration.

Delacroix was vilified for his innovations by those jealous of his artistic ability or simply oblivious to his genius. Any kind of excuse was used to destroy him. Etienne-Jean Delécluze, critic for *Débats*, called his *Dante and Vergil* (1822) "not a picture but a regular hash!" (*tartouillade*).[5] Some stated he could not draw. Such charges, however, were the culmination of a longtime quarrel between the "colorists" and the "draughtsmen," the "Poussinists" and the "Rubenists." Delacroix wrote:

> The forms of a model, be they a tree or a man, are only a dictionary to which the artist goes in order to reinforce his fugitive impressions, or rather to find a sort of confirmation of them. Before nature itself, it is our imagination which makes the picture.[6]

[3] Herbert Read, *The Meaning of Art* (New York: Praeger Paperbacks, 1972), p. 183.
[4] Dorothy Bussy, *Eugène Delacroix* (London: Duckworth, 1912), p. 8.
[5] Bussy, p. 33.
[6] Claude Roger Marx and Sabine Cotte, *Delacroix* (New York: George Braziller, 1971), p. 29.

Color, form, and texture nourished Delacroix's imagination and sense of wonder, filled his tempestuous yet serious temperament with new approaches to painting, which he noted in his *Journal* (1848):

> I am at my window and I see the most beautiful landscape: the idea of a line doesn't occur to me. The lark sings, the river shimmers like a thousand diamonds, the leaves murmur; where are the lines that produce these charming sensations?[7]

Delacroix also had his supporters: Théophile Gautier, writing for *La Presse* and *La Revue de Paris*; Gustave Planche of *La Revue des Deux Mondes*; Jules Janin for *Le Constitutionnel*, whom Baudelaire quoted in his *Salon de 1846*, had predicted as far back as 1822 that judging from the canvas *Dante and Vergil in Hell*, Delacroix's future would be a great one.

Delacroix's "concision," "intensity," and "concentration," Baudelaire wrote, enabled him to reach bedrock: within the *temenos*, or sacred center, out of which he constructed his pictorial edifice frequently pyramidal in structure, existed a storehouse of color combinations and harmonic overtones (p. 1126). In describing Delacroix's inner artistic balance, his steady keel, Baudelaire cited Emerson: "The hero is he who is immovably centered" (p. 1116).[8] The balance that Delacroix possessed allowed him to reach out into space, to seize hold of those forces that served him best, to knead and mold and finally bring them into existence in identifiable form.

It was Delacroix's extraordinary imagination that earned Baudelaire's greatest admiration, all else being subordinate to this one fulgent force. For this reason, he believed that Delacroix belonged to the elect: "Heaven belongs to him as does hell, as does war, as does Olympus, as does voluptuousness" (p. 1122). Imagination during the seventeenth and eighteenth centuries had been deprecated by such philosophers and metaphysicians as Pascal, Spinoza, and Malebranche, and this had caused a concomitant shift in the outlook of art critics and practitioners. Art had evolved into a copy of nature, an ornament, a diversion, and was no longer an evocative, suggestive feat of magic that transported the beholder into primeval or sacred domains. For Baudelaire, the work of Delacroix, the *peintre-poète*, coexisted with mystery, was suffused in an acausal world of probabilities and potentialities.

[7] *Ibid.*, p. 67.
[8] Emerson's essay is entitled "The Conduct of Life."

Imagination, "the Queen of Faculties" for Baudelaire, did not imply the replication of realistically viewed images, a technique used with felicity by the Neoclassicists and Idealistic schools of painting — David, Ingres, Vernet, Chasseriau, Ary Scheffer (p. 1036). Imagination was the way of reforming and shaping eidetic vision, of perceiving the outer world in terms of inner subjective experience, thereby freeing the painter from the constraints imposed upon him by the phenomenological world and its conventional codes and concepts. Imagination for Baudelaire was an *aggressive* faculty. It comported movement in time and space, an ability to depict physical action as well as calling and recalling past, present, and future. Imagination thus might be compared in some ways to meditation techniques used by Hindus and Buddhists for centuries. The *yantra* image, for example, the center of visual focus, activates the unconscious, arousing archetypal images in the process, those "unknown motivating dynamisms of the psyche,"[9] which alter mood and temper, temporal and atemporal conditions, bringing on the *numinosum*. As Baudelaire stated:

> It [imagination] is both analysis and synthesis... It is that, and it is not entirely that. It is sensitivity, and yet there are people who are very sensitive, too sensitive perhaps, who have none of it. It is imagination that first taught man the moral meaning of colour, of contour, of sound and of scent. In the beginning of the world it created analogy and metaphor. It decomposes all creation, and with the raw materials accumulated and disposed in accordance with rules whose origins one cannot find save in the furthest depths of the soul, it creates a new world, it produces the sensation of newness. As it created the world (so much can be said, I think, even in a religious sense), it is proper that it should govern it. (p. 1038; tr., p. 234)

Imagination implies philosophical and spiritual factors: aspiration — the awareness of aerated or nonformal spheres, invisible sound and light vibrations, rhythmic patterns. Imagination presupposes intuition — the experience of a transpersonal dimension that encourages leaps into a pleromatic realm, there to face the void — that terrible maw, the mystic's nothingness, zero or naught. Once the image is implanted in the creator's mind, it evolves, grows, expands, takes on momentum, crystallized in the canvas or the poem. Imagination involves a kind of mutation between the "real" landscape envisaged by the Neoclassical academic painters (who sought to replicate objects

[9] Edward Edinger, "An Outline of Analytical Psychology," unpublished, p. 12.

by fixing their structure and determining their number and color) and the "unreal" sphere of the imaginative artist (who feeds on both inner and outer space, replete with musical and visual discords and harmonies).[10]

Paintings such as *Mary Magdalene in the Desert, Marcus Aurelius's Last Words, Dante and Vergil in Hell, The Taking of Constantinople by the Crusaders, Ovid Exiled among the Scythians, The Death of Sardanapalus* were manifestations of Delacroix's formidable imagination — his genius — at work; for Baudelaire, the celebration of a living mystery.

[10] René Huygue, *Les Puissances de l'image* (Flammarion, 1965), pp. 129-30.

Anteros, Son of Cain?

JOHN W. KNELLER

The Chimeras of Gérard de Nerval continue to fascinate us because they are both hermetic and startlingly clear. These sonnets invite us to wonder about their sources, their genesis, and their hidden meanings. They move us by the cogency of their own poetic statement.

Unlike Wordsworth, Coleridge, Shelley, Hugo, and Baudelaire, Nerval did not write about theories of poetry. Even if he had, he probably would have departed from the generalizations and principles he had developed as he went about the practice of poetry. Here and there throughout his prodigious and varied literary output he scattered traces which have been pursued with sometimes successful and sometimes uncertain results. If it is true that no gap separates Nerval's sources from his writings — or his writings from one another — it is also true that none of the mythological, historical, or biblical figures that stand out in his poems conforms to the accepted characterization of that figure. Their names may well be Artemis, Amor, Phoebus, Orpheus, Isis, or Daphne, or even Caesar, Pilate, or Christ — in which instances we had better know our Sir James George Frazer or our Bible. And if their names are Myrtho, Kneph, Lusignan, Biron, or Delfica, we ought to scurry to more recondite source books. To attempt, however, to resolve these figures into their antecedents is to be guilty of the genetic fallacy.

No belief or attitude of Nerval exists prior to or after any of his works. His figures are new. At the moment of creation, they assume an existence quite apart from their historical, literary, or mythological models and quite apart from the poet himself.

Although Nerval developed no theory of poetry, he did leave us two important passages which can serve as lanterns to guide us through the labyrinth of images in *The Chimeras*.

At the end of *Aurelia*, in the "Memorabilia," he writes:

> I resolved to fix my dream-state and learn its secret. I wondered "Why should I not break open those mystic gates, armed with all my will, and master my sensations instead of being subject to them? Is it not possible to overcome this enticing, formidable chimera, to lay down a rule for the spirits of the night which make game of our reason?"[1]

This passage states the author's purpose in writing *Aurelia*. The presence in it of the word "chimera" provides a clue not only to the title of the group of sonnets in which "Anteros" appears, but also to the experimental, exploratory nature which the sonnets share with the prose narrative.

Another passage, earlier in *Aurelia*, is even more explicit: "Then I saw plastic images of antiquity vaguely taking shape before me, at first in outline, and then more solidly: they seemed to represent symbols, whose meanings I grasped only with difficulty" (*Oeuvres*, I, 392). This sentence tells us much about the process that crystallized out into *The Chimeras*. The process seems to evolve through the following steps: (1) the fixing of an image associated with a vague spiritual state; (2) the molding of the image and the state into sonnet form; (3) the independent existence of the poem. Such a succession of steps relies heavily on the recapturing of dream-states and the discovery of their meaning.

But Nerval's sonnets are not simply the artistic ordering of recaptured dream-states. Each one of them is a coherent — albeit obscure — statement. Not the expression of an emotion, but, as T.S. Eliot would later say, "the creation of a new emotion."

By creating a new emotion, rather than reflecting a prior emotion, Nerval parts company with prevailing expressive theories of poetry during the Romantic period. He probably never read Wordsworth's Preface to the *Lyrical Ballads*, and, in any case, would surely have rejected the formulation that poetry "is the spontaneous overflow of powerful feelings." His great appeal for us today is — to modify the last two lines of the "Ars Poetica" of Archibald MacLeish — is that for him "a poem must not only mean but be." His sonnets are the forms

---

[1] Gérard de Nerval, *Oeuvres*, I (Pléiade, 1960), 412.

he gave to his discoveries — the transformed plastic images of antiquity. Our approach to them must respect the unity of each of these forms, the oneness of each experience.

The experience, or new emotion, which concerns us here is metaphysical revolt, about which herewith some background.

Metaphysical revolt was given great currency and put in historical perspective by Albert Camus in *The Rebel*. Camus would have it go back to the Old Testament account of the Lord's refusal of Cain's offering and Cain's subsequent murder of Abel. It is inseparable from the belief in a personal God, who is not only the creator of all beings but also responsible for all evil. Its development in the history of ideas parallels that of Christianity in the western world. The New Testament, according to Camus, can be considered "as an attempt to reply in advance to all the Cains of the world by mitigating God's countenance, and by creating an intercessor between God and man."[2] In Camus's logic, Jesus Christ came to solve the two principal concerns of the world's rebels — evil and death: "Only the sacrifice of an innocent God could justify the long, universal torture of innocence."[3]

Metaphysical revolt during the Romantic period merges into satanism and owes much to the writings of John Milton, particularly as emphasized by William Blake. Blake's interpretation of *Paradise Lost* may very well be challenged today; he nevertheless set the keynote of the Romantic attitude when he declared in *The Marriage of Heaven and Hell* that Milton was "of the Devil's party without knowing it." This interpretation was probably never questioned by the Romantics themselves, who noted that Satan, not Adam, was the central figure of *Paradise Lost*, and that after the fall he was — in Milton's own terms — "majestic though in ruins." By espousing the right of human beings to redeem themselves, by making an apology for the right to revolt, and by placing humanity at the center of the universe, Milton, with Blake's assistance, opened the way to Romantic satanism.

The affinity for Satanism and metaphysical revolt, as Mario Praz and Max Milner have shown, appears almost everywhere from the end of the eighteenth century on: in Schiller's *Die Räuber* (1781); in Ann Radcliffe's *The Italian, or the Confessional of the Black Penitents* (1787); in Matthew Gregory Lewis' *The Monk* (1796); in Shelley's *Defense of Poesy* (1821); and especially in Lord Byron's *Lara* (1814), *The Corsair*

---

[2] Albert Camus, *Essais* (Pléiade, 1965), p. 443.
[3] Camus, p. 445.

(1814), *Manfred* (1817), *The Giaour* (1813), and *Cain* (1821).[4] Jean Richer and Max Milner have discussed these works and their influence on Nerval.[5]

There can be little doubt that Gérard, more often than not, adhered to Romantic satanism — that, like so many of his contemporaries and immediate literary forbears, he denied that the devil was wicked, that he considered evil as an active force produced by energy, and traditional good as a passive element whose principal characteristic was to follow reason. The sonnet, "Anteros," first published in *Daughters of Fire* (1853), is — and expresses — Nervalian satanism in its purest form.

Because "Anteros," like all other poems of *The Chimeras*, is complete in itself and in its order, we shall present it in the original French, which the reader will, we trust, read along with our English approximation and our comments.

ANTÉROS

Tu demandes pourquoi j'ai tant de rage au coeur
Et sur un col flexible une tête indomptée;
C'est que je suis issu de la race d'Antée,
Je retourne les dards contre le dieu vainqueur.   4

Oui, je suis de ceux-là qu'inspire le Vengeur,
Il m'a marqué le front de sa lèvre irritée,
Sous la pâleur d'Abel, hélas! ensanglantée,
J'ai parfois de Caïn l'implacable rougeur!   8

[4] Mario Praz, *The Romantic Agony* (New York: Meridian Books, 1956), pp. 55-81. Max Milner, *Le Diable dans la littérature française: De Cazotte à Baudelaire*, 2 vols. (Corti, 1960). Milner gives an exhaustive account of satanism in Nerval in two chapters of this book: "Pandémonium romantique" and "Gérard de Nerval, fils du feu." He sums up Nerval's "Faustian vocation," then follows Satan through *Le Monstre vert*, *L'Imagier de Harlem*, *Robert le diable*, *Histoire de la reine du matin*, *Aurélia*, and "Antéros."
[5] Gérard de Nerval, *Expérience et création* (Hachette/ 1963), pp. 139-51. The entire chapter entitled "La Race rouge," provides a rich setting for any study of "Antéros." In a curious article entitled "Diorama," published in the September 15, 1844, issue of *L'Artiste* and reproduced by Jean Richer in his *Gérard de Nerval et les doctrines ésotériques* (Le Griffon d'Or, 1947), pp. 65-70, Nerval treats one of the principal themes of this poem, the division of the world into two races — the race of Cain (humanity) and the race of Abel (children of God). Protestantism supposedly translated "children of God" by "angels" and this translation inspired Thomas Moore's *The Loves of the Angels* (1823) and Byron's *Cain* (1823). Nerval concludes that the apocryphal Book of Enoch influenced Milton's *Paradise Lost* and Lamartine s *La Chute d'un ange* (1838).

Jéhovah! le dernier, vaincu par ton génie,
Qui, du fond des enfers, criait: "O tyrannie!"
C'est mon aïeul Bélus ou mon père Dagon...

Ils m'ont plongé trois fois dans les eaux du Cocyte,   12
Et protégeant tout seul ma mère Amalécyte,
Je ressème à ses pieds les dents du vieux dragon.

The Anteros of the title has, of course, a mythological ancestor. The Greek Anteros does not appear in early myths. He seems to have been shaped late in the cult of the Gymnasia when the ancients, wishing to depict the struggle of passionate instincts which attract or repel, divided Eros into two gods: Eros as consummated love and Anteros as unfilfilled love. The name, which means literally "against love" — ant(i)-Eros — lends itself admirably to ambiguity, since it connotes the negation of love as well as the reciprocity of love. Anteros was the quintessential *deus ultor* ("avenging god") — the avenger of those whose love has been spurned. As such, he had an altar dedicated to him by the metics, or alien residents, in Athens. On this altar, according to Pausanias, artistic figures told a legend. The Athenian, Meles, was loved by Timagoras, a metic, but returned the love only with scorn and according to his whims. One day he dared Timagoras to plunge from the rocks of the Acropolis. Timagoras was accustomed to gratifying the young man's every whim; feeling in this instance that he should prove his love at the expense of his life, he threw himself headlong to his death. Meles was so shocked and ashamed that he too climbed the rocks to die in the same manner.

Nerval read the consulted Pausanias. He could therefore have known this legend. He might also have seen the passage in which Pausanias describes a bas-relief in a palestra of Elis showing Eros and Anteros wrestling, the former holding a palm branch and the latter trying to get it away from him.[6] He could have seen a marble relief in Naples and especially a bas-relief in the Palazzo Colonna depicting Eros and Anteros wrestling during a torch race. But even granting some prior knowledge on his part of myths or legends concerning Anteros — especially those depicting wrestling matches with Eros —

---

[6] I have consulted the French translation of Pausanias' work by l'Abbé Gedoyn, *Voyage historique, pittoresque, et philosophique de la Grèce*, 3 vols. (Debarle, 1797). The Elis voyage is described in vol. I, book vi, ch. 23, p. 107. The Timagoras-Meles legend appears in vol. I, ch. 30, pp. 214-15.

and acknowledging that some familiarity with the stories can enrich our understanding as readers, it is fruitless to see the meaning of Anteros and other figures of this poem beyond the poem itself.

(1) You ask me why my heart rages so (2) And why my head remains unconquered on my flexible neck; (3) It's because I am sprung from Antaeus' race, (4) I hurl back the darts against the conquering god. Who is the *tu* of the first line? An anonymous interlocutor? The *Jehovah* of verse nine? If *tu* is an indefinite person who has asked Anteros the question which has inspired the poem, then the point of view must necessarily shift from the two quatrains, in which Anteros would be speaking of this *tu*, and the tercets, in which he unambiguously addresses Jehovah. But if we let the *tu* of the first line be the Jehovah of line nine, the poem acquires not only unity of point of view, but richer connotation.[7]

The mingling of Greek mythology with Old Testament religion becomes more acceptable if we remember that Anteros — and, later, Antaeus — are avatars of their Classical prototypes, playing fresh roles in the world of this poem. The muffled fury of the first two lines goes far beyond Genesis 4:5-7: "but for Cain and his offering he had no regard. So Cain was very angry and his countenance fell. The Lord said to Cain, 'Why are you so angry and why has your countenance fallen?'"; and even beyond Isaiah 48:4, when the prophet berates the people of Israel: "Because I know that you are obstinate, and your neck is an iron sinew and your forehead brass..."[8] The neck and the head become symbols of his revolt. The neck may have been all too ready to yield, may not have been invincibly rigid; but the head, unabashed, unsubdued, bespeaks eternal resistance to the power of Jehovah.

---

[7] A strong case for the interpretation of *Tu* as anyone within earshot of Anteros — and not Jehovah — has been made by Jacques Geninasca in his *Analyse structurale des "Chimères" de Nerval* (Neuchâtel, 1971), pp. 223, 269.

[8] For all Old Testament and New Testament quotations, I have referred to the Oxford Annotated Bible (Revised Standard Version) ed. Herbert G. May and Bruce M. Metzger (New York: Oxford University Press, 1962). For Old Testament references in French translation, I have employed the Pléiade edition in two volumes (Gallimard, 1961-1962). The French text of Genesis from this edition reads: "Or Iahvé eut égard à Abel et à son oblation, mais à Caïn et à son oblation il n'eut pas égard. Caïn éprouva une grande colère et son visage fut abattu. Alors Iahvé dit à Caïn: 'Pourquoi éprouves-tu de la colère et pourquoi ton visage est-il abattu?'" The Isaiah quote: "Car je savais que tu es obstiné, que ton cou est en nerfs de fer et que ton front est d'airain."

Throughout the rest of the poem, Anteros gives his reasons. His heart seethes with rage, first, because he is descended from Antaeus. Son of Poseidon and Gaea—God of the Sea and Mother Earth—Antaeus, let us remember, was the giant Libyan king and wrestler whose strength revived every time he touched the earth. Heracles took him on and soon realized that the only way to beat the giant was to lift him high into the air and thus prevent him from renewing contact with Mother Earth, the source of his strength. Holding him aloft, Heracles succeeded in strangling him. Heracles, son of Zeus, kills Antaeus, son of Mother Earth—by trickery. But Antaeus lives on as do all creatures whose destiny was to be slain by the God of Heaven or his delegates, Anteros, descendant of Antaeus, does not shoot arrows at potential or actual lovers; he hurls them back at the "conquering God," who is not Eros but the archetypal embodiment of the victorious sons of heaven.

(5) Yes, I am one of those whom the Avenger inspires, (6) He has put a mark on my brow with his angry lip, (7) Beneath Abel's—alas!—blood-stained paleness, (8) I sometimes show (literally: have) the implacable redness of Cain!

To say that the Avenger of verse five is the conquering god of the previous line is to accuse the poet of redundancy.[9] The Avenger is on the other side. He drives Anteros to revolt against Jehovah, to fling back the arrows and javelins against the conquering god. He has branded Anteros with his angry lip.

Nor can he be the Cain of verse eight. "The Avenger" is indeed an epithet frequently applied to Cain during the Romantic period. Byron so regarded him in *Cain: A Mystery*, which was lavishly praised by Goethe, Shelley, and Scott, as well as by Nerval. But, again, if Nerval had wanted the Avenger to be Cain, he would have found a better way to do it. The Avenger is the personification of all the meanings of that word—a new figure created by the poet. He is the progenitor of the race of Antaeus, the one from whom Anteros is sprung.

"Cain-colored" is red, since the color of Cain's hair is reputedly red—just as Judas' beard is supposedly red. The Cainites are a heretical

---

[9] R. Faurisson, *La Clef des "Chimères" de Nerval* (Pauvert, 1977), p. 39. François Constans identifies the Avenger as the fallen angel of the Bible in "*Artémis, ou les fleurs du désespoir*," *Revue de Littérature Comparée* (1934), pp. 356-57. J. Vianey discusses the use of the term "the Avenger" in connection with Cain in *Les Sources de Leconte de Lisle* (1907), p. 289.

sect of the second century, so-named because they held that Cain was created by a powerful force (fire) and Abel by a weak one (heaven). The Cain-Abel opposition parallels the Avenger-Jehovah struggle. Abel's paleness, or whiteness (the color of heaven) has been bloodied over and over again by the wrathful Jehovah of this poem who has unleashed great evil upon innocent people. Perceiving humanity as being divided into two groups, the chosen and the damned, the sons of Abel and the sons of Cain, Anteros declares his filiation from Cain/Antaeus and his opposition to Abel/Heracles. That his brow should be marked by the Avenger's angry lip is a nice twist. If the Almighty could set a mark on Cain to provide divine protection from physical harm to the first son of Adam, then why couldn't his rival, the Avenger, do the same for Anteros? The Almighty's power to bestow immunity is stolen from him, just as the sacred fire was stolen from Zeus by Prometheus. The mark of Anteros guarantees protection from the despotic abuse of celestial authority. It assures that his head will be unbowed.

Although the entire poem is addressed to him, Jehovah does not appear until verse nine. In this run-on position at the beginning of the first tercet, he serves as a semantic and syntactical linchpin holding the parts of the sonnet together. (9) Jehovah! the last one conquered by your spirit (literally: genius), (10) Who, from the depths of hell, cried out: "O tyranny!" (11) Is my grandfather Belus or my father Dagon...

The last one to be conquered by Jehovah — *le dernier* — has been identified variously as Dante's, Milton's, or Blake's Satan, and as Julian the Apostate.[10] But a careful reading of the tercet provides a more accurate identification. He is, as Anteros clearly states, Belus — a Babylonian cognate of Baal — or Dagon. Baal is the name used throughout the Old Testament for the deity or deities of Canaan. Among the many biblical stories on this subject, the one depicting the contest between Elijah, representing the God of Israel, and Ahab, fighting for the Canaanite Baal is especially pertinent. Ahab's prayers were ignored, while Elijah's supplication was answered by the "fire of the Lord." Thereupon Elijah ordered the prophets of Baal to be killed and ran seventeen miles before the chariot of Ahab to announce

[10] André Lebois, *Vers une élucidation des "Chimères" de Nerval* (Archives des Lettres Modernes, 1957), p. 19.

to the people of Jezreel the victory over the forces of Baal (I Kings 18:20-46).

One of the nicknames of Baal was Baalzebub (or Beelzebub), which came to mean "lord of the flies" (a mocking distortion of Baal-zebul — "lord of the divine abode") and was used in the New Testament as a synonym for Satan. This association and the various biblical stories depicting the struggles between the God of Israel and Baal provide a rich historical background for Belus, whose identity is shaped by the context of his poem.[11]

Dagon was an ancient Semitic deity whose cult was adopted by the Philistines. Although he was originally thought to be a fish-god, it is more probable that he was an agricultural deity — the root meaning of the word being "grain." According to many authorities, Dagon is supposed to have taught the use of the plough to humanity; he was considered germane to agricultural fertility.[12] His connection with Cain and Antaeus is thus apparent. Like Gaea, he causes the earth to yield its strength to them. According to most accounts, Dagon was the father of Baal, not vice versa, as in some other versions, and in this poem. But *aïeul* and *père* can each mean "one who is the head of a long line of descendants" (*Littré*) and this meaning makes the most sense here. Jehovah may have vanquished them, but their seed survives in Anteros.

(12) They have plunged me three times into Cocytus' waters, (13) And, quite alone, protecting my Amalekite mother, (14) I sow anew at her feet the teeth of the ancient dragon. By some miracle, Belus and Dagon have immersed Anteros in the wailing waters of the Cocytus, the river tributary to the Styx, in order to protect him from the wrath of Jehovah and to safeguard the smoldering fires of his revenge. This act of triple immersion has, of course, nothing to do with the Christian ceremony of baptism, which is for the remission of sins. It is more akin to the dipping of Achilles in the Styx by his mother, Thetis, in order that Achilles be rendered invulnerable —

---

[11] In Greek mythology, Belus is one of the twins the nymph Libya had by Poseidon, the other being Agenor, who is the father of Cadmus (see verse fourteen). The myth of Belus and the Danaids "records the early arrival in Greece of Helladic colonists from Palestine, by way of Rhodes, and their introduction of agriculture into the Peloponnese... Belus is the Baal of the Old Testament, and the Bel of the Apocrypha; he had taken his name from the Sumerian Moon-goddess Belili, whom he ousted" (Robert Graves, *Greek Myths* [London: Cassell, 1961], p. 202).

[12] *Oxford Annotated Bible*, p. 337, note.

except at the heel, by which he was held. But instead of being protected by his mother, as Achilles was by Thetis, Anteros defends *her* against extinction. As with other figures of this poem, we must not try to place an identification tag on this mother. For Anteros, she is the one who takes from the earth, not from heaven, the fiery principle of the Avenger and passes it on from generation to generation.[13] She is an Amalekite, a member of an aboriginal people descended from Esau. Since Esau sold his birthright to his brother Jacob for pottage, he is a proper ancestor for the world's disinherited. The Amalekites waged constant war against the Hebrews until they were wiped out by the Hebrews during the reign of Hezekiah.[14]

On the order of Athene, the goddess of wisdom, Cadmus sowed the dragon's teeth in the soil, whereupon Sparti (or "Sown Men") sprang up and looked menacingly at the hero. Cadmus tossed a stone among them, and each of the Sparti accused the other of having thrown it. The javelins began to fly and in the battle that ensued only five survived. These five offered their services to Cadmus.[15]

In another sonnet of *The Chimeras*, "Delifca," "the conquered dragon's ancient seed" sleeps in the cave, which is "fatal to rash visitors," and "the Sibyl... lies asleep under the arch of Constantine." These images signify the eternal return of religious ideas and they are implied but not clearly stated in "Anteros."

Anteros is silent about slaying dragons and about the role of Athene. But he knows that if he plants the dragon's teeth in the earth mother — or, more precisely, at her feet, as she lies asleep (like the Sibyl) — she will give birth to warriors who will fight on his side against Jehovah, the oppressor.

The sonnet "Anteros" is, thus, a second sowing of the dragon's teeth. No commentaries or prose equivalents can ever explain the enchantment of these fourteen lines. The enchantment can, however, be

---

[13] Jean Richer sheds light on the origin of this image by referring to the articles "Amlak," "Arab," and "Saba" of Barthélemy d'Herbelot de Molainville's *Bibliothèque orientale* (La Compagnie des Libraires, 1697), and concludes: "Cette mère amalécyte est donc une formidable entité, à la fois Harmonie, Dragon femelle, Lilith, et Balkis, goule et fée" (*Expérience et création*, pp. 155-56).

[14] I Chronicles 4:41-43 and Oxford Annotated Bible, p. 350, note.

[15] In his *Nerval: Expérience et création*, pp. 153-54, Jean Richer states that the last verse refers implicitly to two passages of Ovid's *Metamorphoses*, which recount the sowing of the teeth, first by Cadmus and second by Jason. He stresses the fact that a civil war followed the rising-up of the Sown Men. He also refers to another passage in

transformed into deeper pleasure and appreciation by a proper interpretation of the poem's discursive meaning. Such an interpretation must be enriched by an understanding of the mythological, historical, or biblical forbears of the images, symbols, metaphors, and myths which figure in this the best balanced and the most tightly constructed of all the sonnets of Nerval.

Anteros is indeed a son of Cain. He prefigures Camus's rebel. He is the man who says no. He says no to the conquering god, to Abel, and to Jehovah. No to the chosen, but yes to the damned. Yes to Antaeus, to Cain, to Belus, to Dagon, to his Amalekite mother, and, above all, to the Avenger.

The sonnet "Anteros" may not negate, but certainly does contradict, important passages of *Aurelia*, where the narrator appears to have opted for Christianity. It is the stone and marble of Gérard de Nerval's metaphysical revolt.

---

the *Metamorphoses* in which Cadmus and his wife Harmony are themselves transformed into serpents.

The sources of the Cadmus and Jason myths are, however, legion. For Cadmus alone, Pierre Grimal lists sixteen authors (*Dictionnaire de la mythologie grecque et romaine* [Presses Universitaires de France, 1951], p. 71). Moreover, the adding of the teeth-sowing incident by certain mythographers is considered by Robert Graves inappropriate to the Jason story (*The Greek Myths*, p. 602).

Mallarmé and Rimbaud in Crisis

ÉLÉONORE M. ZIMMERMANN

When discussing the major French poets of the second part of the nineteenth century, Baudelaire, Mallarmé, Verlaine, and Rimbaud, one is often led to speak of them as though they were neatly arranged on a genealogical tree. Three branches grow from the trunk Baudelaire: Verlaine and Rimbaud are drawn as contiguous, because of their close personal and poetic relationship; Mallarmé is on the other side of Verlaine since, although each went his separate way, they read and admired each other's work. Mallarmé and Rimbaud are thus always seen as furthest apart. How could it be otherwise when Mallarmé seems to be the very incarnation of the intellectual poet, while Rimbaud appears as all uncontrolled spontaneity; when the major part of Mallarmé's work presents itself in neatly aligned alexandrines, often in sonnet form, whereas Rimbaud's soon breaks out of such restrictive molds into a kind of rhythmic prose? Isn't Mallarmé the elderly pundit holding weekly meetings in the Rue de Rome where all young poets dream to be admitted, and Rimbaud the vagabond who wrote much of his work before he was twenty years old and became poetically silent after twenty-four at the latest? While Mallarmé married early, worried over the family income, grieved over the death of his son and wrote adoringly about his daughter, Rimbaud attacked the family and wanted to reinvent love. To support himself and his family, Mallarmé went dutifully every day to the *lycée* and taught his English classes, whereas Rimbaud fulminated against the "travailleurs," refused all work, advocated the use of alcohol and, possibly, of drugs, and never ceased to search for freedom from all constraints.

I do not wish to deny or even to minimize these and other major differences between the two poets. And yet Mallarmé and Rimbaud had at least one thing in common: a total faith in the poetic enterprise. Because of this, however far apart they may have been otherwise, they lived through a similar period of trial and initiation. And while other poets may have known comparable experiences, Rimbaud and Mallarmé left us a record of theirs.

The story of Rimbaud's search has received more attention, partly because it is essential to the vision we have of him as a youthful, iconoclastic genius, partly because it plays a proportionately greater role in his short life as a poet. He wrote about his search and discoveries first to his teacher Izambard and his friend Demeney in two letters of May 1871, which have come to be known as "Lettres du voyant." We then find echoes of the same experience in the section of *Une Saison en enfer* entitled "Alchimie du verbe," where he says he has given up the experiments started at the time of the two letters and, in all probability, continued during the following two years. Thus, we have a record of his feelings only at the beginning and at the end of the experiment of "voyance." For Mallarmé, on the other hand, the letters he wrote his friends between April 1866 and March 1871 from Tournon, Besançon, and Avignon, allow us to follow, almost month by month, the development of what I shall argue is a similar experience;[1] we see it develop from his first discovery of "le Néant" at the time he was working on *Hérodiade*—when he also begins seriously to fear for his health—to the despair and disarray reflected in two almost incoherent letters of May 1867 and, finally, his announcement, four years later, that the "matinées de vingt ans" have returned after a last "hiver d'anxiétés et de luttes" (*Corr.* 342, HC, March 3, 1871).

However the records of events may differ, both poets move from a willed and, in Rimbaud's case, joyous search to a feeling of helplessness when they come to fear that this very search entails a destruction of the self which may precipitate them into madness. While Rimbaud introduces "Alchimie du verbe" by the words, "A moi.

---

[1] These letters are available to us in Stéphane Mallarmé, *Correspondance 1862-1871* (Gallimard, 1959), which will be referred to as *Corr.* followed by page number. Henri Cazalis and Eugène Lefébure were the recipients of most of the letters we have, and their names will be indicated by their initials, HC and EL.

L'histoire d'une de mes folies,"[2] and the *Saison en enfer*, of which it is a part, by: "J'ai joué de bons tours à la folie" (R. 219), Mallarmé writes his friends:

> Ma pensée... perdait sa fonction normale: j'ai senti des symptômes très inquiétants causés par le seul acte d'écrire et l'hystérie allait commencer à troubler ma parole. (*Corr.* 299, HC, April 4, 1869)

> Je passe d'instants voisins de la folie entrevue à des extases équilibrantes. (*Corr.* 273, EL, May 3, 1863)

The intensity of the experience could not be sustained, and both poets, frightened by its consequences, are finally willing to climb down from heights recognized as too perilous. Mallarmé claims he is resigned to becoming a simple "littérateur" (*Corr.* 342). Both write in terms of having possibly been only intermediaries, whose search will be continued by others (*Corr.* 273, EL, May 3, 1868; R. 271).

What was to become a crisis had been, first of all, a conscious attempt to reach the outer limits of poetry. Both poets were young, with youth's uncompromising and total commitment to their visions.[3] "Je me suis reconnu poète" (R. 268), wrote Rimbaud, and Mallarmé was no less certain of his calling. As poets, both wanted first of all to move beyond the quotidian, to invent a new form of poetry. The purpose of the true poet, according to Rimbaud, is to reach "l'inconnu." Mallarmé, in a less Baudelairean idiom explains to Cazalis that in relation to the "Scène" from *Hérodiade* (which he dismisses as "ces vieux vers"), "ce que j'ai dans le front est non moins rare, tout à fait inconnu" (*Corr.* 323, April 1870). Like Rimbaud, who feels limited even by the term "poet" and wants to go beyond, to become "voyant," Mallarmé is full of faith in what his poetic search can achieve:

---

[2] Arthur Rimbaud, *Oeuvres complètes* (Pléiade, 1963), p. 232, subsequently to be referred to as R. followed by page number. Similarly, the Pléiade edition of Mallarmé's work will be referred to by M. followed by page number, and that of Baudelaire by B. followed by page number. The editions used are Stéphane Mallarmé, *Oeuvres complètes* (Gallimard, 1945); Charles Baudelaire, *Oeuvres complètes* (Gallimard, 1961).
[3] We are used to exclaiming over the youthful precociousness of Rimbaud. Indeed, when his "Lettres du voyant" were sent, he was not yet seventeen years old. But it may be worth stressing that Mallarmé in April 1866, had only just turned twenty-two and had already composed many of his major poems, including *Hérodiade* and *L'Après-midi d'un faune.* He, too, had started writing when he was very young. Though now more experienced as a poet, he cannot by any means be seen as a settled old man.

Je veux me donner le spectacle de la matière, ayant conscience d'être
et, cependant, s'élançant forcenément dans le Rêve qu'elle sait n'être
pas. (*Corr.* 207, HC, end of April 1866)

Mallarmé has entered the realm of ontological questioning through
his focussing on language. It has brought him personal anxiety as
well as exultation: "Malheureusement, en creusant le vers à ce point,
j'ai rencontré deux abîmes, qui me désespèrent. L'un est le Néant," —
implying doubt about his very spiritual being (the other is his poor
health) (*ibid.*).[4]

Indeed, while they advance, fascinated, to explore the heights or
the abyss — both images are used — Mallarmé and Rimbaud fall prey
to a sense of depersonalization which they will later experience as
madness. Rimbaud's formulation has become famous: "JE est un autre"
(R. 268, 270). It is so central to his thinking at that time that he repeats
it to both his correspondents. The poet is outside of himself: "J'assiste
à l'éclosion de ma pensée: je la regarde, je l'écoute" (R. 270, to
Demeney); "C'est faux de dire: Je pense. On devrait dire: On me
pense" (R. 268, to Izambard). Mallarmé seems to have felt something
similar — the formula is less striking, but more far reaching and
mysterious: "Ma Pensée s'est pensée" (*Corr.* 240, May 14, 1867), he
writes Cazalis, adding: "je suis maintenant impersonnel et non plus
Stéphane que tu as connu, — mais une aptitude qu'a l'Univers spirituel

---

[4] Certainly, a contributing factor to his crisis was his feeling of despair at what he
considered the senseless duties he had to perform teaching English to unruly children,
at the precarious livelihood he was eking out, at the cold and morose winters remote
from friends and from all intellectual stimulation. Maybe the news of Baudelaire's
final illness, which reached him in March 1867 (*Corr.* 207, n. 1), contributed to it
also. As for the form it was to take, his confrontation with Nothingness, it may in
part have been determined by conversations with Lefébure (*ibid.*). Mallarmé claimed
in a letter to Cazalis that he arrived at the conception of Nothingness "sans connaître le bouddhisme" (*Corr.* 207), but on May 3, 1868, he wrote Lefébure about
his "fréquentation [de l'absolu] de deux années (vous vous rappelez? depuis notre
séjour à Cannes)" (*Corr.* 273), and we know that the egyptologist Lefébure was interested in Buddhism and knew Hegel. Finally, one might wish to ask what unconscious needs were served by the search which Mallarmé undertook, and the same
question could be asked of Rimbaud. The answers could lead to further comparisons
between the two poets. They have not been found by Jean Fretet, in spite of the
title of his book (*Aliénation poétique* [J -B.-Janin, 1946]). Its loose argumentation has
been convincingly criticized by Charles Mauron in *Introduction à la psychanalyse de
Mallarmé* (Neuchâtel: A la Baconnière, 1950), ch. 2.

à se voir et à se développer, à travers ce qui fut moi" (*Corr.* 242, *ibid.*).
To Villiers de l'Isle Adam he confides: "Pour l'Avenir... mon âme
est détruite. Ma pensée a été jusqu'à se penser elle-même" (*Corr.* 259,
September 24, 1867).

The state of consciousness both poets were to reach recalls those
which can be induced through drugs. Thus Baudelaire writes about
the "hachish" takers who gain the faculty of observing themselves (B.
340), of wine drinkers who give birth to a third person, the first two
being the drinker and the wine (B. 333). But while Rimbaud alludes
to his drinking and seems to advocate the taking of drugs, we have
no reason to believe Mallarmé's reliance on wine was excessive nor
that he experimented with drugs.[5] His experience seems to illustrate
what Baudelaire, quoting Barbereau, wrote in his conclusion to *Du
Vin et du hachish*: a state similar to that induced by hashish could be
reached "par le pur et libre exercice de la volonté" of those who are
gifted with an "esprit poétique."

As a consequence of their intense meditation, both Rimbaud and
Mallarmé see their self as having been destroyed. While Mallarmé
believes he has touched truth, he feels sad and even guilty: "car tout
cela n'a pas été trouvé par le développement normal de mes facultés,
mais par la voie pécheresse et hâtive, satanique et *facile*, de la Destruction de moi" (*Corr.* 246, HC, May 17, 1867). The bourgeois Mallarmé
would not, like Rimbaud, advocate the "dérèglement de tous les sens"
(R. 268, 270), yet though the vocabulary differs, the experiences must
have been comparable. For Rimbaud, "toutes les formes d'amour,
de souffrance, de folie; il [le poète] cherche lui-même, il épuise en
lui tous les poisons, pour n'en garder que les quintessences" (R. 270),
while Mallarmé observes: "Je n'ai créé mon oeuvre que par *élimina-
tion*, et toute vérité acquise ne naissait que de la perte d'une impression qui, ayant étincelé, s'était consumée" (*Corr.* 245-46, EL, May
17, 1867). Later, in notes so disjointed they recall at times the "Lettres du voyant," Mallarmé, writing as though in a trance on the subject of women, courtesans, fatness, and various bodily functions,
remarks: "Je suis véritablement décomposé, et dire qu'il faut cela pour
avoir une vue très — une de l'Univers!" (*Corr.* 249, *ibid.*).

The sense of depersonalization entails terrible suffering from the
start. Rimbaud — mindful, possibly, of the curse following the eating

---

[5] All we know is that he may have repeatedly been given medication containing
arsenic for his bronchial complaints (*Corr.* 229, to Mme Mallarmé, August 12, 1866).

from the tree of knowledge — wrote to Demeney in a prophetic mood of the poet's "ineffable torture," which would require "toute la foi,... toute la force surhumaine" and would make him "le grand malade, le grand criminel, le grand maudit, — et le suprême Savant! —" (R. 270). In *Alchimie du verbe* he retraces the actual events. As with Mallarmé, physical joins with spiritual torture, and reality and dream are no longer clearly separated:

> Ma santé fut menacée. La terreur venait. Je tombais dans des sommeils de plusieurs jours, et, levé, je continuais les rêves les plus tristes. J'étais mûr pour le trépas, et par une route de dangers ma faiblesse me menait aux confins du monde et de la Cimmérie, patrie de l'ombre et des tourbillons. (R. 237)

Mallarmé mentions his sufferings again and again: "Tout ce que, par contrecoup, mon être a souffert, pendant cette longue agonie, est inénarrable" (*Corr.* 240, HC, May 14, 1867); "mon cerveau, envahi par le Rêve, se refus[ait] à ses fonctions extérieures qui ne le sollicitaient plus" (*Corr.* 301, HC, February 18, 1869). In December he mentions his "absences cataleptiques" (315). In May 1868, after he had hoped to overcome his despair and to recover his health only to be struck down again, he writes: "Je suis dans un état de crise qui ne peut durer" (*Corr.* 273, EL).

When the anguish, the suffering, the fear of losing control had led the poets to withdraw from their experiment, a sense of renewal remained. In concluding "Alchimie du verbe," Rimbaud writes: "Cela s'est passé. Je sais aujourd'hui saluer la beauté" (R. 238). Mallarmé, less concisely, expresses his belief that "La première phase de ma vie a été finie. La conscience, excédée d'ombres, se réveille, lentement, formant un homme nouveau" (*Corr.* 301, HC, February 18, 1869). He becomes a small child again (*Corr.* 300, HC, February 4, 1869) and will be reborn through the Dream which destroyed him (*ibid.*, 299). Even as they were struggling with their new insights, both poets were writing — although Mallarmé was constantly complaining of his inability, literally, to set pen to paper — and their poems reveal some of the changes in their conception of poetry.

Most strikingly perhaps, the communication of a message, or even of an expressible meaning, no longer enters the realm of their concerns. While a poem like "Le Bateau ivre" still has a recognizable narrative line, this gets lost in *Derniers Vers* as Rimbaud had foreseen in his letter to Demeney: the poet "arrive à l'inconnu, et quand, affollé, il finirait par perdre l'intelligence de ses visions, il les a vues!" (R. 271). This he later describes in "Alchimie du verbe": "Je finis par trouver sacré le désordre de mon esprit" (R. 234). The "Scène" from *Hérodiade, L'Après-midi d'un faune,* and the earlier poems may be difficult, yet they all have a plot or a story line. But as the crisis deepened, Mallarmé's interest shifted perceptibly, and at the time when he wrote that he had gone far beyond *Hérodiade,* he was composing the mysterious "sonnet en ix" ("ses purs ongles"), which he was to refer to as a "sonnet nul" (*Corr.* 279), in a letter to his friend Lefébure, whom he asks for the meaning of the word "ptyx." His comments have received much attention: "on m'assure," he writes, "qu'il n'existe dans aucune langue, ce que je préférerais de beaucoup afin de me donner le charme de le créer par la magie de la rime" (*Corr.* 274, May 3, 1868). When he sends the sonnet to Cazalis, at the latter's request, he writes:

> Il est inverse, je veux dire que le sens, s'il en a un (mais je me consolerais du contraire grâce à la dose de poésie qu'il renferme, ce me semble) est évoqué par un mirage interne des mots mêmes. En se laissant aller à le murmurer plusieurs fois, on éprouve une sensation assez cabalistique. (*Corr.* 244, May 14, 1867)

Of course, Mallarmé had been moving away from a primary interest in meaning for a long time; the concern he showed about his friends not understanding "L'Azur" (*Corr.* 104, HC, January 1864) never appeared again in the letters which we have. Instead, his poetic interest had shifted toward absolute control of the word. About *Hérodiade* he wrote to his friend Lefébure in February 1865:

> La plus belle page de mon oeuvre sera celle qui ne contiendra que ce nom divin *Hérodiade...,* et je crois que si mon héroïne s'était appelée Salomé, j'eusse inventé ce mot sombre, et rouge comme une grenade ouverte, *Hérodiade.* (*Corr.* 154)

A few months later, in December 1865, Mallarmé wrote to Henri Cazalis about the same work: "n'ayant que les nuits à moi, je les passe à en rêver à l'avance tous les mots" (*Corr.* 180). *L'Après-midi d'un faune* requires no less of an effort:

> Mais si tu savais que de nuits désespérées et de jours de rêveries il faut sacrifier pour arriver à faire des vers originaux... Quelle étude du son et de la couleur des mots, musique et peinture par lesquelles devra passer ta pensée, tant belle soit-elle, pour être poétique. (*Corr.* 168, HC, July 1865)

The experiments of Rimbaud lead him to somewhat similar phrasing. In "Alchimie du verbe" he states:

> J'inventai la couleur des voyelles!... Je réglai la forme et le mouvement de chaque consonne, et, avec des rhythmes instinctifs, je me flattai d'inventer un verbe poétique accessible, un jour ou l'autre, à tous les sens. Je réservai la traduction.
> Ce fut d'abord une étude. J'écrivais des silences, des nuits, je notais l'inexprimable. Je fixais des vertiges. (R. 233)

"Ce fut d'abord une étude": it is this intense concentration which for Rimbaud as well as for Mallarmé leads to the exploration of the unknown. Rimbaud, whatever his reliance on stimulants may have been, also started with an "étude" and an attempt to gain total control of language, fighting "le hasard," to use Mallarmé's vocabulary, a control which, as the concentration became too intense and its object dissolved and lost its reality, was to escape both poets.

The concentration on the words, each "rêvé à l'avance" in a desperate search for perfection, may, as he believed, have precipitated Mallarmé's crisis (*Corr.* 207). The crisis, which was linked to a new vision of the universe, in turn changed his relationship to the word. Thus, the correspondence reveals that the words, which previously were "rêvés," "savourés," lose their privileged status as the basic unit of the poem: Mallarmé's creative thinking from now on is directed toward the word in its context, and his endeavor at control is shifted from the choice of words to the interplay between words. In December 1866, he writes Coppée:

> *Vos mots vivent un peu trop de leur propre vie comme les pierreries d'une mosaïque de joyaux...* Ce à quoi nous devons viser surtout est que, dans le poème, les mots—qui sont déjà assez eux pour ne plus recevoir d'impression du dehors—*se reflètent les uns sur les autres jusqu'à paraître ne plus avoir leur couleur propre, mais n'être que les transitions d'une gamme.* (*Corr.* 234, Mallarmé's emphasis)

Some twenty years later, in *Crise de vers*, the formulation remains similar:

> L'oeuvre pure implique la disparition élocutoire du poëte, qui cède l'initiative aux mots, par le heurt de leur inégalité mobilisés; ils s'allument de reflets réciproques comme une virtuelle traînée de feux sur des pierreries. (M. 366)

Inevitably, the poet himself, who had appeared to Mallarmé already in 1865 as a "vaine forme de la Matière," would disappear, while the words, joined according to his will, would live their own lives without interference.

Rimbaud, who condemned subjectivity so vehemently in his letter to Izambard and who vividly expressed his sense of depersonalization, does not, in his *Derniers Vers*, eliminate the "I" to the same degree as Mallarmé in his poems after 1865.[6] The inner revolution of the "voyance," while effecting some changes, does not suppress tendencies long present in his poetry, such as the primacy of sensation, usually of a narrator. One of his very first poems was entitled "Sensation"; it describes a happy "je" feeling the wheat, the grass, the wind: "Je ne parlerai pas, je ne penserai rien." The poet-voyant may abandon narrative, but part of his endeavor remains linked to his previous conception of poetry. He will search for a language to translate the insights he brings back from "l'inconnu" into sensations:

> [le poète] devra faire sentir, palper, écouter ses inventions; si ce qu'il rapporte de là-bas a forme, il donne forme; si c'est informe, il donne l'informe. Trouver une langue; — Du reste, toute parole étant idée, le temps d'un langage universel viendra!... Cette langue sera de l'âme pour l'âme, résumant tout, parfums, sons, couleurs, de la pensée accrochant la pensée et tirant. (R. 271)

Sensation, while mentioned in Mallarmé's correspondence, is used much more vaguely (*Corr.* 137, 151, 161). After Mallarmé's plunge into the "Néant" and his subsequent discovery of the Universe, it was relegated, once and for all, to a subordinate role. Rimbaud wants to filter the discoveries of the beyond through sensations, translated into a language which makes them accessible to all; Mallarmé only uses sensation, the tool of the poet, to project himself into the Universe:

> Toute vérité acquise ne naissait que de la perte d'une impression qui, ayant étincelé, s'était consumée et me permettait, grâce à ses ténèbres dégagées, d'avancer profondément dans la sensation des Ténèbres absolues. (*Corr.* 245-47, EL, May 17, 1867)

[6] The critics still do not agree on the time of composition for *Les Illuminations*. Was it, or was it not, part of the experience of the "voyance"? The "je" is less prominent in them than in *Derniers Vers*. Verlaine, from prison, writes about "Le système" and about an objective poetry, which may be related to Rimbaud's views. But, as the critics have repeatedly argued, all the examples given by Rimbaud in "Alchimie du verbe" are from *Derniers Vers*, although this may be so because, relying on his memory, Rimbaud could more easily quote verse. The fact remains that we can only be absolutely sure that the *Derniers Vers* were written during the period of "folie" which Rimbaud abjures in *Une Saison en enfer*.

Vous serez terrifié d'apprendre que je suis arrivé à l'Idée de l'Univers par la seule sensation (et que, par exemple, pour garder une notion ineffaçable du Néant pur, j'ai dû imposer à mon cerveau la sensation du vide absolu). (*Corr.* 259, to Villiers de L'Isle-Adam, September 24, 1867)

The movement clearly is from the sensation to the abstraction, an abstraction which, as I shall have the occasion to stress later, keeps a barely perceptible but essential concrete coloring. In the letter to Villiers, the sensation functions as a means of reaching the idea of the Universe, indeed, of appropriating it.

It is at this point that the conception of "Le Livre" suddenly takes on life in Mallarmé. "Le Livre" is a poetic form of the Universe, which all poets, consciously or not, are writing (M. 662-63). Mallarmé's work is not, from now on, to be a fragmentary rendering of a fraction of reality. He wants it to be in tune with the Universe, for

J'avais, à la faveur d'une grande sensibilité, compris la corrélation in-time de la Poésie avec l'Univers, et pour qu'elle fût pure, conçu le des-sein de la sortir du Rêve et du Hasard et de la juxtaposer à la concep-tion de l'Univers. (*Corr.* 259, see above)

Thus, it is at the very time when the word, in Mallarmé's new con-ception of poetry, is no longer to be looked upon in isolation, but is seen in its interaction with other words, that the poem ceases to be a haphazard fragment, isolated, and complete in itself. As one first reads the *Correspondance*, one may find it strange that while over-whelmed to the point of despair by his new vision of the world, Mallarmé still makes plans for writing. Yet there is no reason to doubt his sincerity in reporting that his depressed state makes writing difficult for him. Once more we are reminded of Baudelaire's report on the effect of hashish: after such a "grande dépense de fluide nerveux... vous avez jeté votre personnalité aux quatre vents du ciel, et mainte-nant vous avez de la peine à la rassembler et à la concentrer" (B. 341). What fills the pages of Mallarmé's letters is not the report of poems written, but of plans for writing them, and the vision of the task ahead is synchronous with his vision of the universe. His comments on the shape his work is to take appear in all the important letters we have from these five years, and range from the sublime to the near-ridiculous, from equating his task with the *Grand Oeuvre* to a wishful counting of how many books and poems it will comprise. One of the key letters, that of May 1867, shows this sequence clearly: the necessary rising to the level of the Universe, without which the poet feels himself sinking into the Nothingness he has discovered; the appropriation of the Universe; and the resulting vision of his work:

> J'avoue du reste... que j'ai encore besoin... de me regarder dans cette glace pour penser et que si elle n'était pas devant la table où je t'écris cette letter, je redeviendrais le Néant.
>
> Fragile comme est mon apparition terrestre, je ne puis subir que les développements absolument nécessaires pour que l'Univers retrouve, en ce moi, son identité. Ainsi je viens, à l'heure de la Synthèse, de délimiter l'oeuvre qui sera l'image de ce développement. Trois poèmes en vers, dont *Hérodiade* est l'Ouverture,... et quatre poèmes en prose, sur la conception spirituelle du Néant. (*Corr.* 242, HC, May 14, 1867)

Mallarmé is in turn optimistic and despairing as he envisages his new task:

> Je travaille à tout à la fois, ou plutôt je veux dire que tout est si bien ordonné en moi, qu'à mesure, maintenant, qu'une sensation m'arrive, elle se transfigure et va d'elle-même se caser dans tel livre et tel poème. Quand un poème sera mûr, il se détachera. Tu vois que j'imite la loi naturelle. (*Corr.* 222, to Th. Aubanel, July 16, 1866)

Thus, about the "sonnet en ix," which for him does *not* belong to the "Oeuvre," he writes:

> J'ai pris ce sujet d'un sonnet nul et se réfléchissant de toutes les façons, parce que mon oeuvre est si bien préparé et hiérarchisé, représentant comme il le peut l'Univers, que je n'aurais su, sans endommager quel-qu'une de mes impressions étagées, rien en enlever. (*Corr.* 279, HC, July 18, 1868)

The experiences of Rimbaud and Mallarmé, then, were often parallel — even merged at times — as they attempted to reach beyond the everyday meaning of words. We do find, however, that their paths diverge as they come to deal with the revelations that their search has brought. Rimbaud's verse mirrors his experience of "hallucination simple," the substitution of one reality, at times including himself, by another ("Je devins un opéra fabuleux," R. 237).[7] The reality he

---

[7] Baudelaire tells of a person who, while smoking after taking hashish, feels he is being smoked ("Vous croyez être assis dans votre pipe et c'est vous que votre pipe fume; c'est vous qui vous exhalez sous la forme de nuages bleus" [B. 338]). Mallarmé's "Ma Pensée s'est pensée" reflects a similar experience, tinged with terror.

now creates is still linked to direct perceptions and sensations, albeit in a totally unexpected, constantly surprising sequence which will shake and jar the imagination of the reader. Mallarmé, as we just saw, is more concerned with reflecting the structure, the order of the newly sensed universe, through the totality of his writings. Within the individual poem he will not strive to transpose sensation directly. As the Universe is re-created through the juxtaposition of his individual writings, so poetic reality is to arise out of the interstices between words; it partakes both of the idea and of transcended sensation. The idea of Nothingness acquired its reality for him through sensation; similarly, he will create a flower beyond all flowers — "l'absente de tous les bouquets," more real than any one flower perceived only through our senses — by replacing a fugitive exterior reality with an indestructible word, a name ("Je dis: une fleur!"), and finally an abstraction ("idée même"), but one that is endowed with the characteristics of concreteness ("et suave") (M. 368, *Crise de vers*).

A glance at the two poets' treatment of time will reveal some of the differences between them. It is well known that the sense of time suffers alteration under the influence of drugs and mystical experience. Baudelaire writes that hashish causes the sense of time to disappear (B. 339), and indeed Mallarmé states repeatedly in his correspondence, occasionally with amusing self-mockery, that he has come to live outside of time, in Eternity (*Corr.* 240).

Rimbaud deals most directly with the experience of Time in a well-known poem from *Derniers Vers*, "L'Eternité":

> Elle est retrouvée.
> Quoi? — L'Eternité.
> C'est la mer allée
> Avec le soleil.[8]

As an answer to the question of the second line about the *locus* of an abstract concept, Eternity, two concrete elements are evoked. They have, it is true, a possible abstract connotation — "mer" can be linked to infinite expansion in space, "soleil" to the diurnal rhythm of time. But what Rimbaud suggests first and with greatest force are sensations of color ("mer" — see "Voyelles" or "Le Bateau ivre"), of light ("soleil") and of fusion ("allée avec"). In the following stanzas, the soul in search of eternity liberates itself of all awkward constraints, of duties,

---

[8] The variant from "Alchimie du verbe" reads: "C'est la mer mêlée / Au soleil."

the past, hope—human and abstract—to plunge again into sea and sun in the closing four lines, which repeat the first.

We cannot here do justice to the complex problems of the sense of time in either Rimbaud or Mallarmé, but the marked change it undergoes after the onset of their crises must be stressed. "Le Bateau ivre" had a clear sequential narrative line. This disappears in *Derniers Vers*, even in those poems where the past is mentioned as such. The prose poems *Les Illuminations* are, with a very few exceptions, tableaux written in the present. Similarly, in Mallarmé, poems such as "L'Azur," "Apparition," "Brise marine," "Don du poème," even *L'Après-midi d'un faune* and "Scène" from *Hérodiade* have clear time zones in which they develop. The "Ouverture ancienne" reaches toward a synthesis of past and present. But the poems written during the prolonged crisis cannot be read with the same assumptions.

"Le vierge, le vivace et le bel aujourd'hui" is, next to *Igitur*, the one poem which, like Rimbaud's "L'Eternité," deals most explicitly with time. Here past, present, and future are compressed, even fused. In it, the future ("Va-t-il nous déchirer," 1.2) appears to be quickly dismissed, as is the wide open space, bare of all image of flight or conquest ("Tout son col secouera cette blanche agonie / Par l'espace infligé à l'oiseau qui le nie," 1.8-9). The past invades the present to the point of killing the life, the "future" quality of the present, as the "aujourd'hui" of the first line, "vierge," "vivace," gets changed into the Fantôme of the second tercet. Indeed, "le vivace... va-t-il nous déchirer" was the expression of a hope that "aujourd'hui" would be projected into the future. It appeared "vierge," new, not marked by the past. But of the "vierge," only the association of whiteness lingers on in the poem, and already the third and fourth lines, with the frozen lake, the "givre," the "glacier," displace the suggestion of whiteness toward words associated not with new life but with rigidity ("dur," "n'ont pas fui"), while "hante" more explicitly refers to the permanence of the past. "Hante" prefigures the "Fantôme" of line 13. The "pur éclat," which might have characterized the "vierge aujourd'hui," then the "glacier" of the past, is now attached explicitly to the Fantôme, and the future is not to be found in action ("déchirer") but consists in a lasting immobility of the present (the whole last stanza is in the present) fused with the past—"Fantôme"—shorn of its concreteness—"Cygne" (1.14) not "cygne" (1.5), "signe" of the bird. The last word of the poem, "Cygne," suggests a constellation, the immortalizing transformation of Greek myths, but the implied "signe" points to the mediation of the word to achieve the immortalization. The image of the long-necked white bird had to give way to the abstract sign of itself to receive, outside of concrete and measurable time, a new life, but, characteristically, it is not without the suggestion of other images, such as that of stars, which give a visual quality to the abstraction.

Thus, Mallarmé's poem, in contrast to Rimbaud's, moves away from concreteness to an abstraction defined by sensory notations, a sense of eternity created by abolishing in turn the future, the present, and the past, and by disincarnating the metaphor which first embodied it.

The preoccupation with time can be sensed as clearly in the "sonnet en ix" and in *Igitur*, both poised in anguish at midnight, a momentary and fragile present between yesterday and tomorrow. The "sonnet en ix" closes with a "scintillation" of death which again becomes "fixée," as did the Cygne. In *Igitur*, the descent into death does take place. This movement toward immobility is an attempt to eliminate chance, the "hasard" which is equated to life (M. 442). Midnight, the hour at which it occurs, is given the same quality of the present and of nonconcreteness as the "Fantôme" which remains at the end of "Le vierge, le vivace...":

> Que de l'Infini se séparent et les constellations et la mer, demeurées, en l'extériorité, de réciproques néants, pour en laisser l'essence, à l'heure unie, faire le présent absolu des choses. (M. 435)

It is the

> Rêve pur d'un Minuit, en soi disparu... [il] subsiste encore le silence d'une antique parole proférée par lui, en lequel, revenue, ce Minuit évoque son ombre finie et nulle par ces mots: J'étais l'heure qui doit me rendre pur. (M. 435)

The present, fused with the past, will again be immobilized into pure eternity:

> L'heure se formule en cet écho... "Adieu, nuit, que je fus, ton propre sépulcre, mais qui, l'ombre survivante, se métamorphosera en Eternité." (M. 436)

We find here the same presence of the past overwhelming the present, and the striving toward purity which characterized "Le vierge, le vivace..."

If carried further, the comparison between Rimbaud and Mallarmé might help elucidate the different nature of their poetry's "difficulty." A similar search brought both men to a parallel fundamental experience: their intense focussing on words led to a sense of depersonalization and indeed to the edge of madness. It also changed their poetry: rational comprehensibility became irrelevant, time, events, and perception appeared as nonlinear and nonsequential. Thus, both poets came to reject basic poetic conventions. However, the differences between them remain marked, as they translated their new insights according to their own personal bent. I have given examples of the sensuousness of Rimbaud's poetry, which often seems like juxtaposed visionary blocks. A hypnotic, song-like quality is also characteristic of *Derniers Vers*. One of Mallarmé's chief concerns, on the other hand, was that his poetry mirror what he had perceived as the structure of the universe. This structure was to be reflected in his work as a whole, through the careful placing of each poem in relation to the others. In this vast plan Mallarmé failed: "Le Livre" was never completed. But the structuring principle is also basic to each individual poem, as in a microcosm. Mallarmé, as we saw, was deeply concerned with the words' relations to each other, and on that plane he succeeded in incorporating into his poetry one of his basic insights about the nature of the universe. Moreover, we learn through one of his letters to Villiers that the concept of the Universe only became apprehensible to him when he linked it with sensation. This peculiar experience is also reflected in his writings at the time: his very personal poetic universe takes on its life through the predominance of the abstract, indissolubly fused with the concrete. Finally, one might note that, in a letter to Henri Cazalis, Mallarmé relates how his crisis and revelation began with a hard struggle against God, whom he finally managed to kill (*Corr.* 241, May 14, 1867). Thus, there may also be a reflection of his vision of the universe in his envisaging the disappearance of the poet from his work, even though all his initial efforts were directed to an absolute, god-like control of his creation.

Finally, Rimbaud's "translation" of his insights generated by his experience was much more direct than in the case of Mallarmé. This may explain why Rimbaud was able to write more during and immediately after the crisis he underwent. By contrast, Mallarmé, who found it difficult at first to express himself in accordance with his new aesthetics, saw his work sustained through many more years as he patiently explored the complex ramifications of a new conception of poetry.

From Mallarmé to Breton: Continuity and Discontinuity in the Poetics of Ambiguity

ANNA BALAKIAN

Separated by half a century, Stéphane Mallarmé and André Breton follow each other like two milestones on the path of modern poetics, and their roles as heads of literary schools, symbolism and surrealism, invite comparison. Their positions as masters in the throes of the poetic activities of the avant-garde of their respective times had gained for them a cosmopolitan following in Paris, clusters of poets who were as much affected by the stature of their two personalities as by their pronouncements. By associating poetics with the processes in the other arts, such as music and dance in the case of Mallarmé and painting in the case of Breton, they succeeded in reducing the distance between poets and other categories of artists but also increased the gap between poetry and the other forms of literature, particularly in the dislike both expressed of the narrative form. At the end of their careers both reached advanced forms of writing, Mallarmé with his *Un Coup de dés jamais n'abolira le hasard*, Breton with his *Constellations*, surpassing the models they had first created and the variants adopted by those who had imitated them and followed in their paths.[1]

But the first level of the parallel between Breton and Mallarmé in its most obvious aspects stops here. Before looking in depth at other levels of connection, let us look at some obvious differences.

Mallarmé became a master among disciples who were some twenty years his juniors. Breton, on the other hand, became a leader among

---

[1] Stéphane Mallarmé, *Un Coup de dés jamais n'abolira le hasard* in *Oeuvres complètes* (Editions de la Pléiade, 1956), pp. 455-77; hereafter abbreviated *OC*. André Breton, *Constellations* in *Signe ascendant* (Gallimard, 1968), pp. 127-71.

117

his contemporaries, despite the fact that he was identified as the "Pope" of surrealism. The concepts that constituted Mallarmé's *ars poetica* were handed down *a posteriori*, after he had practiced them in his poetry for some twenty years, after his aesthetics had been put to the test in his works, recognized and appreciated even if only by a limited number of readers. On the other hand, Breton had made his declarations of theory at an age when he had written little and proved nothing. His doctrines were chosen and pronounced *a priori* and accepted on faith. Mallarmé's manner was quiet, nondogmatic, his aspirations qualitative rather than quantitative. He had said that if he could catch the attention of one person in each city of France he would be quite satisfied. Breton's concepts took the form of Manifestoes, and like political manifestoes aimed to reach the many, with the firm conviction that poetry was a human necessity.

In a recent book called *Poetry and Repression*, the American critic, Harold Bloom, states — perhaps in reaction to the analytical studies of literature in isolated fragments — the importance of placing every writer in the current which reaches him.[2] Every act of poetic creativity, he insists, is actually a form of revision of previous poetic achievements, and consequently, there exists in literary history a flux and reflux in the course of literary phenomena and periods. This is, of course, another way of saying that the greatest influences are the negative, reactionary ones. Gide had made the same observation a while back. One can explain much about symbolism and surrealism on the basis of the theory of reactions. Although André Breton at age sixteen was writing Mallarmean sonnets, he was soon to attack the artifices of the symbolists, their withdrawal from the lifestream, their protracted introspections, their espousal of an ontology of fiction. The reaction of the surrealists to these postures is readily evident in the surrealist behavior and the revisionist character of the early poetry that ensued. The interiority of the poetic stance, which had become traditional, was reversed as the surrealists emerged from the expected shell to project themselves and their work into the concrete world and to try to transform it instead of turning their backs to it. The chamber is abandoned in favor of the street. Instead of withdrawing from exterior reality they wanted to come to grips with it and to manipulate it. One of the first poems of Breton is nothing more than a rebuttal of the

---

[2] Harold Bloom, *Poetry and Repression* (New Haven, Conn.: Yale University Press, 1976).

symbolist mystique. Let me quote a few lines from the excellent translation of Kenneth White:

> Rather life than those prisms without depth even if
>   the colors are purer
> Rather than that always clouded hour those terrible
>   wagons of cold flame
> Than those soft stones
> Rather this triggered heart
> Than that murmuring mere
> And that white cloth singing in the air and in the
>   earth
> That nuptial blessing linking my brow to the brow
>   of absolute vanity
> > Rather life
> > *Clair de terre*[3]

On the level of symbols, the revision of the symbolist vision is also very obvious. The preponderant image of the symbolist lily is transformed into banal and common flowers, such as the wild rose and the sunflower. The swan is replaced by the high flying and more resilient egret or eagle (not yet considered an endangered species!), and if a certain difficulty of interpretation of discourse is preserved as we pass from symbolism to surrealism, it is no longer due to lexical rarefactions and semantic intricacies but to a vocabulary that is replete with words that have never been associated with each other before, which are innocent of previous poetic connotations, having been culled from the fields not of literature but botany and biology. Even in the choice of mythological figures, reaction to the standard choices brings back from the past some of the ones that have had less visibility in modern literature: Leda fades away; she was a favorite of the symbolists because she suggested to them the human being in whom divine seed is put by the embrace of a god. She is replaced by Melusine, suggesting on the contrary the divine being who aspires to become and to stay human in the interpretation of Breton. Hérodiade, Mallarmé's version of that fascinating Salome of the symbolists, is sterile in her static existence, and we know to what terrible violence her sickly narcissism was to lead her. The character of Esclarmonde in Breton's *Les Etats-Généraux* is a revolutionary heroine chosen

---

[3] André Breton, *Clair de terre*, tr. Kenneth White, *Selected Poems of André Breton* (London: Jonathan Cape, 1969), p. 19.

from the medieval history of the religious wars of France; she is also violent but her violence is part of her martyrdom caused in the course of her quest for the common salvation of her people.

The examples could be multiplied to prove that reaction and revision were part of the passage from symbolism to surrealism, and this element has indeed been recognized in the commentaries of literary history. And on that level there is no need to comment further on differences already noted.

However, as soon as we detach Mallarmé from the symbolist framework, and Breton from the surrealist label, an analysis more closely applied to these two poets reveals elements that bring them closer together and which go beyond the purely aesthetic considerations to enter the field of ontological inquiry. What is poetry? What is its field of interaction? How is it a factor in the apprehension of reality? What is the nature of symbol?

Breton tells us in an article called "Fronton-Virage" that he was familiar with the cryptic sonnets of Mallarmé. And in his autobiographical *Entretiens* (published in the later years of his life) he explains in retrospective meditation that of course it was normal for an activist group like the surrealists to reject what came before them and free themselves from ancestors. But what surprised him, he said, was the fact that the official body of literary historians did not seem to recognize the fact that there was a chain of transmission that linked the two movements. How did they fail to notice that there were threads that knit together an underground tradition? an esoteric tradition that linked all across Europe from the early nineteenth century the poetic preoccupations of poets such as Novalis, Hoelderlin in Germany, Blake and Coleridge in England, Nerval and Baudelaire in France, and reached a peak with Mallarmé?[4] In this hermetic tradition, the need for the marvelous and the imponderable remain constants among the variations in style related to passing literary schools, but the symbols changed, and certain natural phenomena took turns in functioning as mediations between human imagination and a reality which wavers behind certain common appearances. In this current which manifests successive foils for concealment and eventually reaches him, Breton recognizes the most fruitful indices of modern poetics. And in the case of Mallarmé, there had occurred a strange paradox. The agnostic

---

[4] Breton, "Fronton-Virage" in *La Clé des champs* (Sagittaire, 1953) (written in 1948), and *Entretiens* (Gallimard, 1952), p. 78.

little bourgeois that Mallarmé was in his personal life had carried on a sustained search for gnostic revelations and had made him dream of a future when "the instinct for heaven which resides in each human being" would be stirred by the poet who would have assumed the role of "mystagogue." But Mallarmé's mistake, according to Breton, was to have cultivated mystery for its own sake, simply to become difficult. Said Breton: "I know nothing so puerile as Mallarmé's compulsion not to let any text of his be read which might be too easily understood without injecting into it some shadow of mystification" (in "Le Merveilleux contre le mystère").[5] He found in this type of artificial mystification a form of weakness unworthy of Mallarmé and more characteristic of the minor symbolist poets. For this artificial mystery Breton wanted to substitute the marvelous, which is veiled only so that it may be unveiled, in the spirit of the operations of the alchemists who had found the same basic linguistic root in the word "veil" (*voile*) as in "revelation" and whose every effort for veiling carried in itself the clues to the unveiling and then to the reveiling of significations. Thus, the veil that in the eyes of the Romantic poets was the barrier between the real world and the supernal, and in the case of the symbolists "trembled" at the temple of Isis and became torn with Mallarmé and in Yeats; more and more permanent fissures became visible in the so-called impenetrable cloisters into which retreated the symbolists. The marvelous to which the symbolists sometimes yielded almost unconsciously became for Breton a form of reception, total and englobing, through which human beings could reach each other over and above the limitation of time and space.

Breton's criticism of Mallarmé is not altogether fair. If it is true that Mallarmé told the poets around him to work with mystery, he meant exactly the same thing as when Breton declared in his Second Manifesto that the surrealist must engage in deep occultation. Both meant that the poet had to work in silence and secrecy with the patience of an alchemist and be aware of the process of poetic creation. The admonition implied the difficulty of the process of writing poetry; it suggested that poetry required infinite care and undisturbed monitoring of the altered state. This awareness is manifest in all of Mallarmé's writings from the mysterious *Igitur*, the creation of which almost drove Mallarmé out of his mind, to the obsession he had in the last years

---

[5]Breton, "Le Merveilleux contre le mystère," in *La Clé des champs* (Sagittaire, 1953), pp. 11-12 (written in 1936); the translation is mine.

of his life to write the Book, in the guise of a Magus and adept in the use of a magical language of hieroglyphics. In fact, this sense of a language of high power is the basis of the link between Mallarmé and Breton over and above the variety of poetic forms they adopt. Both feel that the mysterious powers of language enlarge consciousness and deepen the sense of existence. Mallarmé expressed this sense in his famous sentence: "The orphic explanation of the Earth, which is the only duty of the poet and the only literary play that counts."[6] This literary maneuver of language changes, according to both poets, the functioning of the logical, linear train of thought, and it is this change which distinguishes the new poetic form from all other forms of writing whether written in verse or prose. One of the most important propositions that Mallarmé made in the domain of poetics was that language was henceforth to be not a conveyer of thoughts but a container or thesaurus of poetic images whose disposition or precipitation or even tension with each other created poetic states or phenomena. Language thus became for him a pursuit and an end in itself. In his last poems as well as in his much studied last will and testament, *Un Coup de dés*, Mallarmé had discovered a secret inaccessible to most of his symbolist colleagues, and that he seems to have passed directly to Breton: that language contains in its sounds and words and in its morphological contours a great number of meanings that can be utilized simultaneously; this character of language was indeed the source of the ancient enigmas, or the rebus, or the oracle, and could be adapted to a polysemantic harmony in modern poetry. When we say that symbolism cultivated ambiguity in poetry, the word "ambiguity" is itself ambiguous. There is the kind of ambiguity you can find in the poetry of Verlaine, what he called "la chanson grise," the gray song, which creates a general sense of mystery inviting each reader to find his own interpretation of Verlaine's state of being, or substitute one of his own parallel to Verlaine's. The ambiguity of Mallarmé, which was to be passed on to Breton and to a few other surrealists is a systematic construction of associations of words which interplay, which create different states of meanings in synchronized structure, begin a series and suggest to the reader, through clues, how to continue the scale. It is a system which he called architectural and premeditated like the work of the alchemist to whom he compared himself. And contrary to the very spirit of this

---

[6] Mallarmé, "Autobiographie," *OC*, p. 663; the translation is mine.

type of poetic construction, learned readers have been trying to decode a single meaning, to untangle the so-called difficulty, when the target of reader-critic should indeed be to discover and appreciate the *process* that creates a multiplicity of meanings. As early as 1923, when his own poetic writings were still ahead of him, Breton realized that there was much to be discovered about Mallarmé's poetics that was avant-garde and not to be confused with his conservative life-style. He also believed that it would take some time to sort out and understand his achievements: "It will be some time before Mallarmé will be discovered, the work of Mallarmé which the person of Mallarmé still hides from us, and eyes will be turned particularly in the direction of *Un Coup de dés* (letter of December 8, 1923). Breton meditated along the same lines as Mallarmé when he asked in his article on Raymond Roussel in "Fronton-Virage": how can one hide something in such a way as to invite possibilities of eventual deciphering? He came to the conclusion that this attitude which was of half-deceit, and at the same time somewhat engaging, was strictly conforming to the discourse of hermetic philosophers (*La Clé des champs*, p. 192). Both poets conclude in the same manner: that the occult does not reside principally in a particular philosophy but in the depths of language itself with its hide-and-seek quality, and if this quality is integral to language it means of course that the hermeticism is inherent in all thought that reaches beyond the surface of consciousness, the movement from the first layer of the self to the next is what Breton called the passage from the *moi* to the *soi*. The search for these facets of language was in fact for Breton, manifesting his belief in the *poetry of language over and above the language of poetry*, the guiding principle of his work from his first poems to the majestic ones of his mature period. Although he talked readily about the miracle of automatic writing, whatever psychic provocations he used were a means rather than an end, like finger exercises to the very structured poetics that combined with the aid of carefully chosen words and their fortuitous gravitations several registers of poetic states, generally one having to do with the immediacy of life, one on a mythological universal plane, and one digging into unconscious desire or dream, the synchronization suggesting a complex reality in the manner in which Mallarmé had evoked through the meditations of a Faun that unforgettable afternoon. And the timid school teacher that Mallarmé was, had crystallized desire, universal throughout the ages, through the miracle of a language that fused dream, fiction, and reality. He had pushed the art of the polysemantic much further on to a cosmic plane in the *Coup de dés*. For instance, the word that means in French pen and wing, *plume* brought together writing and flying, and the word veil and sail, *voile* associating sea and obstruction communicating human frailty and poetic power simultaneously, replaced linear thought with a system of analogical circularity going beyond allegory or even symbol.

Thus, poetry becomes a provocative guessing game, in principle inexhaustible, and in which the message that each person can pick up is apt to surpass the projections that the poet might have had in mind, creating an activity of the mind which can well illustrate the statement that the poet Aragon made in *Le Paysan de Paris*: that the very idea of limit is the only concept that is unacceptable to the human mind.[7]

But if both Mallarmé and Breton believed in the polysemantic character of language as a base for poetic activity, there is a basic difference in the search for the multiplicity of meaning. Mallarmé went about finding this multiplicity in a methodical manner, with etymological dictionaries, and relied on his knowledge of foreign languages — in his case English, his means of livelihood! Many of his findings (*trouvailles*) in polyvalence were put to use in a somewhat artificial manner and their hidden meanings were acceptable only in a fictitious world. Breton, however, thought etymological significations inert, unfunctional. He sought polyvalence in the subconscious functioning of language, such as in the speech of mediums or the deranged, on through the process of automatic writing, or dream transcription. That is why it is not paradoxical or contradictory to claim that Breton's poetry is both automatic and structured. Automatism is a state of grace for him, a state in which he can spontaneously make discoveries about language that hours of reflective study may fail to achieve. In retrospection he tells us this in his *Entretiens*: "Automatism, under whatever form you may want to envisage it, does not come upon demand." It is most likely to come, he says, to those who have an intimate relationship with the natural world; it is spontaneous, in the case of primitive societies, desired and sought by revolutionaries "who have believed in and who believe in the restauration of man in a world from which he has ceased to be alienated."[8]

[7] Louis Aragon, *Le Paysan de Paris* (Gallimard, 1926).
[8] Breton, *Entretiens*, p. 257.

In a short article called "Le La" Breton compared the role of the automatic phase to the "A" of the orchestra when it tunes up in preparation for performance.[9] For the poet, the "A" of automatism is the pure unmitigated data catalyzing the artistic work; this parallel between the musicians who prepare to perform and the poet who sharpens his imagination is a distinction which to my knowledge no one has shown except Breton and in a more subtle way Mallarmé before him in *Afternoon of a Faun*. In Breton's opinion it is the spontaneous process of automatism that breaks the shackles of inhibition and thereby permits the poet to collect the materials with which he will then *consciously* create his work of art. His essential work will consist of blending the spontaneous or fortuitous with the deliberate.

Meditating on the spontaneously creative power of words, Breton associated his efforts of course with those of Rimbaud, adventurer in poetics as in life-style. What Breton found noteworthy in the famous sonnet of the "Vowels" was not simply the polysemantic play with words and the discovery of their associations but the manner in which Rimbaud had "turned the word away from its duty to signify." This comment occurs in an early article entitled "Les Mots sans rides" in which Breton speculates about magnetic fields that make certain words gravitate toward others not only on the basis of associative meanings but by their spacial qualities and cognitive tensions. Words, he says, are creators of energy, and "the expression of an idea depends as much on the appearance of the words as on their meaning. There are words that work against the idea that they presume to express."[10] What he is saying is that once you have exploited the riches of meanings, once you have — in modern terminology — *deconstructed* their ordinary and mechanical connotations, you reach a point zero *but you don't stay there* — at least if you are a poet. You assign new significations to them. Mallarmé had had the same idea when he said that the "Aim of language is to become beautiful, and not to give preference to the expression of the beautiful over everything else."[11]

In "Les Mots sans rides," which was a work of his youth, Breton placed on the same level of theoretical conjecture what Mallarmé had already tried and tested concretely in his untitled sonnet "Le vierge, le vivace, et le bel aujourd'hui," in which the process he used is precisely

[9] Breton, "Le La" in *Signe ascendant*, pp. 174-75 (written about 1960).
[10] Breton, *Les Pas perdus* (Gallimard, 1924), p. 133.
[11] Mallarmé, *Diptyque: Une Méthode, OC*, p. 853.

to let the meaning of words and their analogical sonorities as well as morphological parallels spill on to each other and in a cumulative movement create the synthetic, virtual (as opposed to real) image of a swan, all the while crystallizing on the semantic register the physical and psychological state of the poet. This poem is the perfect example of Mallarmé's theory of the interaction of words in the creation of a substitute reality. He stated this notion in his preface to the theoretical work of a co-symbolist, René Ghil. He said in the preface to his *Traité du verbe*: "Contrary to a face value, easy and representative, as handled by the masses, Discourse is before anything else, a dream and song, which finds in the hands of the poet, because of the necessary constitution of an art dedicated to fictions, its own virtual image."[12] The dexterity needed to accomplish this feat of recreating the universe with the aid of language, Mallarmé characterizes it as a linguistic one attained through the cultivation of the possibilities of the interplay of words. His theoretical writings are widely interspersed with expressions such as "language in its play," "word play," "literary play." We might say that the game theory of language is at work, and that its work is a verbal play activity. When we come to Breton, however, "play" is too lowly a word to characterize what he considers the high mission of the destiny of language. The analogy is no longer confined to play but aims at *love*. Words make love with each other, subjected to all the traps and perils of chance, desire, attraction, copulation, and procreation. "From the moment when words are appreciated from a more and more emotional angle, from which we lend to their association, under certain forms, a power of deep, unique relationship, between one being and another, better still in which we dream thanks to them of reaching essence, it is clear that behavior in terms of language, will tend more and more to follow the pattern of behavior in love" (*La Clé des champs*, p. 12). The association of words includes the factor of the "emotional" here which is never mentioned in Mallarmé.

Onward from the major poem of his early period, "L'Union libre" to the series of love poems called *L'Air de l'eau*, and on and up to his last series of prose poems, *Constellations*, in which he departs completely from the verse line as Mallarmé had done in *Coup de dés*, the dominant pattern of Breton's poetry is that of verbal alliance paralleling

---

[12] Mallarmé, *Traité de verbe, OC*, p. 858.

intimate protoplasmic and cosmic alliances, with the broader structure of the erotic embrace. "Poetry is made in bed like love / Its rumpled sheets are the dawn of things" ("Sur la route de San Romano").[13] The mixing of metaphors is not a failing of rhetoric but a conscious effort to suggest the intermingling of spheres of human, natural, and cosmic activity such as human movement synchronized with snowing, soaring of birds, convulsion of earthquake: "Your flesh sprinkled with the flight of a thousand birds of paradise / Is a high flame lying in the snow."[14] Sometimes when the central word of the image has more than one meaning in French, it does not come off in English translation. The following lines in French do not carry across their double identity into English even in the expert hands of Kenneth White: "En partant j'ai mis le feu à une mèche de cheveux qui est celle d'une bombe / Et la mèche de cheveux creuse un tunnel sous Paris / Si seulement mon train entrait dans ce tunnel" rendered as "On leaving I set fire to a lock of hair which was the fuse of a bomb / And the lock of hair is hollowing out a tunnel under Paris / If only my train could enter that tunnel" (*Clair de terre*). The trouble is that the sensuality of hair and the explosive character of bomb which are integrated into the verbal polyvalence in French where "mèche" means both lock of hair and bomb, do not carry over into English and the hair-meaning cannot penetrate the bomb-meaning and vise versa although the translator can suggest a parallel on a linear level ("Aigrette"). The reason Breton loved the sunflower, "tournesol," so much is because his own poetic movements were like the physical ones of the sunflower and could be called "heliotropic." The words he chose gravitate like the sunflower toward fire (and explosion) whether of a human or cosmic nature. That is indeed the broad meaning of his last sentence in *Nadja*: "Beauty must be convulsive or not at all."

The dexterity Breton developed in making verbal alliances in close step with human concordances with the rhythms of nature, reached its peak with the prose poems called *Constellations*, and this structural pattern is evidenced in the number of words that are signifiers of conjunction and function as links in the interplay. The central character is a prestigitator whose success depends on the combination of dexterity and chance, the very attributes that Breton manipulates one against the other in the creation of poetry.

[13] Breton, *Signe ascendant*, p. 122 (the translation is mine).
[14] Breton, *L'Air de l'eau* in *Clair de terre* (Gallimard, 1966), p. 160 (original date of the poem 1934).

What is most significant in all this over and above common interests in language, is the fact that the problems of writing are directly associated both by Mallarmé and by Breton with the crucial problematics of life although the circumstance of life are not the same for the two poets. Above all the interest in the functioning of language is motivated by the thought that man finds his liberty in the use he makes of language; the other side of the coin is that if he does not find his liberty through language he may well risk finding his bondage in using language in the stilted way society can induce him to do. Breton moreover believes that there is a strong carry-over from man's effort to emancipate his language to that of emancipating his life. Thus is language in its poetic function integrally tied to the notion of existence in both poets in their awareness of the power of language to burgeon with thought rather than simply to express it. According to Breton, the last great French poet to have used language in its traditional way to convey thought rather than generate it was Baudelaire.

But despite this important parallel between Mallarmé and Breton in the composition of a poem and the central significance of language, we are obliged to recognize that distance between a poem of Mallarmé and one of Breton is not narrowed. If some of the means to the poetic objective are similar, if some of the techniques are handed down from the one to the other over the heads of a host of lesser poets of imitative nature, the objectives or intentions of the poetic activity envisaged, desired, reflect the differences both of their individual characters and the separate epochs in which they were nurtured. In their pursuit of liberty, both are obsessed by the forces of chance. Mallarmé spent a lifetime confronting and combatting chance in the context of the human will. Unable to cope with the struggle on the philosophical level, he posits it on the level of poetry. *Un Coup de dés* is the monument to the great battle he waged against chance. The artist/writer cannot abolish chance but in the very utterance of that statement he causes chance to stumble; in the spaces of the book even as in the spaces of the cosmos his presence and his effort to daunt the forces leading him to sure catastrophe compel him to engage with those forces and consider the possibility of survival through language. In the broad literature that emanates from symbolism, with which Mallarmé's name is so closely connected, I am aware only of two poets who tackle this cosmic problem, although many have used the exterior format of the *Coup de dés*. They are two Latin-American poets,

Aldo Pellegrini of Argentina in *Distribución del silencio* and the Chilean Vincente Huidobro in *Altazor*.[15]

Breton was of an age that had had time to accept chance as a substitute for providence. Some of his contemporaries succumbed to that acceptance and developed an *écriture* that reflects not the struggle of Mallarmé but a diffidence and a begrudging imitation of the indifference with which chance strikes and passes. Theirs is the world of the absurd, as we all know. But Breton's stance is neither that of Mallarmé nor of the absurdists. Instead of thinking like Mallarmé that chance intrudes into the ordered scheme of the mind, he invites it with open arms; he sets out to seduce it, to court it, to appropriate its powers for his own ends whether along the lines of poetic discoveries or in questions of love as important to him as his poetics.

Both poets were rebels against the conditions of the society of their time, but they compensated for their dissatisfaction in quite different ways. Mallarmé turned his back on society, Breton attacked it with the notorious but symbolic revolver shot which he characterized as the typical surrealist attitude of alarm and anger in relation to the ills of society. Mallarmé's introverted rebellion reflected the spirit of decadence of the time. Writing became a refuge for him, an act of interiority, and the communication of a poem to others was likened by him to the dropping of a visiting card at someone's doorstep to say: "I came by but you were not there." The assumption was, of course, that symbolically speaking he was unlikely to be received by those on whose doors he knocked; that is to say, the poetic message would be subject to an absence of reception. But the retreat was not only vis-à-vis the readers, whom he assumed to be sparse. The withdrawal was also manifest in the kind of lexicon he chose, a lexicon which created for him a synthetic existence, a fictitious one, in which would flourish the flower absent from all bouquets, or that Hérodiade, enclosed in stone and tapistry, removed in time and space from any possibility of historical identification, a Salome intentionally misnamed to add a fictitious character beyond even legendary identification. With Mallarmé something new happened, and in this respect he was to have many followers into the modern world: he creates the fiction of the poet, ever more removed from reality than ever the fiction of the novelist was or has been, in which life itself finds a substitute

[15] Aldo Pellegrini, *Distribución del silencio* (Buenos Aires: Ediciones "A partir de Cero," 1957), p. 27. Vicente Huidobro, *Altazor* in *Obras completas*, I (Zig-Zag, 1964).

in the undecipherable book (*le grimoire*). Biographers of Mallarmé have observed that he was sexually inhibited and repressed because of a very early marriage and a structured bourgeois life. That may be so; I am not here to dispute the conjectures of psychocriticism. But the sexual repression found vivid compensation in a language-oriented eroticism, in the *virtual* rather than real world, audacious and isolated, moving in the direction of the Septentrion, which he conceived as a dead star. There he can do all that he does not dare to do within the narrow confines of his life. Language in its liberty and generosity makes it possible for him to make love with two nymphs simultaneously, and if Beauty is on the wane in the real world, he shows us in that cryptic poem called "Prose pour Des Esseintes" a "Pulcherie" who survives thanks to the fictitious hyperbole of a gladiola too tall for this world but quite comfortable in "a world that did not exist."[16] In the pursuit of this fictitious world of new alliances of signifiers with signified his following is immense and international: Yeats, Valéry, Rilke, Stevens, to name some of the greatest.

André Breton's sense of the meaning of liberation was quite different. Here we have a philosophy of life which makes of man and the human experience of living a triumph over the artist, or, as he said it himself, makes art reversible to life. Rebellion, even as Mallarmé's refuge, is manifest in language which instead of crystallizing in a swan caught in ice, or a golden bird of Byzantium, plunges into natural phenomena to find there the hyperbole that surpasses the fictitious. Over and above all the exterior lables that his poetry has acquired, he characterized poetry as the result of "exceptional intensity of man before the spectacle of life."[17] He felt this as he viewed the activity of the Martiniquan poet, Aimé Césaire, in a country where the savage eye which Breton had sought to cultivate in his own Parisian environment had a much better chance to realize its potential. In a "Dialogue créole" which he conducted with his artist friend André Masson he observed: "One can wonder to what degree the poverty of European vegetation is responsible for the escape of the mind toward an imaginary flora. Should we not try to escape from that particular perception of what falls under our senses when we return to less favored places?"[18]

[16] Mallarmé, "Prose pour Des Esseintes," *OC*, p. 55.
[17] Breton, "Un Grand Poète noir," in *Martinique, charmeuse de serpents* (Pauvert, 1972), p. 105.
[18] Breton, "Dialogue créole," *ibid.*, pp. 18-19.

In conclusion, I will reiterate some of the points I have tried to make about the Mallarmé/Breton axis as they relate directly to current preoccupations with polysemantics, symbolization and writer/reader relationships. The impact of Mallarmé and Breton has been in three categories as we might conclude from my discussion, moving poetics toward a redefinition of the sacred, toward the reconsideration of the question of human relationship with nature, and the writer's relationship to the reader.

Mallarmé and Breton belonged to an era of philosophical transition, Mallarmé at its beginning, Breton at its closure. They were both intent on using poetry as an adjustment factor. In that respect, as they saw the divine being dislocated from its erstwhile association with the arts as a supernal presence, participating in the process of artistic creativity, they tried to preserve the notion of the sacred by appropriating its power.

Mallarmé's so-called "virtual reality" was such an attempt to capture the sacred. The artifact he created with high intellectual lucidity did not englobe him but was endowed with a certain autonomy from circumstantial strictures. Nothing is clearer than the analogy he makes in that early poem, "Le Don du poème," in which he compares the birth of a poem with the birth of a child. After difficult and prolonged labor, it is born and *given*, i.e., severed from the one who begot it. All we hear about the process is that it was "horrible" and if we look at the years Mallarmé spent correcting his works, we know that he was not exaggerating about the difficulties of creating. Lately he has been quoted repeatedly from *Crise de vers* where he says that his "I" disappeared into the poem.[19] In truth, it disappeared from the poem as well, leaving in its trace a multiplicity of potential "I"'s. The notion of the "sacred" surfaces in the manner in which a sacerdotal ritual is performed in the symbolization process whereby the earthly bread incorporates divine spirit. Mallarmé saw himself performing that type of ritual over and over again as he distilled material entities into ideations containing in their contours an infinite series of reidentifications. For Mallarmé, the word "Verbe" is sacred, as opposed to languages which are subjected to changing codes and mores. The poet is a mediator between the Verbe, with its integral meaning, and the languages of comprehension.

---

[19] Mallarmé, *Crise de vers, OC,* p. 366.

Breton also saw a desperate need in the modern world to preserve the notion of the sacred while rejecting its supernatural character. His solution was different although like Mallarmé he claimed a whole line of predecessors. He attached the creative process to that of analogical thinking which he found at the basis of all magical operations. But his major objective was not the production of an artifact endowed with a sacred character reinterpretable through the ages. For Breton, the process of creativity was more important than the ultimate product, and not something horribly difficult to do but rather supremely enjoyable. Influenced by the esoterism of the ages, and by contemporaries such as Pierre Mabille who was studying voodoo ritual, and Malcolm de Chazal engrossed in the rituals of Eastern cultures, he saw the transfer of the sacred into the notion of *volupté*, i.e., a vertiginous reception of physical reality and the effervescent participation of the poet in the universal intercourse amongst beings, things, animal, vegetable, mineral, human existences. Because this flow was evident not only in the primitive but in modern poetic perceptions — and he drew his examples from among the great poets of the nineteenth century in particular — he believed that it was a permanent manifestation which the polysemantic character of languages supported. The resulting artifact was part of the life experience, a provocation for other creative activity, i.e., everyman's rite of passage from surface reality to deeper levels where antinomies ceased to exist. The symbolization was not confined to the work of art but in the pool of language available to all. We proceed thus from the notion of poetry as an elitist activity to poetry for all. In this respect, the intentionality, so often the very subject of Breton's writings, is as important a text as the work of art that may arise to implement it. In fact, three of his major prose writings: *Nadja* (1928), *Les Vases communicants* (1932), and *L'Amour fou* (1937) are expressions of that intentionality. They are projects, instigations for works of greater proportion open to others. In these times, when the discussion of intentionality of the writer is frowned upon in critical circles, it is important to realize that in the case of surrealist writings it is at the heart of the matter and part of the transformational process of the work of art.

Like Mallarmé, Breton had that sense of delivery of the work of art to the reader except that for him the catalytic power (or sacred character) resided in the process of production rather than in the work produced. That is why sharing his intentions with the reader was so important. In the case of Mallarmé, the value of the work is to be judged empirically through the reception of the work itself; in the case of Breton it is the creator's communication of the altered state of ap-perception that has to be received along with the work itself, i.e., the transfer of emotion, of a sublimation.

What light do Mallarmé and Breton throw on the altered relation-ship of man with nature? In the case of Mallarmé, as I pointed out earlier, much of his work presents a rupture with the ordinary flow of natural states and phenomena. His garden is artificial, in a coun-try that does not exist; his planet is dead except as it is cultivated by language creating artifacts on an empty and indifferent canvas. Nature in no way contributes to the sacralization of the poet's universe. He has deconstructed what was there before projecting his interiority onto a tangible exteriority. His negation of the gods involves also the nega-tion of the principal sites where they had established correspondences. On this matter, he concurred with George W. Cox, whose work he rendered into French in his *Les Dieux antiques*, a work in which Cox had demythified ancient mythology by reducing the powers of the gods to natural movements of earth, sun, stars, etc.[20]

But the blank space, depopulated of its gods, does not thereby return to a void. Mallarmé does not deal in abstractions. His images are very concrete but the composite, derived from culling of physical im-ages, no longer functions in its natural and original habitat. Instead, it is staged in a new space totally controlled by the stage directions of the poet. He is not alienated as a creator although he may well have been exiled as a human being.

Breton had the same preoccupation: how to revise modern man's relation with nature. Like Mallarmé, he considered his answer of primary importance to his role as poet. But his proposed solution was quite different. He made himself permeable to the larger and unpredictable movements of the physical world which work toward integration rather than separation of man in relation to nature. He could reach this sense of monistic integration by developing as we have already mentioned, the mental activity involved in establishing analogies. Every symbol created through analogy is integrated in a pool and only provisionally detached from the matrix where it cor-relates with an infinite number of others.

---

[20] Mallarmé, *Les Dieux antiques*, *OC*, pp. 1159-276.

Now we might think that this resembles belief in a Swedenborgian network of correspondences except for the very important fact that nature is not viewed as a temple, intermediary between earth and an unknowable heaven; instead, we might say that it is a cauldron ever productive and attainable. The mission of the poet is not to make a break but to enter into the "synthetic comprehension of the world and to make man enter into this knowledge," as expressed by Pierre Mabille and quoted by Breton in one of his last essays, entitled "Pont Levis," which was published in the posthumous collection of Breton's prose, *Perspective cavalière.*[21] The fact of the matter is—and this is the basic quality of modernism as I see it—that correspondences are no longer recognized as preexisting to the artist's recognition of them; they are established by the artist himself, and their impact on human consciousness is strictly monitored by the artist. The aleatory character of natural and human phenomena is captured and vigilantly structured into the artifact.

To come to the third question: the relationship with the reader, Mallarmé and Breton united in their recognition of the writer's responsiblity vis-à-vis the reader. Their position preempts that of modern hermeneutics in the assumption that interpretation is a creative activity and conducive to what Breton called "a perplexed lucidity." Both opened their works to the uncertainty and multiplicity of interpretation. Mallarmé based his polysemy on the strategic composition of the poem aimed at creating ambiguity. Breton relied on the inherent riches of the analogical content captured by both writer and reader through the practice of nonlinear reading. This procedure is not identifiable with modern poetics of criticism although the works of both poets have served as objects of the critical exercise in hermeneutics which decodes and recodes so-called "texts" through the practice of logical discourse. One of the basic distinctions Mallarmé and Breton made between poetry and other forms of writing was poetry's inherent hermeneutic function. In making this broad separation between *poésie* and prose, they had thought that they had liberated poetry from what Breton called the "yoke of Greco-Roman logistics." Poetry's subjection to methodologies applicable to expository writing would have struck them as paradoxical, indeed as a threat to the very survival of poetry.

---

[21] *Perspective cavalière* (Gallimard, 1970), p. 201.

Modern analytical, empirical criticism has encouraged the confusion between informative communication and esthetic coexperience. In the climate of the modernism here discussed, language was interesting only as a resource or pool for the creative process. Language is important only as it illuminates the poetry; when the tables are turned around, poetry becomes interesting only as it illuminates language. The inverted importance may be beneficial to the development of the skill of analytical thinking, but poetry's first concern is esthetic. The epistemological concerns of both Mallarmé and Breton were encrusted, were incapsulated in their esthetics because at that point in time poetry had become much more than a way of writing about beautiful things. It was a counterproposal to ordinary life; and in trying to emerge from the linguistic labyrinth, they thought they were leaving the poem, not as a testimony to their struggle with language, but as an opening to lead others toward the light. So the poem itself was not an exercise in analysis but a cameo of synthesis, not an object reflective of the writer, but provocative of the reader's own self-identification and power to enrich universal wisdom.

Mallarmé's "La Gloire"

JAMES R. LAWLER

> On a eu le tort de ne voir dans cette obscurité de
> Mallarmé qu'un dessein prémédité et un jeu
> intellectuel...
>
> Henri Peyre

La Gloire! je ne la sus qu'hier, irréfragable, et rien ne m'intéressera
d'appelé par quelqu'un ainsi.

Cent affiches s'assimilant l'or incompris des jours, trahison de la lettre, ont fui, comme à tous confins de la ville, mes yeux au ras de
l'horizon par un départ sur le rail traînés avant de se recueillir dans
l'abstruse fierté que donne une approche de forêt en son temps
d'apothéose.

Si discord parmi l'exaltation de l'heure, un cri faussa ce nom connu
pour déployer la continuité de cimes tard évanouies, Fontainebleau,
que je pensai, la glace du compartiment violentée, du poing aussi étrein-
dre à la gorge l'interrupteur: Tais-toi! Ne divulgue pas du fait d'un aboi
indifférent l'ombre ici insinuée dans mon esprit, aux portières de wagons
battant sous un vent inspiré et égalitaire, les touristes omniprésents
vomis. Une quiétude menteuse de riches bois suspend alentour quelque extraordinarie état d'illusion, que me réponds-tu? qu'ils ont, ces
voyageurs, pour ta gare aujourd'hui quitté la capitale, bon employé
vociférateur par devoir et dont je n'attends, loin d'accaparer une ivresse
à tous départie par les libéralités conjointes de la nature et de l'Etat,
rien qu'un silence prolongé le temps de m'isoler de la délégation urbaine vers l'extatique torpeur de ces feuillages là-bas trop immobilisés

136

pour qu'une crise ne les éparpille bientôt dans l'air; voici, sans attenter à ton intégrité, tiens, une monnaie.

Un uniforme inattentif m'invitant vers quelque barrière, je remets sans dire mot, au lieu du suborneur métal, mon billet.

Obéi pourtant, oui, à ne voir que l'asphalte s'étaler net de pas, car je ne peux encore imaginer qu'en ce pompeux octobre exceptionnel du million d'existences étageant leur vacuité en tant qu'une monotonie énorme de capitale dont va s'effacer ici la hantise avec le coup de sifflet sous la brume, aucun furtivement évadé que moi n'ait senti qu'il est, cet an, d'amers et lumineux sanglots, mainte indécise flottaison d'idée désertant les hasards comme des branches, tel frisson et ce qui fait penser à un automne sous les cieux.

Personne et, les bras de doute envolés comme qui porte aussi un lot d'une splendeur secrète, trop inappréciable trophée pour paraître! mais sans du coup m'élancer dans cette diurne veillée d'immortels troncs au déversement sur un d'orgueils surhumains (or ne faut-il pas qu'on en constate l'authenticité?) ni passer le seuil où des torches consument, dans une haute garde, tous rêves antérieurs à leur éclat répercutant en pourpre dans la nue l'universel sacre de l'intrus royal qui n'aura eu qu'à venir: j'attendis, pour l'être, que lent et repris du mouvement ordinaire, se réduisît à ses proportions d'une chimère puérile emportant du monde quelque part, le train qui m'avait là déposé seul.[1]

Glory! I did not know it until yesterday, ungainsayable, and nothing called thus by anyone will interest me.

A hundred posters absorbing the day's misunderstood gold, a betrayal of letters, have fled, as to every limit of the city, my eyes drawn level with the horizon by a rail departure before meditating in the secret pride given by a forest at the time of its apotheosis.

So discordantly amid the hour's exaltation did a cry falsify the familiar name of Fontainebleau, unfolding the continuity of slowly vanishing peaks, that I was on the point of breaking my compartment window and seizing the interruptor by the throat: Be silent! Do not, by an uncaring yelp, expose the shadow here insinuated in my mind to the carriage doors banging in an inspired egalitarian breeze, having spewed forth the omnipresent tourists. A fictitious calm of rich woods suspends hereabouts an extraordinary state of illusion, what do you answer? that these travellers have today left the capital for your station, good employee who vociferate in duty's name; far from monopolizing an intoxication offered to all by

[1] Stéphane Mallarmé, *Oeuvres complètes* (Pléiade, Gallimard, 1945), pp. 288-89. Hereafter cited as *OC*.

the joint generosity of nature and state, I ask of you nothing but a silence as long as it will take for me to isolate myself from the urban delegation toward the ecstatic torpor of leaves too still for them not to be soon scattered upon the air by a crisis; here, without my encroaching on your integrity, take this coin.

A heedless uniform inviting me toward some barrier, I mutely hand over my ticket, instead of the corruptive metal.

Obeyed nonetheless, yes, seeing only asphalt spread out bare of footsteps, for I cannot yet conceive that in this magnificent and exceptional October none but I of the million lives that range their emptiness in the likeness of the enormous monotony of a capital city whose obsessive presence will vanish here with the whistle blast in the mist, has escaped, feeling that there are, this year, bitter and luminous sobs, many an uncertain floating idea falling from chance like leaves from branches, a particular shimmering, and that which makes us think of autumn in this world.

No one, and the arms of doubt have fled like one who also bears a secret splendor, a trophy too precious to appear! but without immediately plunging into the diurnal vigil of immortal trunks pouring superhuman floods of pride onto a single person (for must not its authenticity be attested?) or crossing the threshold on which, in solemn guardage, torches consume all dreams prior to their brilliance, reflecting in a purple image upon the sky the universal consecration of the royal intruder who shall only have had to come: I waited, in order to be he, for the train which had left me there alone, at first slowly, then at its customary speed, to be reduced to the size of a childish fancy carrying people somewhere.

In *Les Mots anglais* Mallarmé observes that the letter *g* signifies aspiration toward a spiritual goal which, when joined to liquid *l*—"le désir comme satisfait par l"—expresses joy and light. He does not quote "glory" among his examples but its very omission is revealing: "gloire" is a key word in his vocabulary and can hardly but have served as a point of reference in his idiosyncratic analysis of English. Thus his poems evoke a work of genius ("la gloire ardente du métier"), the triymph of a painter ("la nymphe sans linceul / Que lui découvre ta Gloire"), the brilliance of a woman's hair ("le cri des Gloires..."), the grandeur of a sunset ("Tison de gloire"). At the heart of the usage is an association with traditional representations of Christ to which he links the gloria of the liturgy, directly echoed in his early piece "La Prière d'une mère." These, then, are the elements that, summoning the history of the word, convey beauty as illumination, whether the artist's "aveuglante gloire" or as spiritual absolute.

First published in Verlaine's *Les Hommes d'aujourd'hui* in 1886, "La Gloire" is no doubt the most resonant of the Mallarmé prose poems.

It points back to the reveries of Rousseau, Chateaubriand, Lamartine, Hugo, Baudelaire, Verlaine himself whose violins—"Les sanglots longs / Des violons / De l'automne"—we hear in these "amers et lumineux sanglots." But Mallarmé's predecessors had treated autumn as a figure of nostalgia, whereas he enunciates a supreme goal and purpose celebrated in the name of all, "le sens (notoire, le destin de l'homme),"[2] "les splendeurs d'un holocauste élargi à tous les temps pour que ne s'en juxtapose à personne le sacre vain."[3] Here is the bitter-sweet drama of universal desire, the end of which is to achieve the mutation into an idea. Mallarmé renews the Romantic topos by expressing it within the framework of a rigorous poetics. For more than twenty years October at Valvins was the highlight of his year in which he read a sign; but nowhere, I think, did he elaborate language with a mastery greater than that of the page we are reading.

The first sentence has an energy that separates it from the rest of the poem.

> La Gloire! je ne la sus qu'hier, irréfragable, et rien ne m'intéressera d'appelé par quelqu'un ainsi.

A lapidary statement brings together past, future, implied present: it contains in a way all that can be said, so that the five other paragraphs will be variations rather than development. The reader's attention is forced by exclamation, capitalization, inversion, displacement of the epithet, dislocation of the adjectival phrase which resembles a single new word—"d'appelé par quelqu'un ainsi." The use of the past definite is also surprising, like that of "savoir" instead of "connaître"; but immediacy of impact is translated by the verbal tense, while clear-eyed awareness is emphasized above and beyond experience by "savoir." Held in isolated suspense by punctuation, the erudite "irréfragable" designates a radical truth that cannot be gainsaid, a fiction that confounds refutation. Thus a proud flourish introduces "un éclat triomphal trop brusque pour durer," its generality resuming an unelaborated valorization: to have known beauty is to scorn petty fame.[4] The poet's only concern must henceforth be to recover orphically an absent fullness.

---

[2] "Crayonné au théâtre," *OC*, p. 299.

[3] *OC*, p. 300.

[4] See "Le Mystère dans les lettres," *OC*, p. 384: "On peut du reste commencer d'un éclat triomphal trop brusque pour durer; invitant que se groupe, en retards, libérés par l'écho, la surprise."

Focus changes from the general to the particular as a line of discovery is traced in the more casual *passé composé*.

Cent affiches s'assimilant l'or incompris des jours, trahison de la lettre, ont fui, comme à tous confins de la ville, mes yeux au ras de l'horizon par un départ sur le rail traînés avant de se recueillir dans l'abstruse fierté que donne une approche de forêt en son temps d'apothéose.

Observant, self-conscious, the narrator turns from vulgar publicity to arcane rite: the rare "abstruse" points to a secret that requires penetration. But instead of transforming golden day into new radiance, the posters absorb — as dark colors absorb — that which has not been understood and thereby betray the role of language that gives voice to reality's meaning. The glance that sees opaque lettering is not provoked: monotony prevails in the first half of the sentence with insistent assonance, relatively short phrases staked out by commas, images of flatness. However, the second half leads beyond banality to mysterious mutation into the divine. A process opposite to that of the first sentence occurs: where "La Gloire!" introduced the text with panache, this paragraph goes from plainness to ornament and from rhythmic restriction to sumptuous expansion. We recognize a thought and its dynamics that bends objects to a personal philosophy and plays the concrete against the abstract.

After the initial affirmation and description, the third paragraph consists of an inner monologue in which humor is paramount.

Si discord parmi l'exaltation de l'heure, un cri faussa ce nom connu pour déployer la continuité de cimes tard évanouies, Fontainebleau, que je pensai, la glace du compartiment violentée, du poing aussi éteindre à la gorge l'interrupteur: Tais-toi! Ne divulge pas du fait d'un aboi indifférent l'ombre ici insinuée dans mon esprit, aux portières de wagons battant sous un vent inspiré et égalitaire, les touristes omniprésents vomis. Une quiétude menteuse de riches bois suspend alentour quelque extraordinaire état d'illusion, que me réponds-tu? qu'ils ont, ces voyageurs, pour ta gare aujourd'hui quitté la capitale, bon employé vociférateur par devoir et dont je n'attends, loin d'accaparer une ivresse à tous départie par les libéralités conjointes de la nature et de l'Etat, rien qu'un silence prolongé le temps de m'isoler de la délégation urbaine vers l'extatique torpeur de ces feuillages là-bas trop immobilisés pour qu'une crise ne les éparpille bientôt dans l'air; voici, sans attenter à ton intégrité, tiens, une monnaie.

The poet imagines himself turning on the stationmaster who, by his cry, appears to want to draw a crowd, since each syllable of "Fontainebleau" is thrown into relief like a line of mountain peaks; he is tempted to break the window and throttle the crier for it seems that a host of travellers will spill out on the platform, with carriage doors banging in democratic spirit; but he reminds himself that the employee is merely doing his duty, and that nature is not a gift made to himself alone: he would wish only to be allowed to precede the crowd that will march forth in a cluster like so many urban envoys. The tone, then, is witty, light, self-caricatural in its very earnestness. Yet the lyrical note is not abandoned as the wonders of the site of pilgrimage are spread before our eyes: "l'ombre ici insinuée dans mon esprit" is the sacred sense of nature; "une quiétude menteuse de riches bois" is the illusory dream of beauty that veils the void; "l'extatique torpeur de ce feuillages" is the perfected ecstasy after which there can be nothing but dispersion. In this fashion humor and lyricism work together to fill out the broad rhythm of two periods composing the longest section of the poem. On the one hand, a gesture; on the other, a mute request fantasized: in the poet's mind the discordant cry is silenced, then postponed by means of an imaginary gratuity. The paragraph does not have the brio of the first, nor the dramatic antithesis of the second, but it composes with an abundance of good spirits the dual curve of agitation calmed. In keeping with this progression the syntax is marked by long apodoses that show to advantage the elegant line of the voice as it encompasses question, indirect speech, vocative, qualification, inversion, subordinate clause, and terminates, after sustained expectancy, on the familiarity of a command.

A brief sentence replaces the fantasy and brings a witty return to the real.

> Un uniforme inattentif m'invitant vers quelque barrière, je remets sans dire mot, au lieu du suborneur métal, mon billet.

It is not the employee himself who is confronted but rather an impersonal uniform that, patently, has not attended to the poet's unspoken desires. The attitude is courteous and conventional, and the poet responds with similar formality. The contrast between monologue and description is thereby made in the space of a moment as humor comes from the change of rhythms and from the self's wordlessness after ample internal eloquence. The two halves of the sentence thus record the observance of a code in a silent ballet of conventions.

The language of the fifth paragraph is that of abstract thought, the self having turned to reflection and the meanders of musing.

Obéi pourtant, oui, à ne voir que l'asphalte s'étaler net de pas, car je ne peux encore imaginer qu'en ce pompeux octobre exceptionnel du million d'existences étageant leur vacuité en tant qu'une monotonie énorme de capitale dont va s'effacer ici la hantise avec le coup de sifflet sous la brume, aucun furtivement évadé que moi n'ait senti qu'il est, cet an, d'amers et lumineux sanglots, mainte indécise flottaison d'idée désertant les hasards comme des branches, tel frisson et ce qui fait penser à un automne sous les cieux.

The first word looks back to the imperatives of the previous interior monologue which now finds its desired result in a platform unencumbered. It is as if there has been magic intervention, since how else can one understand that people should willingly absent themselves from the forest's wonder? The empty station recalls the multitudinous emptiness of life in the vertical city ("étageant leur vacuité"), its huge sameness ("une monotonie énorme de capitale"). Yet this brooding image will disappear with the stationmaster's whistle for none but the poet has come to profit from the season("ce pompeux octobre exceptionnel"), none but he has answered the call of intermingling brightness and melancholy as beauty reaches its peak which is also its coming extinction ("d'amers et lumineux sanglots") and as ideas appear in their mature ambiguity like leaves wafted from branches or necessity born of chance. The moment is one of essential breeze, shimmering light, convergence of increase and decline that the symbolic imagination resumes in the word autumn ("ce qui fait penser à un automne sous les cieux"): Abstraction is allied with emotion, allegory with image. A single sentence of dazzling poise — its main verb elliptically reduced to a past participle, its syntax playfully deferring resolution — sets forth its several layers like a musical development whose echoes linger to the last. A gradual clarification takes place in the contrasts of sense and sensibility, vacancy and plenitude.

In a mode that recalls the opening words of the text, "Personne" is thrown into relief at the start of the closing sentence, yet with none of the phonetic and semantic brilliance of "La Gloire!" This is the primary term that will resonate in the paragraph until a final phrase brings the balance: presence will answer absence, the self will verify beauty.

Personne et, les bras de doute envolés comme qui porte aussi un lot d'une splendeur secrète, trop inappréciable trophée pour paraître! mais sans du coup m'élancer dans cette diurne veillée d'immortels troncs au déversement sur un d'orgueils surhumains (or ne faut-il pas qu'on en constate l'authenticité?) ni passer le seuil où des torches consument, dans une haute garde, tous rêves antérieurs à leur éclat répercutant en pourpre dans la nue l'universel sacre de l'intrus royal qui n'aura eu qu'à venir: j'attendis, pour l'être, que lent et repris du mouvement ordinaire, se réduisit à ses proportions d'une chimère puérile emportant du monde quelque part, le train qui m'avait là déposé seul.

Thus the poem concludes on a period of some one hundred and ten words that is no longer reflection but self-description governed by the tense of precise historical action previously found in the first ("sus") and third ("faussa," "pensai") sections, yet containing now the statement of a transcendent election. All else is cast aside — not only the crowd that might have thronged the site, but also the doubts and hesitations that invaded thought as to the possibility of witnessing beauty — so that now the vision can declare itself. Nevertheless, the poet does not go to his supreme pleasure but waits in a mood of pre-ecstasy to savor the time to be. He conceives the nobility of trees pouring forth their bounty like a cup running over, of "orgueils surhumains" crowning the previous references to "quelque extraordinaire état d'illusion," to "ce pompeux octobre exceptionnel," to "abstruse fierté," to "or incompris des jours," to "Gloire." Nature will be translated into words ("or ne faut-il pas qu'on en constate l'authenticité?"), the sacrificial fire will purify previous fictions which, being consumed, constitute the royal purple of a ritual like the mantle of the sky. The sentence achieves balance — solemn language, assured rhythm, continuous assonance — which shows Mallarméan prose at its most subtle. Emotion, intellect, imagination are brought together and the poem can conclude on a calm note, reaffirming the contrast between religious expectancy and the train's quotidian departure. In a span that moves from anonymity to authenticity, from "personne" to "seul," the sensibility comes to realize its function and found its truth.

"La Gloire" shows, then, not so much obscurity as density, and not so much obliqueness as orchestrated thought. Indeed, it is the metaphor of music that commands the style as Mallarmé plays with language in the most complex ways: first, by phonetic interweaving such as that of the anagrammatic "gloire" - "irréfragable," "glace," "gorge," "gare," "délégation," "sanglots," "orgueils," "garde," and of "or" – "discord," "extraordinaire," "torpeur," "suborneur," "énorme," "porte," "immortels," "torches," "ordinaire," "emportant," and of closed *o*, and of *i*; by rhythmic variety of a constantly inventive kind such as an emphatic terseness followed by fluidity in the first paragraph (2, 5, 4, 8, 8), or the balance of the fourth which ends on a mischievous trisyllable (7, 8, 7, 8, 3), or the sinuous light-footed elegance of the other sentences; or syntactic modulation like a compositional problem that is at long last solved, then discarded in order to be solved anew with each following sentence; or the tone moving between wit, self-irony, lyricism, high seriousness; or the vocabulary that allows puns ("mes yeux... *traînés*," where the participle evokes the train itself, or "existences *étageant* leur vacuité," which suggests the multistoreyed dwellings of the crowd, no less than rare or learned associations ("ir-réfragable," "abstruse," "diurne"); or the rapid appearance and disap-pearance of images caught in a single expressive wave, with concrete words losing their weight through the dominance of abstractions, through adjectives preceding nouns, through main verbs hidden or absent.

All this is clear; but I would wish to underline an aspect of the or-chestration that is no doubt less apparent. The poem produces its sense according to a set of binary oppositions of a plainly musical sort: it proceeds by ornament and not argument. We recognize a creative method that moves out from its central tensions as, in the first paragraph, "La Gloire" is contrasted with that which may normally be considered under the same name but which is dross. The distinc-tion between true and false provides a dominant statement which is a model of the structural polarities to come. Thus, in the second paragraph, "l'or incompris des jours" stands against the true gold and secret pride of the poetic imagination as city stands against forest, banality against apotheosis, dull absorption ("s'assimilant") against proud self-absorption ("se recueillir"). The third paragraph, with its involuted rhythm and syntax, is no less unified: the primary opposi-tion is between noise and silence—on the one hand, the cry ("si discord... un cri...," "aboi," "vociférateur"), which is analogous to the phonetically similar crisis ("crise") that will scatter the leafage, on the other, desirable calm ("tais-toi," "quiétude menteuse," "rien qu'un silence") which culminates in the intellectual and sensuous delight of nature's stillness ("exaltation de l'heure," "extatique torpeur"). At the same time, a contrast is drawn between noble secrecy and vulgar diffusion, between private delight and public pleasure. Mallarmé controls what at first sight seems an overlong paragraph by way of compressed Latinate constructions that trace an arabesque around a single point. The fourth paragraph ends too abruptly in self-irony for any subtle development, yet turns on the contrast of base reality with symbol, money with ticket. Now, however, in the last two paragraphs, the poem has once more recourse to length and breadth: the first paragraph measures the obsessive idea ("hantise") of the city with an ideal conception of autumn ("ce pompeux octobre exceptionnel," "ce qui fait penser à un automne sous les cieux"), checks visible emptiness with emotional suggestion; the second hinges on the polarity of doubt and faith as pointed up by a daring ablative absolute ("les bras de doute envolés comme qui porte un lot d'une splendeur secrète") and developed in the contrast between vanished dreams ("tous rêves antérieurs"), vanishing image ("chimère puérile"), present beauty ("orgueils surhumains," "universel sacre"). The entire sequence is, then, the fluid movement of proposition and counterproposition, which shows Mallarméan desire in a delicate and constantly changing relationship with its opposite, like two motifs of a fugue. The concrete becomes the harmonic condition of the abstract, the referential that of the nonreferential, nature — that of the poem.[5]

---

[5] Claudel was harsh in his judgment of Mallarmé's last works which, in his eyes, do not have the necessary inner tension of masterpieces: "Non, il ne fallait pas diviser. Il fallait garder actif le ferment intérieur, le principe de contradiction vivifiant." On the contrary, I would think that certain of Mallarmé's sonnets are less good than others, not because they ignore the law of contradiction, but rather because they overuse it. This is clearly not the case in "La Gloire" which conducts all with brio, the prose enabling Mallarmé to reinsert the real into his ideal language.

The Meaning of Surrealism, and Why It Matters

MARY ANN CAWS

> And this object should be, first of all, what mat-
> ters; it matters in a way quite different from the one
> in which it looks like the sky, or like blood.
>
> André Breton, *Point du jour*[1]

1. Mattering

Mattering matters, outside of reference; it is essential to the spirit of surrealism, perhaps more than to any other of the literary and artistic movements which characterize the early part of the twentieth century. The surrealist fact that whatever is chosen to be imagined as real is assumed to become so is paralleled by the surrealist fact that what is chosen to become important indeed becomes so. Unembarrassed, the surrealist writer or reader, actor or observer, decides to have as a matter of concern the fact of being concerned, however unfashionable; this is quite as important as the meaning or meanings we might ascribe to the movement.

I am speaking as a surrealist reader, trained over a number of years by the texts I confront. Equally important to such a reader is the scope of interpretation: if, in the title of this essay, I put "meaning" in the singular, that singularization cannot be or at least should not be read

---

[1] André Breton, *Point du jour* (*Idées*/Gallimard, 1970), p. 147. Hereafter referred to as *PJ*.

146

as a dogmatic narrowing in. In surrealism, no image is tied down, but all are free:

> Jamais le ciel toujours le silence
> Jamais la liberté que pour la liberté
> Breton, "Non-lieu," *Clair de terre*[2]

This does emphatically not mean ever that surrealism means *a*, and not *b*. But it does mean, on the other hand, that whatever I take it to mean, or you take it to mean, or X takes it to mean, that it means. These meanings in fact are indeed the matter not with but of surrealism. To quote Breton: "Nothing is inadmissible, in my opinion" (*PJ*, p. 26).

An "open realism," as he defines surrealism, coincides with the "open rationalism" he sees in modern science, disturbing the sensibility (*PJ*, p. 102). A plural meaning, and a serious matter; these are indeed the basic tenets of an open surrealism as I view it now. As we move into what does, I think, mean most and how, and why, I shall give subheadings like would-be landmarks to the mattering of my main heading, and shall be, however implicitly, signaling what, from my viewpoint, does indeed matter intensely about surrealism's meanings, from this viewpoint to the next. First and foremost, surrealism teaches relations and the arts of interacting and relating.

2. Relating and Bridging

The unique relation made to the listener or the viewer or the reader by the bearer of the surrealist message is at once a relation of, and a relation between. The relation of a meaning, or a meaning of meanings assembled, gathered, and made quintessential, already defines the bearer of that meaning as a describer and an interpreter.

Creating and evoking are the relating to the outside of a new power within, whose continual expression it is the highest duty of the surrealist to faithfully relay and relate:

> I have never appreciated in myself anything other than what appeared to contrast drastically with what was outside, and I have never had any misgivings about my interior equilibrium. That is why I consent to keep some interest in public life and, in writing, to sacrifice to it a part of my own. (*PJ*, p. 27)

---

[2] In André Breton, *Poèmes* (Gallimard, 1948), p. 109. Hereafter referred to as *P*.

This relating role relates, I think, to the other relating role, that of bridging objects in the world and their perception, the very feel of them and of their own essential message substantially incarnated, and of the spectators who perceive them, which is to say, ourselves. Our selves as relaters, tellers, describers, interpreters, critics, and writers, are essentially and providentially related to our selves as sensitive speakers of an interchange between human and natural forces which is best called bridging, or interfering.

3. Intersecting and Interfering

Breton describes Dali as "one of those who arrive from so far off that when you see them enter, and only enter, you have no time to see them. He places himself, without saying a word, in a system of interferences" (*PJ*, p. 67).

In the surrealist notion of the sublime point, the notions of interference, net, and intersection are triumphant already: the point condenses, the sight rays converge, and angles, twists, and curves are all shaped in a subjective pattern: "If we talk here of the highest point, it is only because we wish to clarify those curves whose intersection produces this point with its peculiar significance and to attempt to place it in relation to the coordinates of time and place" (*PJ*, p. 95).

The surrealist temperament bridges love and death, high and low, action and dream, day and night, these communicating vessels spilling over into each other, until they join in a supreme or sublime point:

> Everything I love, all I think and feel, inclines me towards a particular philosophy of immanence according to which surreality is contained in reality itself and is neither superior nor exterior to it. And reciprocally, for the container is also the contained. It can be considered as a communicating vessel between the containing and the contained.[3]

"The poet to come," reads another Bretonian text, "will overcome the difference..."[4] A poet to come, and the reader already present: but in surrealism, by a further twist, they are identical. A metaphor

---

[3] André Breton, *Le Surréalisme et la peinture* (Gallimard, 1965), p. 69. See *Les Vases communicants* themselves (Gallimard, 1955), and my discussion in *André Breton* (New York: Twayne, 1971), pp. 59-61, of the interconnections and, *passim*, of the point sublime, and also in *The Poetry of Dada and Surrealism* (Princeton: Princeton University Press, 1970), pp. 71 ff., of the *fil conducteur*, and the communicating vessels.
[4] André Breton, *Les Vases communicants*, p. 198.

such as the communication of the vessels makes evident the possible communicability of future with present as of humans with one another. By the outpouring and inpouring of meaning, a special interference is established of solid as of liquid states, of the real as of the emotional objects: this is for perception, and for their expression, all of language is to be remade. One of the most powerful questions ever to be posed by surrealism arises here: "Isn't the mediocrity of our universe a function of our language?" (*PJ*, p. 22).

Speaking and writing are already making and remaking; the power of analogy, first perceived, then described, at last incorporated, is such that not just the marvelous tends to become the real, but that, perhaps more important still, the real becomes, incontrovertibly, the marvelous. Perishable, mortal, ephemeral, no more enduring than Vinteuil's little snatch of melody in Proust, no larger than the little patch of yellow wall: but what could endure longer, or better render to mortals the conviction of immortality through art?

4. Doubting and Desiring

Now Descartes's doubt was provisional. Many of us who started out in philosophy came, I think, to doubt that doubt, and for that very reason. It seemed poised there at the entry of his system, providentially chosen and not inflicted; it seemed of short term, and infinitely disposable. But surrealist doubt, grave always, is related to a personal unrest, a profound discomfort at the depth of a feeling surrealism is quick to draw out, and slow to let go. Despair is lyricized, understated, and convincing, as in Breton's "Le Verbe être":

> I know despair in its great lines. Despair has no wings, it does not necessarily remain seated at a table cleared upon a terrace, in the evening beside the sea. It is despair and it is not the return of a mass of little facts like seeds leaving one furrow at nightfall for another... In its great lines, despair has no importance. It is a burden of trees to make still another forest, a burden of stars to make still another day less, a burden of days less to make my life still again. (*PJ*, p. 120)

What is not said, but only hinted at, is often just what, in other movements, would be said aloud or shouted; in Eluard's poem called "Deafman's Eye," the title is already indicative of the compensatory impulse (not hearing, thus seeing). We might associate this with some philosophy of accommodation, were it not for the poem itself, as it stutters along:

OEIL DE SOURD

Faites mon portrait.
Il se modifiera pour remplir tous les vides.
Faites mon portrait sans bruit, seul le silence
A moins que – s'il – sauf – excepté –
Je ne vous entends pas.

Il s'agit, il ne s'agit plus.
Je ne voudrais ressembler –
(Eluard, *Capitale de la douleur*)[5]

The poem is not finished, but left open for the insertion of all resemblances, and yet its very stuttering speech casts doubt ultimately upon our understanding, upon our making of portraits, our interrogations of ourselves and of them, and even and especially our understanding itself. Our portrait of ourselves is often made complete by our taking on of other roles, which, in their very strangeness, in their distance from us, become part of ourselves.

> Oh eternal theatre, you require that we put on the mask of another, not just to play his role, but even to say of what it consists, and that the mirror in front of which we are posing should give back a strange image to us. Imagination has every power except that of identifying us in spite of our appearance with someone other than ourselves. (*PJ*, p. 8)[6]

What we resemble, however variously, modifies us, and increases not just our doubts about our ordinary costumes, but our assurance of our own continuing and refreshed desires, refusing boredom.

Not spelled out, never defined, surrealism's desires, which are supposed to be captured in their very fluctuation, may read like some vague manual of self-intensification combined with an intensification of the world around us: to act in a way appropriate to the lyric relation of person and universe (that "lyric comportment," with which Breton identified surrealism) or to change the world and the word ("change the Word," said Rimbaud, "change the world," said Marx; change both, says surrealism in its highest moments).

But doubt always was to surface, all along the way. There resides in this very uncertainty turned upon itself the very thing some of us

[5] Paul Eluard, *Capitale de la douleur* (*Poésie*/Gallimard, 1966), p. 49.
[6] For the theatrical concept, see also such texts as "Devant le rideau" and "Rideau rideau."

persist in valuing above all else. To this tone we might ascribe our affection for surrealist writing and its violent appeal of contraries. "It is time perhaps, to turn back," says Breton, at the height of his marvelous encounter with the recipient and the giver of Mad Love. And, walking together with his new-found heroine so loved, among the garbage scraps tossed on the sidewalk at midnight, he has a moment of uncertainty. This high lyric passage, extreme in its fluctuations of despair and exaltation, ranks with the greatest moments of surrealism and is marked by their unique stamp. It is at once self-questioning, assertive, and meditative; it is poetry at its highest point. It is, like the point of juncture in surrealist philosophy, sublime, a true "point sublime":

> Of what am I finally capable? How shall I not be undeserving of such a fate?... All sorts of defenses become visible around me, clear bursts of laughter rise from the past to finish in sobs, under the great beatings of grey wings in an uncertain spring night... Who goes with me at this hour in Paris without guiding me, whom, moreover, I am not guiding? I never remember having felt such weakness. I see the bad and the good in their crudest state, the bad winning out by all the ease of suffering. Life is slow and we hardly know how to play it... Who goes with me, who goes in front of me once again tonight?... There would still be time to turn back.[7]

How can humans swear their faith, make their promises of lasting fidelity beside the ruins of nature? The same questions asked by the romantics are re-asked, and answered differently. Everything flows, rushes, crumbles, and we with it. What, then, is immortality, asks the questioner, or what, then, is any promise, or then, death? And the answer, given among others, by Desnos among the greatest, takes its initial term from what seems most trivial, from an advertisement for a brand of soap, with a baby continually wreathed in smiles. From this unpromising beginning, seeming not to matter at all, it soon works out its juxtapositions of reality, irony, and lyric understatement:

> It's Baby Cadum, eternally smiling on the wall, it's Robespierre's sublime sentence: "Those who deny the immortality of the soul are doing themselves justice," it's the laurel tree yellowing at the foot of a column truncated on purpose, it's the reflection of a bridge, it's an um-

---

[7] André Breton, *L'Amour fou* (Gallimard, 1937), p. 55.

brella glistening like a sea monster spied on a rainy day from some fifth floor.[8]

Definitions redefine always, and repeatedly, in surrealism, and each new one at once raises doubts, desires, and consciousness. Desnos, himself the inspired author of a Third Surrealist Manifesto, himself the greatest imaginer — eyes closed or open — was not its least great thinker or its least modern mind. This theoretician of the film, this truly great novelist, this poet of the most heartrending texts, sees and sees what matters.

Love is, he continues here, mixed with death in a marvelous concoction, a new potion of Liebestod drunk by whatever lovers surrealism may sponsor, never guaranteeing permanence, but only the mattering of what goes by, like Baudelaire's celebrated "passerby": ("O toi que j'eusse aimée, / O toi qui le savais..."), loved because the meeting could not last, the love not be put to the trial of endurance.[9]

Desnos explains:

> The past and the future are subject to matter. Spiritual life like eternity, is conjugated in the present.
>   If death touches me, it is nevertheless of no concern to my thought or my mind, which are not rolled along by even the noblest hearse, but concern rather my senses. I can imagine no love without the taste of death mixed in, stripped of all sentimentality and all sadness.[10]

This is not provisional doubt, but real awareness of mortality, heightened and intensified to the level of exalted lyricism heard at the moments of greatest surrealist expression, never devoid of that awareness, but rather taken through it to a state far on the other side of pragmatic movements in which other things than mattering come to mind. "The limits assigned to expression are exceeded once again" (*PJ*, p. 145).

5. Perception and Revolution

An odd aspect learned from surrealist writing in surrealist reading is the enforced vision or the peculiar focus. Amid the details of what

[8] Robert Desnos, "La Mort," in *La Révolution surréaliste*, no. 1 (December 1, 1924), p. 22.
[9] Charles Baudelaire, "A une passante," in *Les Fleurs du mal* (Colin, 1958), p. 103.
[10] Desnos, p. 22.

seems an ordinary description, the sight is made to concentrate, in a space progressively narrower, upon an element of singular nature, like some condensation of plot or character traits. The view of the onlooker — obliged to compactness or compacity and obliged with that, to an intensity and clarity not always available to a wide-range vision — is trained upon the detail, moving in closer and closer.

Take this quite unhidden passage found at the end of Dali's *Hidden Faces*: "All things come and go. Years revolved round a fist more and more obstinately closed with rage and decision, and this fist, since the character was sitting in a large armchair with his back to us, was the sole thing which it was given us to see."[11] Here the fist controls our vision with its own intrinsic violence.

Now the point of the surrealist revolution is to upset the forces of stability, of sedentary-mindedness, of a world, as Artaud puts it, "delivered to the forces of dessicating reason, to the copying tendency struck in the mud of centuries."[12] The flatness and dullness, the boredom and certainty of a world to whose perceiving we are too accustomed to see it afresh is attacked by exactly this concentration upon one odd point, with the "concrete irrationality" recommended by Dali, as it mixes with his "irremediable lyric contagion," in a dialectic far removed from the static and reasonable madness we might want to appropriate, and to use.[13]

Surrealism refuses, as we know, to be used. Present surrealist reading refuses to separate one tendency from the other as outlawed or unsurrealist in nature. Meanings are all present in the delirious image, one of the finest offsprings of convulsive beauty. Ecstasy — the counterpart of delirium — depends on the vivid and the vividly expressive, the totally consuming and consumed experience. An experience both convulsive and occasionally comestible: "So it was a question of building a habitable building (and furthermore, as I saw it, edible) with the reflections of lake waters, this work displaying the maximum of naturalist rigor and trompe-l'oeil. Let us shout what a gigantic progress this is over the simple submersion practiced by Rimbaud, sinking a salon in the depths of a lake."[14]

From there to the most rapid conversions of sight into taste, the most drastic appropriations of the universe by the all-appetited

[11] Salvador Dali, *Hidden Faces* (London: Picador, 1975), p. 301..
[12] Antonin Artaud, *Oeuvres complètes*, I (Gallimard, 1956), 251.
[13] In *Minotaure*, nos. 3-4, December 10, 1934, p. 76.
[14] *Ibid.*

devourer, is only a step. At the feast table in *Hidden Faces*, the sadistic Grandsailles is seen

> bringing the light very close as if in calling attention to the budding curves of Solange de Cleda's breasts exposed above her décolleté. Here her skin was so fine and white that Grandsailles, looking at her, cautiously dipped his dessert spoon into the smooth surface of his cream cheese, taking only a small piece to taste it, snapping it adroitly with the agile tip of his tongue. The slightly salt and tart taste, evoking the animal femininity of the she-goat, went straight to his heart. (*HF*, p. 37).

The brilliant and deforming rage of the host transforms nature into the unnatural, twisting the images of the guests into "their own animality. As if in an instantaneous demoniac flash one saw the dazzling teeth of a jackal in the divine face of an angel, and the stupid eye of a chimpanzee would gleam savagely in the serene face of the philosopher" (*HF*, pp. 32-33). But the absorption of the outer universe in the interior world of the transformative senses leads eventually to the same despair of boredom at having absorbed too much, eaten too avariciously, seen too lustingly, for the lust to last.

This grave despair gnaws at the heart of surrealism. All the glorious rage of revolution leads to the inglorious and halting speech: "I have seen," says Breton, Tzara without words to order matches in a cafe; and "one might well say to the woman loved and found again after a year's absence, not Bonjour, but Adieu."[15] I want to propose this very irresolution, paradoxically, as one of the summits of surrealism, and of the surrealist revolution in perception and feeling.

For the uncertainty of self-identification coincides often with the uncertainty about oneself as it seems to the other. René Crevel, committing suicide, taped to his wrist his name in large letters: "René Crevel." For whom? A signal full of meaning, or an empty signal, to use a term of Eluard? To name oneself after death as oneself is surely an obsession with inscription as ascription; Crevel is ascribed to Crevel, just as he is named.

Artaud dying with his shoe in his hand, that shoe with which he beat out the rhythm for the incomprehensible words he shouted; Crevel naming himself at the moment of death; Jacques Rigaut propping up his wrist upon a satin pillow so that his firing hand would not tremble as he directed it upon himself; Jacques Vaché, used to drugs and

---

[15] André Breton, *Les Pas perdus* (Gallimard, 1924), p. 76.

knowing their use, overdosing with two friends as if by accident—which of these is a tragic death, and which is an inscription by will and by design upon a universe desperately appropriated, if at all, by this poetic plan? We do not now make those large gestures, not those of us grown older in reading of them, inscribed as they are now only in their own time. What we ourselves do with texts, what we do with tragedies for others and ourselves may indeed seem to have nothing to do with surrealism and its signals, empty or full, with surrealism as it sung itself in his heroic period, which we may now vicariously see as our own.

But what we do with what we read is surely the question, and cannot be turned aside. Not how we admire, or even what we emulate or put off, or turn away from, but what, in fact and in our freedom to judge and to be and to write, we do. For each of us, I have to suppose, there is a separate answer. To the extent that we absorb what we have as it is most lasting, not making of it our property, but rather our inner life, to that extent, what we choose to read matters just as what we are becomes coincident with what we choose to be.

Reading matters, then, like being.

6. Being

Surrealism is never less than realism, and always more. When Breton accuses his age of what he calls "miserabilism," it is an accusation of settling for the less instead of the more. He turns towards an intensity luminous and resonant even in its strangeness, so willed and chosen often so far off.

> Orient, victorious Orient, having only a symbolic value, dispose of me, Orient of anger and of pearls! In the turn of a sentence as in the mysterious strain of a jazz melody, let me recognize your manner in the next Revolution, radiant image of my dispossession, Orient, lovely bird of prey and of innocence, I implore you from the depths of the kingdom of shadows! Inspire me to be the one without shadows from now on. (*PJ*, pp. 28-29)

And yet, in close and even ardent contact with the real, the surrealist sensitivity draws near to the object even when mystifying it, rather than taking its distance.

> That this bunch of flowers I am about to smell or this catalogue I am leafing through seems in advance to exist should suffice for me; but

it does not. I must be assured of its reality, as we say, I must make contact with it. (*PJ*, p. 11)

This is, clearly, a hands-on movement, quite unlike some of the other twentieth-century movements such as the existentialism that follows so closely on its heels. To contrast the two, we have only to compare the attitude of Sartre's Roquentin in *La Nausée* toward those viscous pieces of matter that bring the nauseated feeling for the touch, and even the kill, with Dali's hero Grandsailles in *Hidden Faces*, rolling the piece of cork tree between his palms, delighting in the very matter of the tree:

> And in passing he would tear off a handful of cork-oak leaves from a low branch, squeeze them tightly and roll them in the hollow of his hand, enjoying the sensation against his fine skin of the prickly resistance of their spiny contact whose touch alone sufficed to isolate the count from the rest of the world. (*HF*, p. 17)

The surrealist leans forward, chooses, touches, and believes him or herself, as Breton puts it, unique and selected to carry a message out toward the world from the world inside and from the world outside to the world in.

> Beyond all sorts of tastes I know myself to have, affinities that I sense, attractions I feel, events which happen to me and only to me, beyond all sorts of gestures I see myself making, emotions I alone endure, I try, in relation to others, to ascertain in what my difference consists, without even knowing why. Doesn't my consciousness of this difference govern my self-revelation about what I alone have come into this world to do, and what unique message I bear for which I must be responsible, at my own risk?[16]

7. Seeing and Revealing

This common butterfly forever halted near a dry leaf, I wondered one whole afternoon how it happened to confer this special importance on the tiny canvas that I had seen that very morning in Picasso's studio. The objects towards which I had subsequently turned, objects which I appreciate among all others, had seemed to me freshly illuminated

[16] André Breton, *Nadja* (Gallimard, coll. Livre de poche, 1964), p. 11.

by it—I wondered how it came about that this unique emotion depended upon its perfect incorporation into the painting which, once it takes hold of you, provides incontrovertible evidence of a sudden revelation. (*PJ*, p. 144)

Picasso's canvases are directed, says Breton, toward the complete consciousness of self, but also toward the revolutionary goal of making the universe conform with that self ("Picasso dans son élément," *PJ*, p. 151). And yet, no matter how extraordinary the revelation made to us by such canvases, or by the *papiers collés* in their joyous brilliant abandon miraculously or at least marvelously—like "le merveilleux"— identified as works of triumph, no matter how unlike the Dada abandon and the statement it makes, no matter anything at all, the perishable so sung perishes.

I want to make what I suppose can be heard as mostly a personal statement: we all read surrealism, as we read anything else, differently from each other, and from ourselves as time takes us on. Time, said Dali, that most surrealist element. When I first worked on surrealism, over twenty-five years ago, I read it as what I then thought it was, a youthful protest, a revolutionary statement against all that was over-academic and chilled, against research and resolution and structure and system, a statement whose excess was its delight, and which was over-heated if anything, and had nothing of the academic about it. The particular irony of "making one's career" (a quite peculiarly dreadful expression in any case) by writing and speaking and thinking about such a statement was its own statement, funny and flawed, the one as it was the other, or then the triumph of trying both at once. But then I never thought of surrealism as other than that lyric comportment Breton guaranteed it to be, and have never read it otherwise.

Yet I no longer read surrealism the way I read it then in one sense; that is, I now locate its high lyricism at points other than those in which I used to locate it. Let me continue on the theme of the perishable, as one of the things that endures, ironically and magnificently, in surrealism, and quote to you what Breton sees, afterwards, in the traces of Picasso's works on paper. As I do so, I hope it will be hard for you not to remember that, after all, all we others do, as artists of the everyday, is also doomed to this fate, whether we write on paper or in actions or both. Because it may be fated too, to this kind of aging.

The twenty years which have passed over them have already made these scraps of newspaper go yellow, those scraps whose fresh ink went a long way in 1913 toward the insolence of the magnificent *papiers collés* of that epoch. The light has faded and dampness has in some spots deformed the great blue and rose cutouts. That is the way it should be. The stupefying guitars made of inferior wood, real bridges of fortune tossed day by day across song itself, have succumbed to the headlong course of the singer. But everything is just as if Picasso had counted on this impoverishment, this weakness, even this dismembering. As if, in this unequal struggle, in this struggle whose outcome is in no doubt, but which is waged even so by the creations of the human hand against the elements, he had wanted to bend ahead of time, to reconcile to himself exactly what is most precious, because it is ultra-real, in the very process of perishing. (*PJ*, p. 152)

This is the response to the doubts that plagued the Night of the Sunflower, the crisis of wondering about turning back in the midst of the wanderings of Mad Love. Nothing endures at its colorful height or its rate of initial speed, which is not to say that nothing keeps its promise. The promise kept is the promise earned, and not just granted. If I defend surrealism as one of the highest forms of humanity, it is — you can be sure of it — not because of its bravado: going down to shoot the first person in the street was no more Breton's real program than it is ours, and the great menaces proferred in the manifestoes were less manifest than the intensity of the positive style and the reach.

And in this response to what perishes as to what endures, it is in this too that surrealism speaks to us now, as we ourselves are, in some sense, of a fading light and a diminishing color, as even our revolutionary instincts are dampened and our energy slowed. It is by this means too that lyricism triumphs over life itself, by loss itself, and, especially, by love. Breton chose that way, certainly, like Picasso, and like the poet he was. What Magritte lights up in the painting called *The Light of Coincidence*, with his candle still burning, after all the paintings of *vanitas*, of the *memento mori* theme from ages past, is not de La Tour's *Magdalene by Her Vigil Lamp*, rather a lady less whole, if you like, selected and framed differently, yet no less luminous. No particular lady, having neither face nor name nor nationality, being, then, all of us or our idea. Only a part of a lady, you may say, as in his *Representation*, similarly framed. But this is indeed a case where the part exceeds the entire person: what is represented is as much as what all of Proust's desperate and enduring search for lost time represents: life as art.

8. Integrating

The poetic spirit, over whose demonstrations there fly two flags, black and red, is thus inscribed under the signs of anarchy and revolution. These form the "collective myth" to be flown as the standard of our generation and its successors: "Poetry and art will always keep a special place for everything that transfigures a person... Whether we like it or not, there flies — above art, above poetry — a flag now red, now black. There too things hurry by: we must take all we can from human sensitivity."[17]

Bearing just as surely a witness to sensitivity as to a violent concern with noninstitutional truth, this spirit marked with a double sign language is an integrative one. It gathers, unites, resolves. For all conflict exterior to the surrealist temperament, the person possessing it, described by Breton, is to be the resolution, having become what he terms a poet: how could we find a better term?

> Nevertheless, poets over the ages have provided us the sensitivity which alone can restore us to the heart of the universe, abstracting us for a moment from the kind of adventures which dissolve the personality, reminding us that we can be, for every sorrow and joy outside of us an always more perfect place for resolution and echo.[18]

Integrity combines exteriority with interiority, and puts a high moral value on the combination; but the mixture is anything but adaptable to our rigid structures of church and state. Surrealism as revolution was first termed "The Surrealist Revolution," then, "Surrealism in the Service of the Revolution," and then "Surrealism, Itself." That last says it all, and I would stick with this all-inclusive, all-integrating term, already containing, as vessel, and communicating, as one of the vessels which express exactly that prolongation into the heart and mind and spirit of all that surrealism was ever to be and to mean.

9. Manifesting and Meaning

If surrealism at its best is permeated with an intensely moral sense, what it manifests is no less dangerous to what the French call *les assis*, or the comfortably seated. And that is, probably, all of us as we read or speak or hear of surrealism, now. Once that meaning is comfort-

---

[17] André Breton, *Arcane 17* (Editions du Sagittaire, 1947), pp. 43-44.
[18] Breton, *Les Vases communicants*, pp. 197-98.

ably absorbed into exhibitions or expositions, explanations or explications, it is itself analogized, and ciphered only to be deciphered.

Is this not, even here, the temptation to rely on what is already seen, as opposed to the surrealist tendency, to thrust toward what has not yet been? "... the constant temptation to confront everything that exists with everything that might come to exist, bringing forth from what has never yet been seen the very thing that might persuade what has already been seen to make itself a little less dazzlingly visible."[19]

Poetic theoreticians hold forth on "The Surrealist Metaphor," linked or not. Poetic imagicians, how far, alas, from what surrealist magicianship could have been, discourse endlessly on "The Surrealist Image." Poetic genre enthusiasts explain "Surrealism as a Non-Genre" or divide its own manifestations up into "The Surrealist Theatre" or "Surrealist Poetry" or "The Surrealist Film" and the like. No movement worth its salt is, of course, to be taken in by such generic nets, by such divisive categories. And yet which of us is not guilty of that divisionism, if it is considered a flaw? I can in no way, for example, count myself outside the dividers, postmovement seers of what there was, genuinely, to see.

Readers are always afterwards, nor does it take any blush off the Bloom to see or to say that. Strong readers or writers or critics are just a little more strongly reactive. What is, among other things, miraculous about surrealist reading of surrealist writing is very precisely its presentness, no matter how after it seems.

> Are poetic creations meant to assume immediately this tangible character, to displace in such an extraordinary fashion the borders of the so-called real? The hallucinatory power of certain images, the real gift of evocation which certain people possess independent of their faculty of remembering, will not go unrecognized any longer. The God dwelling in us is not about to rest on the seventh day. (*PJ*, p. 25)

Surrealism, in rejecting the Fall, rejects, and movingly, all doctrine of sin. It gives back, deliberately, to the apple its prelapsarian taste, forgiving even the fruit. Forgiving it because it is, as we are, perishable, and therefore beautiful. The apple neither condemns, nor, in its inevitable rotting, does it sour: "The poet-to-be will overcome the depressing idea of some irreparable divorce between action and

---

[19] This thrust towards the future is the basic determinant of surrealist optimism, together with the concept of the conducting wire and its connections.

dream, will hold out the magnificent fruit of the tree with the tangled roots and will know how to persuade everyone who tastes it that it has nothing bitter about it."[20]

Or, again, in one of the most radiant poems ever written, Breton speaks of what comes after the Fall, redeeming the apple tree by mingling it with the ever-returning spring and the all-forgiving sea:

> ...la preuve par le printemps
> D'APRÈS
> De l'inexistence du mal
> Tout le pommier en fleur de la mer
> *("On me dit," P*, p. 179)

But then symbols are, like us, transient. We knew that all along, without phrasing it, perhaps, quite in that manner. When we first read in Proust what we are in ourselves, did anyone indicate to us that the madeleine dipped in the tea might someday take on a cast of marble, so ensheathed was it to be in literature and the subsequent literature of literature? When we first read of roses, and how, lest they were plucked in their first crimson by some rowdy poet (Ronsard, I was told, was fortyish, with bad breath, and balding), did we cast them in reddish bronze to make them last? Did that swan of Mallarmé's, so eternally emprisoned in that lake of ice, turn itself to crystal beyond the possibility of flight from out the whitest page? I think not. I believe not, even, for were the sublime and frailest images of literature to become hardened and cast forever in the surest bronze or marble or glass, how would literature endure as emotion in the present?

Surrealist literature and perception, like romantic literature and perception before it, celebrates the transient as transient, refusing its entombment as the permanent. It does not cling to what it creates, nor consider it eternal:

> I see Picasso as great because he has constantly defended himself against those exterior things, even the ones he drew from himself, because he never thought of them as anything but moments of intercession between himself and the world. He has sought out, for themselves, the perishable and the ephemeral, against everything which generally serves the artist's vanity and his pleasure. (*PJ*, pp. 151-52)

---

[20] Breton, *Les Vases communicants*, pp. 169-70.

So there is no after, but only now. So the highest point of surrealist is at its beginning, and consonant at once with its end, therein included.

10. Importing and Ending

Surrealism is always just starting out. How to say this of a movement which began when the century was in its teens and ended, so think some, with its founder, in the late sixties, if not before? Because, were it not to be so, it never was.

Toujours pour la première fois... (P, p. 150)

Surrealism sings not a faith that failed, not an illumination that fades, but the hope of undoing itself, sings, then, "la lumière qui cessera d'être défaillante," the light which will not cease, until it ceases to be failing.[21] This is the "avenging arm" of the great idea, the idea that — some will say — had its time.

But the time it had is not even fully yet; and there are some who would maintain, and with all the force of their most ultimate conviction, that we might all be, or each of us, that "perfect place of resolution and echo," were we so to resolve. Were we each to become, and one becomes in this sense only by believing and being, the poet Breton thought we might indeed be. For Breton's key passage on the real key to the fields, not just where madmen and children roam, but the fields, still more real, of life as it is lived and struggled, won, and finally lost, I give a reading of the key noun: "le poète," and the key pronoun "il," which sets the passage differently but perhaps no less really, for us all, now these many years later. It is my response to the presence now of surrealism, re-read:

> Let all poets look for the key said to be lost, for we have it. We can only rise above those fleeting feelings to live dangerously, and to die. Let us scorn all taboos to use the avenging arm of the *idea* against the bestiality of all beings and things, and one day, vanquished — but vanquished *only if the world is world* — let us greet the discharge of our sad guns like a glorious salvo.[22]

This interpretation of that passage betrays my optimism; not the poet, "he," as Breton would of course have had it, nor even the poet,

---

[21] André Breton, *Manifestes du surréalisme* (Pauvert, 1962), p. 220.
[22] *Ibid.*, p. 221.

"she," as some would have it, nor yet the poets, "they," to be what is often called safe. No, the poet, "we": here my reading of surrealism remains subjective, and thus, I would submit, surrealist in itself.

Whether the world is world, or whether it is not quite only that, surrealism maintains that the becoming of a poet is what will always matter, and that this meaning of surrealism is in the long run, what will most have mattered.

André Breton and Malcolm de Chazal: Perception Versus Opacity

J. H. MATTHEWS

"Qui suis-je?" The opening sentence in André Breton's *Nadja* (1928) asks two questions in one, posed in the first person singular.[1] At once, Breton's text makes clear that he is writing for himself, not for a conjectural reader, whether hypocritical or not. The same is true, essentially, of *Les Vases communicants* and *L'Amour fou*.[2] Although, as readers, we are privileged witnesses throughout the trilogy, Breton never condescends to plead a cause before us. The criterion by which he admits evidence and brings it before us is not its persuasiveness, the weight it might be expected to carry with an audience, antagonistic or submissive, but its compelling appeal for his own imagination. Whether we peruse *Nadja* or one of the two books that followed it, we face the same involvement in private experience, relived at a level of intensity which may or may not affect readers, but which the author of these accounts cannot and does not wish to resist.

From the first, André Breton reserved his attention for aspects of daily existence which, in his phrase, "made him live," that is, gave enriched meaning to his own experience. By the standards he set himself, dealing with existence the way he did in the works cited was a poetic act, presupposing *"entry into a trance."*[3] It was of no impor-

---

[1] André Breton, *Nadja* (Gallimard, 1928), p. 7.

[2] André Breton, *Les Vases communicants* (Gallimard, 1932); *L'Amour fou* (Gallimard, 1937).

[3] Breton's phrase in *Ajours* applied not only to writing, our main concern here, but also to painting. In neither case did it signify the involuntary surrender of evaluative faculties.

tance to him that, to others, self-induced trance might look like proof of self-delusion. Breton did not peer out of his books, either boldly or timorously; he looked inward through them. And when he did so, he was less concerned with simply making sense of what he had seen and gone through than with imposing upon events in his own life a reading that would elevate their significance, in his own opinion at all events.

It is important to acknowledge that André Breton was a man very different from Raymond Roussel, who enjoyed the comfortable assurance of his own genius, full confidence in a sense of superiority over other men which made it impossible for lack of success to dampen his spirits or make him question the viability of his own writings. Breton was acutely sensitive to boredom (something apparently beyond Roussel's comprehension) and well acquainted with the debilitating effects of the enervating burden of ambient reality and contingent circumstance. To come to terms profitably with the world about him, he found it imperative to look in a special way at what happened to him. If he could not see incidents in his own life immediately transformed, then Breton had to regard them as susceptible to transformation, to amelioration. Thus, reality was not to be viewed, from his standpoint, as invariably and inevitably indifferent to man's needs, but as potentially cooperative. If not currently attuned to man's needs, it still must be capable of retuning, so that the hope of adjustment — of environment to man rather than of man to his environment — would live on.

In *Nadja* Breton talked not of having been put in this world but of having come into it, and for a purpose. Yet his sense of destiny was hardly, as it was for Roussel, a *given*, to be taken for granted in any serious evaluation of his effort and its achievement. André Breton's destiny was a product of the will, an object of conquest, and hence no mean accomplishment. Breton the surrealist was his own creation, the embodiment of aspirations for which he provided both motivation and energy, despite everything that seemed to conspire to defeat the purpose he had chosen for himself. The lamented absence of God from the Bretonian universe might have left a vacuum and could have engendered unproductive feelings of nostalgia. Conscious exclusion of God, on the other hand, was for Breton a condition of vitally meaningful activity. It established a reference point for all responsible action, and — no less noteworthy — in the here and now rather than in a hypothetical afterlife.

The parameters of man's search for the meaning of life are restricted, in Breton's estimation, to lived experience. They are laid out by imagination, which alone, he confessed in his October 1924 *Manifeste du surréalisme*, gave him an account of "what can be," thus raising "the terrible interdict" a little.[4] All the same, affirming that Breton looked through his life for the meaning of existence, as through a window, suggests that the window permits an unobstructed view of what he wished or preferred to see. The spectacle we are permitted to witness through the books in which he recorded lived experience leaves us with a distinctly different impression.

André Breton possessed the ability to deduce from events which he judged to be "superdetermined" the operation of forces by which the mundane is refined and transmuted. So what fascinated him throughout his relationship with Nadja was that, as he reported, "near her [he felt] nearer the things near her" (p. 119). The presence of the strange and already quite deranged young woman functioned as a catalytic agent, all the more potent in its effect because of Breton's predisposition and capacity to react imaginatively with it. The selfishness of his pursuit, in Nadja's company, of knowledge which — so he believed — he could hope to acquire only when with her leaves us doubting that he would have sacrificed his own needs even to help preserve his companion's sanity. Ruthless it certainly was, yet André Breton's search for meaning through his brief association with Nadja stands as proof of the single-mindedness with which he tried to surmount depressing aspects of daily living and to uncover behind the façade of existence compensatory patterns capable of renewing and even deepening his faith in the value of life.

The surrealists' position vis-à-vis reality called for something more elusive to which — in defiance of common preconceptions — Breton and his followers attached the label "surreal." To understand the surrealist's attitude, and the conduct it inspired, one needs to appreciate that everything hinges less upon a violent confrontation between reality and the imagination than upon the measure of success he achieved in realizing an ambition highlighted in Breton's "Second Manifeste du surréalisme," first published in December 1929, nineteen months after *Nadja*.[5] Surrealists aimed at reaching "a certain point in the mind"

[4] André Breton, *Manifeste du surréalisme* in his *Manifestes du surréalisme* (Jean-Jacques Pauvert, n. d. [1962]), p. 17.
[5] André Breton, "Second Manifeste du surréalisme," *La Révolution surréaliste*, 12 (December 1929), published separately in Paris by Editions Kra on June 20, 1930.

from which such apparent opposites as real and imaginary, communicable and uncommunicable — supposedly mutually exclusive — cease to be perceived in contradiction.

It is an abuse of André Breton's thought to conclude that his devotion to perception at the expense of observation spared him the frustrating embarrassment of heading into an impasse where he would find himself facing insoluble contradiction. As Breton preached it, surrealism was not a formula for replacing the real with the surreal. It was, more practically, a means for coming to terms with the world which must resolve oppositions by way of subjective perception.

In surrealism the ambition to dispose of antinomies was a long way from being a token of blind faith in some power which surrealists wanted to acquire. It pointed instead to the hope — vitalizing energy of all surrealist creative activity — of seeing things from beyond the level at which contradiction, antinomy, and conflict hold our attention, paralyzing (so surrealists were convinced) both thought and action. The surrealist's aim was to perceive reality in a context where it ceases to appear in contradiction with the world of uninhibited imaginative freedom. The important consideration was not so much whether real and imagined are truly reconciled as whether perception eliminates any sense of conflict between them.

The constancy of Bretonian thinking in this regard comes to light when, putting down *Nadja*, we pick up *Arcane 17* (1944). Here Breton speaks of opacity, calling it "the greatest enemy of man" and insisting, "this opacity is outside him, and it is inside him, maintained by conventional opinions and all sorts of suspect defenses."[6] Surrealism, as Breton conceived it, assigns man the task of liberating himself from opacity, which can be destroyed only through the fruitful operation of subjective perception.

During the years which historians (especially those specializing in twentieth-century painting) are accustomed to consider the postsurrealist period, André Breton continued to argue forcefully for imaginative perception and to stress its exciting distance from mere observation. It was in a 1947 essay on the painting of Jacques Hérold, subsequently reprinted in the definitive edition (1965) of his *Le Surréalisme et la peinture*, that he spoke for the very first time of Malcolm de Chazal. Breton declared that the author of *Sens-Plastique* was "in possession

---

[6] André Breton, *Arcane 17* (1944), in *Arcane 17 enté d'Ajours* (Jean-Jacques Pauvert, aux Editions du Sagittaire, 1947), p. 52.

of a general system of perception and interpretation."[7] The "flash" of Chazal's mind, he asserted, "instantaneously evades the opacity of everything surrounding it" (p. 204). Breton went on to advise his audience to assimilate Chazal's method, "and I do not doubt that we shall have advanced, in the direction of comprehending the world, a giant step." Furthermore, his catalogue preface gave its readers the opportunity to notice that *Sens-Plastique* alludes to what Chazal calls a "sudden flash: man feels something like a hand seizing his eye. The effect of tearing out sight" (p. 204).

As for Hérold, Breton credited the Romanian painter with producing pictures ("of which too much could not be made") reflecting "a parallel intention." The parallel he detected appeared so close, in fact, that Breton deemed certain aphorisms from *Sens-Plastique* to be, unintentionally, a most apt commentary on Hérold's painting. Comparison of excerpts from *Sens-Plastique* aligned next to quotations from Hérold's August 1943 essay for *Le Surréalisme encore et toujours*[8] shows that André Breton's confidence in the power of human perception continued undiminished.

The year Breton wrote his preface for a Hérold show the first postwar surrealist exhibition was held in France, an Exposition Internationale du Surréalisme at the Galerie Maeght. For the occasion, Hérold created one of a dozen *autels* dedicated to mythical figures stimulating to the surrealists' imagination. His *autel* was an object made in tribute to the *Grands Transparents*. The latter had been mentioned for the first and indeed the only time at the end of Breton's *Prolégomènes à un troisième manifeste du surréalisme ou non*, written in 1942.[9]

The *Prolégomènes* speak of placing man in "the modest circumstances of interpreting his own universe" and also of approaching "the structure and constitution" of certain hypothetical beings who "manifest themselves dimly to us in fear and the feeling for chance." These are beings—evidently *Grands Transparents*, though not explicitly identified as such—who exist "above" man in the animal scale and whose behavior is as foreign to Breton as is his own to ephemera or whales. Still without naming the *Grands Transparents*, Breton's text closes on

---

[7] André Breton, *Le Surréalisme et la peinture*, definitive edition (Gallimard, 1965), p. 204.

[8] Special number of *Cahiers de Poésie*, edited in Paris by Jean Simonpoli.

[9] André Breton, *Prolégomènes à un troisième manifeste du surréalisme ou non*, reprinted from *VVV*, 1 (June 1942), in his *Manifestes du surréalisme*.

a question which postulates a new myth for surrealism: "Must we convince these beings that they originate in a mirage or give them a chance to come to light?"

Breton alluded to the *Grands Transparents* at a moment when he was preoccupied with defining a new myth from which surrealism might take further impetus. However, if we examine his 1942 essay called *Vie légendaire de Max Ernst, précédée d'une brève discussion sur le besoin d'un nouveau mythe*,[10] what strikes us more than anything else is that the myth discussed therein is not really new. In fact, it simply underlines the continuity of surrealist thought, as reflected in Breton's writings. When, apropos of Ernst's painting, Breton formulates a *"First Commandment,"* we find it to be the very one by which he was already living at the time of his encounter with Nadja: "Everything must be freed from its shell (from its distance, from its comparative size, from its physical and chemical properties, from its affectation). Do not believe yourself inside a cave, but on the surface of an egg" (p. 162).

The principle of discovery through irruption was well rooted in Breton's mind — where release from depressing restraints was linked with breaking in upon oneself — long before exile brought him to the United States in 1941. Hence, his *"Second Commandment"* is a reaffirmation of a rule by which he himself had lived for more than a dozen years: "Wander, to your sides the wings of augury will attach themselves" (p. 162). Small wonder that André Breton's fourth commandment is a direct though unacknowledged borrowing, the concluding sentence of his book about Nadja: "La beauté sera convulsive ou ne sera pas" (p. 215).

The special value of Malcolm de Chazal's *Sens-Plastique II*,[11] in Breton's eyes, is that it reduces perception and interpretation to a system for evading opacity. In *La Lampe dans l'horloge* (1948),[12] Breton admits to being convinced that Chazal abandons himself to "a divinatory intoxication" (p. 41). He urges readers to ask themselves what force lies in Chazal's work for "breaking through opacity." We are reminded that the seventh (*"and, up to now, last"*) commandment recorded in *Vie légendaire de Max Ernst* is the imperative "Love," as we are assured that the key to Malcolm de Chazal's work is *la volupté*, "in the least figurative sense of the term, envisaged as the supreme

[10] Catalogue preface reprinted in his *Le Surréalisme et la peinture.*
[11] Malcolm de Chazal, *Sens-Plastique II* (Mauritius: privately printed, 1947).
[12] André Breton, *La Lampe dans l'horloge* (Robert Marin, 1948).

place of resolution of the physical and the mental" (p. 42). It does
not take us an instant to grasp the significance of Breton's definition.
For it allows him to propose Chazal's work as an exemplary model
to those, like himself, intent on resolving the differences to be observed
when mental projection—desire, need—comes up against physical
reality, contingent circumstance.

Discussion of sensual pleasure brings Breton back, via a reference
to the climax of the sexual act, to the "point suprême," the point at
which we cease to perceive opposites in contradiction. Like the act
of sex, *la volupté* is said to offer us the good fortune to "apprehend
certain unrevealed aspects of the world from a unique angle." It is
no surprise, therefore, that Breton now attributes special importance
to something he regards as Chazal's "central message." Nor is it surprising to discover that, in 1948, Breton placed Chazal among the
great poets. The latter he saw as in touch, without always being aware
of it, with "les *supérieurs inconnus.*" These can only be the *Grands
Transparents* of whom he had written six years earlier.

Malcolm de Chazal was not the only poet to hold André Breton's
attention at the critical time when he faced the task of regrouping
surrealist forces in the French capital. The year of his return to France
saw publication of *Les Armes miraculeuses* by Aimé Césaire[13] whom he
had praised highly while still in New York. Only a little later Breton
lauded the poems of Magloire-Saint-Aude, not to be published in
France until 1970. Meanwhile, during January of 1948, a month
before he began writing *La Lampe dans l'horloge*, he contributed to the
opening issue of *Néon*[14] his "Signe ascendant," written on December
30, 1947. That theoretical discursion on the poetic image emphasized
his love for images which, like so many rockets during a firework
display, light up "a life of relationships fruitful in a different way,"
by means of poetic analogy. Mention of the latter led Breton to quote
from Fourier, to whom he had dedicated an *Ode* published in 1947,
Baudelaire, Swedenborg, Apollinaire, and Reverdy but from no other
living poets except Benjamin Péret and (the compliment intended was
evident) Malcolm de Chazal.

The depth of Breton's respect for Chazal may be gauged from the
placement of a quotation from his work immediately after and on the
same footing as one from Charles Fourier. The latter's writings had

---

[13] Aimé Césaire, *Les Armes miraculeuses* (Gallimard, 1946).
[14] *Néon*, no. 1, 1948.

been, beyond question, the great intellectually stimulating discovery made by Breton during his years in the United States. What, then, was Chazal's reaction when he found himself approved by surrealism's leader in France even before *Sens-Plastique* had been released in Paris? In a letter to Pierre Demarne, dated March 13, 1948, reproduced in Demarne's *Bref, Etoile* (published in 1951 with a frontispiece by Jacques Hérold),[15] Chazal qualified *Sens-Plastique* as a work in which he had launched an inquiry along "super-personal paths," in search of *his own truth* (p. 13). There is nothing equivocal here. Nor again are we left in doubt when we hear Chazal, careful to draw a distinction between surrealist automatism and his own method, explain that he used the conscious to probe "the surreal life of the mind, which is linked with the surreal life of surrounding things" (p. 14). Malcolm de Chazal need not have concerned himself about verbal automatism, never the exclusive method of surrealist composition for which certain ill-informed critics take it. Indeed, his differences from surrealism stand out less, in his letter, than the points of contact between his views and the surrealists'. One does not have to wait until he has confessed that, writing *Sens-Plastique III*, he came close to falling into a trance in order to appreciate how much Chazal's method must have appealed to Breton and how easy it was for him to assure Breton, in a letter written on December 14, 1949, *"The only man I respect profoundly is you,"* and to add, *"My only spiritual friends in France are the surrealists."*

The special interest André Breton took in Malcolm de Chazal stemmed from his admiration when he examined the work of a writer whom he judged to have at his disposal a general system of perception. There seems to be little reason to question that the final verses, "Sur la route de San Romano" (1948), in Breton's selected *Poèmes* (which, brought out in 1948, appeared the year when the suicide of a friend, Arshile Gorky, affected him deeply)[16] expressed solidarity with Chazal's beliefs, and even perhaps some influence from him:

> L'étreinte poétique comme l'étreinte de la chair
> Tant qu'elle dure
> Défend toute échappée sur la misère du monde

[15] Pierre Demarne, *Bref, Etoile* (Editions de Minuit, 1951).
[16] André Breton, *Poèmes* (Gallimard, 1948), pp. 265-67.

Of course, one is at liberty to draw a distinction of degree, so to speak, between the opacity which, in *Arcane 17*, relates to historical circumstance (its author's enforced exile in a country where — a sad fate for a poet — he was always uncomfortable even with the language, the occupation of his homeland by foreign troops, uncertainty about the future) and the opacity that released depression in him one October afternoon when he would come across Nadja for the first time. On balance, all the same, we cannot fail to notice how remarkably consistent — over a period of two decades and more — remained André Breton's view of the restrictions under which we all live and of the means by which they may be circumvented. Similarly, although it is possible to note certain reservations on Breton's part about the direction taken by Malcolm de Chazal's later poetry, the enthusiasm he voiced for the Mauritian writer just after the Second World War, upon his return to France and a new beginning, is indicative of a receptivity conditioned by concerns which had led him in *Arcane 17* to oppose "innumerable existences closed in upon themselves" with the hope of opening up life in defiance of opacity.

The insistence with which, during the postwar period, André Breton recommended that his audience read Malcolm de Chazal's poetry and learn from it does reveal, nonetheless, some evolution in his thinking or, to be more exact, in his interpretation of the problems with which living confronts us all. Even though *Nadja* indicates that the author of the first surrealist manifesto (soon to write a second) was alert to certain difficulties facing us when we try to come to terms with life, it reveals also that Breton inclined to locate conflict in the apparent opposition of external reality to full realization of the individual's dreams. In the mid-twenties, the blockage appeared to Breton as an expression of antagonism emanating from the world about him. This is why Najda's gift for bringing him "nearer" things was so precious to him. By the mid-forties, however, circumstances had begun to show the situation to be far more complex. André Breton had discovered that the blockage can manifest itself as much inside man as outside. Very soon, his sensitivity to the negative effects of inner opacity would make him particularly responsive to the "central message" he detected in the writings of Chazal, when *Sens-Plastique* appeared within two years of his return to Europe.

It does not matter for our purposes whether Breton's estimate of Chazal's importance, in 1948, was strictly accurate. Chazal himself found it acceptable, at first anyway. Breton's views were to elicit no protest from a poet who, before the end of 1949 — after losing the support of Jean Paulhan (who had prefaced *Sens-Plastique*) and Aimé Patri — was convinced that all doors were closed to him in France. Evidently, at that stage Chazal saw no reason to assert his independence from the only Parisian group on whom, through Breton, he felt he could count. In fact, as late as July 1960, in a "Message aux surréalistes" published in the first number (October 1961) of *La Brèche: Action surréaliste*, he prided himself on his fidelity to surrealism. What matters more is that, when proclaiming Chazal's importance, Breton never took time to explain how he believed Chazal had managed to reduce perception to a system by which opacity can be evaded. One understands well enough that the absence of an explanation goes beyond reluctance to speak openly and is consistent with the position taken in the preface "Braise au trépied de Keridwen," which Breton would write in 1956 for Jean Markale's anthology *Les Grands Bardes gallois*:[17] that poetry and *l'explication de texte* are incompatible. Nevertheless, abstention from even the most rapid commentary has left us with no guidance where it would have been welcome, not necessarily as an explication of Chazal's poetry but surely as an insight into Breton's reasons for looking upon *Sens-Plastique* as systematized perception. All we can do is speculate and perhaps draw an informative parallel.

Not until sixteen years after *Nadja* had appeared did the word "opacity" enter Breton's vocabulary, in the profoundly negative sense ascribed to it in *Arcane 17*. Evidently, Breton continued in the interim to identify chance with a positive, beneficent agency to which he owed his meeting with Nadja and even with his wife Elisa, whose presence illuminates *Arcane 17*. But it is just as plain that Breton could not remain satisfied with being dependent at all times on an outside force for the enjoyment of moments of reconciliation with a world from which man risks being totally alienated. Gradually, and without for all that losing faith in chance, Breton came to see with greater clarity than ever before that "the bars are on the inside of the cage."[18] He came to the conclusion that perception is a key that can ensure release from confinement within the self, one that within ten years of writing *Nadja* he found to be firmly and enviably in Malcolm de Chazal's grasp.

---

[17] Jean Markale, *Les Grands Bardes gallois* (G. Fall, 1956).
[18] As earlier, we may note that Breton's phrase, inspired by his reflections on painting, applies just as well to the pictorial artist as to the writer.

Mauriac's Thérèse: An Androgynous Heroine

DIANA FESTA-McCORMICK

Thérèse is a strange heroine. Her story is that of a quest and the quest is, ostensibly, for a conscience, for a confrontation with a crime that defies her understanding. Although she would like to lay bare the mechanism within her that set her on the path to murder and made it urgent to eliminate an undesired presence, Thérèse does not pursue her quest to the end, her search remains unfulfilled, and her questions unanswered. What I propose to do in the following pages is to resume that search, to follow the heroine along the digressions and the labyrinthine ways of her personality, and lay bare her secret. That secret, I believe, is hidden in her androgynous nature.

Thérèse defies definition in the framework of the novel. The story is not a narrative in the manner of *Genitrix*, nor is it a confession in the French tradition of the "roman personnel." The reader can rely neither on an omniscient author to unravel the heroine's motives, nor on the heroine's own merciless pursuit of her identity in the manner of an *Adolphe*. Both author and heroine point to signs and evidences of hidden purposes; neither clearly establishes or clarifies them. It is up to the reader to undertake the detective work, to assemble all manifest clues in order to arrive at a conclusion.

Thérèse is introduced after her crime, or attempted crime. She is a spiritual prisoner of her own impenetrable urges, caught more relentlessly by them than even by the eventual chains of family life. In a brief foreword, the author announces his intention of revealing

174

her secret to the reader, as if that secret lay in the slow resolve to which she had surrendered, unquestioningly, to poison her "foolish husband." But he then adds almost cryptically, "I know the secrets of the hearts that are deep buried in, and mingled with, the filth of the flesh."[1] The act of poisoning, however, is not *per se* "filth of flesh" and we are implicitly directed to look for Thérèse's secret elsewhere. Mauriac hints at the presence of a deeper problem in her than just the temptation of evil. Yet he does not reveal what is at the source of the chasm separating his heroine from the world of those around her.

The forlorn "she wolf" who will later prowl in the bleak woods of Argelouse is introduced in the opening sentence as poised between freedom and bondage. Thérèse's trip back home after the trial then emerges as a brief and sustained interlude in which the events of the past are measured against the rising consciousness of the present. A vacuum has been created where the nexus between years past and this moment remains suspended, and in that vacuum Thérèse moves hesitantly. The lawyer's words echo the uncertainty of her position. Her trial stands unresolved, her "case dismissed." She "felt the fog upon her face and took deep breaths of it." One would like to think that that avid breathing aims at dissolving the enveloping fog. But Thérèse's search never dares go beyond the boundaries of the visible. The fog is welcome, for it is the barrier she seeks against the world of man, and the mantle to which she clings against the intrusion of untenable truths. It is the symbol of her freedom, comforting and yet precarious and volatile. It is, too, the mirror of her personality, opaque and shadowy. But in the very act of deliberate breathing, Thérèse also reaches toward her nature, and the secret that lies there. Courageously, she sets out on her adventure in deciphering her actions through the invisible signs of her unavowed wishes. That she recoils at each step which could lead to a discovery only points to the impossibility of resolution in a dilemma she dares not name.

In his study of love in Mauriac's works, Emile Glénisson analyzes the sense of shame and repulsion that all physical contact with woman

---

[1] The quotations of Mauriac's *Thérèse* refer to the Gerard Hopkins translation (New York: Doubleday Anchor Books, 1956). Only the page number will be given in parenthesis. Whenever a more literal rendition of the original has been desirable I have acknowledged any departure from Hopkins' text.

seems to inspire to the author's male characters.[2] The psychological imbalance that pushes several of those men to abandon the conjugal bed in an unresolved tension of hatred and desire can only be viewed, he insists, as the unconscious transposition of the mother in the woman at their side. The same need for chastity in spite of the throbbing desire which Glénisson discerns in Mauriac's heroes exists and with greater violence in Thérèse. All that would be needed in order to make his assumption applicable here are a few exterior modifications. The "maternal substitute" seen in the victimized wives of Mauriac's novels would become a "paternal substitute," and the "near impotence" of the heroes would have to be translated into frigidity in Thérèse's case. But I would not insist with Glénisson on the author's own distaste for the assertive demands of the flesh, or yearnings for the primordial purity of the child at its mother's breast, in order to try and clarify Thérèse's behavior. It is not relevant to this study to ask whether Mauriac's tormented heroes were a mirror of his own personal bewilderment in relation to sexuality. All the same, I would not dismiss the link that he himself traced between his own person and the most perplexing of his creations. When writing prefaces for the Pléiade edition of his collected works in 1950, Mauriac confessed to an affinity with Thérèse and, implicitly, to his identification with her solitude and misery.

> She is nevertheless more alive than any other of my heroines; not truly me, except in the sense in which Flaubert said "Madame Bovary is myself"—at my antipodes in more ways than one, but built all the same of all that in myself I have had to conquer, or eschew, or ignore.[3]

It is permissible to wonder about the traits that Mauriac felt compelled to "conquer, or eschew, or ignore," and which he lent to his heroine; it is more pertinent to look at Thérèse directly.

[2] Emile Glénisson, *L'Amour dans les romans de François Mauriac* (Editions Universitaires, 1970), p. 68: "C'est enfin sous le signe du 'dégoût' et de la 'honte' au sein même du mariage, que le protagoniste mauriacien accomplit l'oeuvre de la chair, et il n'en pourrait pas être autrement puisque sa moitié est pour lui un substitut maternel: son dégoût, la quasi-impuissance qui s'ensuit, est l'effet du caractère incestueux de la situation et celle-ci est si évidemment fausse—il joue le rôle féminin, exige de sa partenaire qu'elle se charge du sien—qu'il ne peut pas en éprouver un sentiment de honte; mais il ne se rend pas à l'évidence un instant entrevue, comme en témoigne la rancune, qu'après qu'il l'a grugée, il nourrit envers la femme."

[3] François Mauriac, *D'autres et moi* (Grasset, 1966), p. 253. The translation is mine.

Thérèse steps unaware into the realm of her own unconscious. Her search begins almost casually, out of the need to mend her relation with Bernard once she reaches Argelouse. Confidently, she decides that "all that was hidden must be brought into light." She will tell it all and begin at the beginning. And there, at the very start, she finds the image of Anne. Anne is the key, she intuitively knows, not only to her predicament of the moment but to what is hidden in her very nature.

> Little sister Anne, dear innocent, what an important part yours is in all this story! The really pure in heart know nothing of what goes on around them each day, each night! never realize what poisonous weeds spring up beneath their childish feet. (11)

In her effort to uncover the truth, Thérèse evokes unhesitantly the presence of the childlike Anne, that luminous figure in the implacable summers of her adolescent years.

That Thérèse should immediately think of Anne in wanting to understand and in her desire to explain the events leading to her trial, points both to the honesty of her intentions and to an instinctive knowledge of herself. Outwardly, Anne has little bearing on what has happened; indeed, hardly any. Why then does Thérèse address her as the "pure at heart" who has played "an important part" in her story? That part was invisible, hidden within the recesses of Thérèse's wishes. Yet she must know that the beginning of her story coincides with her passionate yearnings for Anne's arrival in the torrid summers of her innocence. She calls "little sister" the slender silhouette she spied from around the bend in the heated moors, as if to conjure away any other identification in her. Her words are endowed with the rite of prayer, but the tone is one of defeat. It is to herself that she alludes in recalling the "poisonous weed" hidden behind the candor of her friend. "Each day, each night," harried by a nameless desire, Thérèse had lived the endless wait of the lover.

The ambiguity of Thérèse's determination to solve her enigma may well be due to some complicity between her and Mauriac, to what Claude-Edmonde Magny defines as the author's participation in his heroine's dilemma, or his "illegitimate paternity," secret and somewhat shameful.[4] Sartre noted, more pertinently, (in his well known chapter

---

[4] Claude-Edmonde Magny, *Histoire du roman français depuis 1918* (Seuil, 1950), p. 113.

on "La Fin de la nuit" in *Situations*, I)[5] that Thérèse is more in the tradition of a classical heroine of ancient Greece than in that of the modern
novel. She is a tragic figure in whom reason is pitted against nature,
and not a dramatic creation whose contest against bondage revolves
on the pursuit of freedom in its own right. But Sartre's analysis is
concerned with the philosophical and religious axioms of the author,
not with investigating the heroine as such. Magny was not interested
in exploring Thérèse's nature either. But Mauriac throws too many
clues on the "masculinity" of that nature for it to remain thus
undetected. My assumption, indeed, is that the androgynous quality
in Thérèse's personality is not merely latent but obvious, though critics
have been surprisingly silent on that score. I am also convinced that
Mauriac intended it as such and made it, through innuendoes, the
culprit for the diabolical force at the root of his heroine's actions.

Masculinity, or femininity for that matter, is a concept tied to times
and social mores. It is remarkable, therefore, that a young woman's
charm in that earlier part of the century and in a provincial French
setting, should have been drawn not along the traditional demure and
gentle stances expected by her society, but rested in her intelligence
and "strong mind." Clearly, those were male prerogatives, together
with a marked taste for reading (she "devoured" all she could lay hands
on, from Paul de Kock's novels to the *Causeries du lundi* and Thiers'
Histoire du Consulat) and for solitude in the vast and silent country home.
Thérèse could not claim for herself the most coveted of a woman's
assets, beauty; yet "it never occurs to one to wonder whether she is
pretty or ugly. One just surrenders to her charm" (18). "Charm" is
to be translated into seductive intelligence here, or that superiority
of intellect that captivates despite all preconceived assumptions. For
Thérèse's thin lips, enormous forehead and large hands (perennially
holding a cigarette) would have stood her ill in a conventional appraisal of feminine allure. Her more noticeable traits are unmistakably
"masculine," both on the intellectual and physical plane. The text recurs
to those qualities, to the "devastated brow" under the weight of torment-
ing thoughts, to the constant cigarette in a hand that was "a little too
large," and thus confirms their importance in the characterization of
the heroine.

The picture that emerges of Thérèse is that of a young woman who
has always been at odds with her society and whose nonconformity

---

[5] Jean-Paul Sartre, *Situations*, I (Gallimard, 1947), 34.

came to be accepted as a matter of course both by the villagers of Argelouse and by herself. The former, no doubt, made concessions to her social position, and she had never known anything else. She was different, and no identification was possible between the dreams shared by other young persons of her sex and her own solitary prowlings within the vague confines of her intimate world. Only through her retrospective glance to those far away days of her immaculate youth does she understand the meaning of happiness. That past which she had attempted to hold still in the penumbra of a country room while the sun raged outside, now emerges as her only share of joy in life. Yet it was a past with no dreams, no tension toward the future, and in which each day sufficed unto itself. It was a past "unsullied, but lit by a vague and flickering happiness" (19). There is no doubt that the "unsullied" refers to a primordial purity here, to her untouched virginity. Later, the presence of a man at her side, her marriage, would desecrate her and obliterate happiness. Mauriac's condemnation of sexuality through what amounts to religious sophistry might explain, but only on the surface, Thérèse's revolt against the intrusion of a male presence in her life. If the author's assertion that man's love for God is to be exclusive and to remain unshared with any other human being is debatable in itself (in spite of his heavy leaning upon Bossuet's and Pascal's pronouncements)[6] that reasoning could hardly apply to a woman who lays no claim to any religious feelings or mysticism. Nor is that all. Thérèse's nostalgic evocation of long summers past does not stress exclusively the innocence of those days. The emphasis in the text is equally shared between the beauty of "that unsullied season of her past" and another kind of allure at the basis of her "vague and flickering happiness." A question naturally arises, "whence had come all that happiness?" and the answer offers itself: Anne was there, sitting by her side on the sofa, in that "darkened drawing room set in the merciless glare of summer heat."

Desire, or one's conscious yearning for something rests on a basis of experience. Recognition of one's desires cannot occur without a retrospective glance (even if it be of a vicarious kind, through hearsay) of the thrill, or anguish, or hope that accompanies them. Thérèse

---

[6] See "Souffrances et bonheur du Chrétien" in Mauriac's *Oeuvres complètes*, II (Grasset, 1951), 230: "Il existe, dites-vous, des *affections légitimes*: la famille, les amis, j'entends bien. Mais ces affections ne sont pas l'amour; et dès qu'elles tournent à l'amour, les voici plus qu'aucune autre, criminelles: inceste, sodomie."

had no experience and no knowledge that could allow her to identify the nature of her happiness at the side of Anne and of her anguish in Anne's absence. Her imagination was thus not involved in expectation or fear, it did not feed or dash hopes. She lived the phases of her passionate longing through violent sensations alone, surrendering in turn to appeasement or to turmoil. She was never far removed from a lingering inner sense of agitation. The cool atmosphere of the drawing room is evoked, contrasted to the fierce heat of summer at Argelouse, the appeasing presence of the blond adolescent at her side acting as balm against the tumult of the senses. Anne would get up now and then and check if the sun had paled. Thérèse remembers the constant quiver of heat that threatened to invade the room, ready to splutter and to flare like fire. "But through the half-opened shutters the blinding glare would pounce like a great stream of molten metal, till it almost burned the carpet, and all must be again shut tight while human beings went once more to earth" (19).[7] This is the torrid nature that furnishes what O'Donnell calls "the dramatic commentary" or the key to what is most intimate in the characters' personality.[8] I do not believe that it would be driving connotations too far to see in the darkened room a desire for protection against the furor of invading heat and unnamed desires.

It could be argued that Thérèse's need for Anne's presence offers nothing unusual. Friendship between girls—or boys—was and still is often passionate in societies where diversions and social relations are curtailed. But there is a tension in the atmosphere here, there are palpitations only briefly quietened for Thérèse and unshared by her friend, that go beyond the most intense feelings of friendship. In this "land of thirst"[9] the girl's yearning knows a momentary respite only in the other's presence. The walk to the cold stream of La Hure is strenuous along the sandy heath; but there, briefly, peace reigns. These are the images that Thérèse evokes as she sits in the carriage that brings her back to Argelouse after the trial. One must remember

---

[7] The original French is somewhat more explicit in its allusion to the need for blocking away the burning sensation of the outside and finding refuge in the pristine air of the darkened room: "mais, les volets à peine entrouverts, la lumière pareille à une gorgée de métal en fusion, soudain jaillie, semblait brûler la natte, et il fallait, de nouveau, tout clore et se tapir."

[8] Donat O'Donnell, *Maria Cross* (New York: Oxford University Press, 1952), 3.

[9] The Hopkins' translation reads "parched land" here (p. 20) for Mauriac's "dans le pays de la soif."

that these are the clues she seeks to help her unravel the confusion
in her being. In those images thus evoked she relives the assuaging
sensation of the icy waters in which their naked feet dipped for a moment, side by side. The girls did not speak a word; time remained
suspended. But the suspension appears somewhat like the holding of
one's breath, condemned soon to resume the accustomed rhythm and,
for Thérèse, to heighten the pervasive anguish of the protracted wait.

> To have stirred so much as a finger, so it seemed to them, would have
> set scurrying in fright their chaste, their formless happiness. It was
> Anne, always, who moved first — eager to be at the business of killing
> larks at sundown, and Thérèse, though she hated the sport, would
> follow, so hungry was she for the other's company. (20)

The "so it seemed to them" of the quotation resembles a lover's obstinate
belief in a shared experience. What makes it unconvincing that it apply
to both of "them" is not merely that these are Thérèse's thoughts with
not a hint of corroboration found in Anne's behavior. On the contrary, Anne is "always" the one to break the silence and so destroy
the magic of the moment for Thérèse. She is quite predictably eager
to move on, to kill birds with the unconscious cruelty of youth and
youth's thoughtless tenderness, too. Thérèse alone is aware of the plight
of those who are hunted and of their helplessness, for she has probed
the dimensions of suffering. She identifies with the lark whose instant of life and "song of rapture" are already tainted by death, yet
she follows her friend for she cannot do otherwise. She tries to blot
away the cry of the wounded bird and her own pain at the same time,
for she is "hungry for the other's company."

Those excursions in the heat of summer offer the only memory of
happiness Thérèse ever experienced. But at no time did she ignore
that those moments were volatile and in perpetual flight, nor was she
spared the anguish of that knowledge. "Coming tomorrow?" she would
ask, and the "sensible" answer would inevitably ensue, "Oh no — not
every day." Thérèse recalls her dispirited walk home after her friend's
silhouette had disappeared around the bend. Evening and darkness
would have set in. "What was that anguish?" she asks.[10] Why was
she unable to read or do anything except wander back onto the now
empty road? The hiatus of time is here evident in the use of the past

[10] Hopkins' rendition here is "Why so restless" for the original "Qu'était donc cette
angoisse?"

tense, and with it the perspective which through distance could now afford a clearer view of events. Thérèse measures her wretchedness of those days, the morose restlessness that would bring her back to the very spot where Anne had disappeared. She asks the right question, but no sooner has she done so than she drops it. No explanation is sought for the dead silence that would suddenly engulf her when Anne was no longer visible. One cannot, however, simply ascribe Thérèse's oscillations to ignorance, let alone to innocence. It is too late for that. She wants to know, presumably, why she was seized by a pervasive anguish once her companion left. Why does she not pursue the question, the reader may ask, unless it be out of fear of finding an unbearable answer?

If Thérèse could simply be classified as a repressed lesbian, she would surely hold limited interest for us. But there exists in her, together with the unrequited need for Anne's nearness, an undeniable urgency for purity. One could argue that her attraction to a rather insipid adolescent girl who shared not a single one of her tastes is dictated by an intricate defense mechanism, which makes her yearn for somebody who must by necessity remain untouchable. This could become a circular reasoning, however, where cause and effect would be inextricably tied. "Christianity makes no allowances for the flesh; it simply abolishes it," Mauriac affirms in the famous opening words of "Souffrances du pécheur."[11] But the turgid atmosphere in *Thérèse* can only be seen as a strong denial of such a precept, and thus of Christianity itself. In that case, it would of course be the absence of grace that wreaks havoc in the heroine's life. Yet that very absence would then emerge as the craving of the flesh and the stormy sensuality at the base of Thérèse's dilemma. Her nostalgia for the purity preceding her marriage is manifest, particularly in contrast to "the indelible filth" of her wedded life (14). But at the same time she cannot silence her doubts on her own candor as she wonders, "was I really so happy, so innocent of guile?" (14).

Thérèse was never unaware of the need, illogical in her own sight, for being close to Anne. Bernard, on the other hand, had never set her imagination to motion. Why had she married him? "I married because ..." and, irrepressibly, Anne's image comes again to the fore: "There had, of course, been the childish delight with which she had

---

[11] François Mauriac, *Oeuvres complètes*, VII (Grasset, 1951), 228: "Le Christianisme ne fait pas sa part à la chair; il la supprime."

looked forward to becoming Anne's sister-in-law as a result of that marriage" (22). She remembers the days preceding the wedding and her calm wait, not for the traditional fulfillment of her woman's role, but for Anne's presence: "Anne would be coming back from the Saint-Sebastian convent for the wedding."[12] But what she had thought of as peace was only "half sleep, the torpor of the snake within her breast" (24). One wonders what she means by "snake," what shape she would give to evil, if she pursued her search to the end and exacted an answer to her own inquiry. Her memory lingers on the oppressiveness that suddenly rushed upon her and the nightmarish quality of her wedding day. "She had entered this cage like a sleepwalker" (24) and sensed with horror that she would inexorably join "the herd of those who have served" (25). This is not the case of a girl's vague dreams of love being dashed by the brutality of a husband or the banality of family life. Thérèse suffered in anticipation of the fatal embrace of the flesh, of her contact with man. She had for the first time resented the presence of Anne whose visible joy made no allowance for the separation that would soon place them apart not merely in space "but by reason of what Thérèse was about to suffer — of that irreparable outrage to which her innocent body would have to submit" (25). Again, it is not merely the case of a certain anxiety, perturbation, or even fear, which could be explained by a puritanical education (although Thérèse professed independence of mind and no submission to church dogma) or by inexperience. She felt outright horror, an irrepressible revulsion at the very thought of physical contact with the man she had chosen to marry — and who was the best she could have chosen, she still believed.

Perhaps the most revelatory signs of a certain abnormality in Thérèse's nature are to be found in her musings about her nights in Bernard's arms. She had mastered the art of feigning a pleasure she did not in fact experience. Yet her husband's embraces had made her wonder about the happiness of complete abandon: "Much as when looking at a landscape shrouded in mist, we fancy what it must be like in sunshine, so did Thérèse discover[13] the delights of the flesh" (26). Her sensuality was awakened but remained shrouded in the mist

---

[12] Hopkins' use of the past tense here, "Anne was coming home from the convent .." does not fully convey the nuance of wish in the original use of the conditional: "Anne reviendrait du couvent de Saint-Sébastien pour le mariage."

[13] Hopkins gives "contemplate" where I have written "discover" for the original: "découvrait la volupté."

of her own resistance. She never considered the possibility of surrender and joy in her nuptial bed, but now found herself trying to envisage their wondrous beauty, the "sunshine" that remained elusive. She submitted to the laws of matrimony and, possibly, her body involuntarily responded to the pressures of the male at her side. Yet her vagaries pushed her toward an unknown realm of voluptuous experience where she too might discover the total fulfillment of desire. So her honeymoon passed, her "teeth clenched" as the "little pig" at her side sought pleasure in his trough: "and I was the trough" (26)[14] she reflects. Her only comfort during that time: a letter from Anne which she read over and over again. The girl complained that she no longer went to Vilméja so as not to run into the owner of the premises. Young Azévédo had come back and she abhorred consumptives.

For a woman who ignores or chooses to ignore all peremptory calls of the flesh, the imperatives of love must remain empty words in the dictionary of the inane. Thus it is that Anne's subsequent letters with their message of burning passion for Azévédo are found shocking. Thérèse's violent and cruel reaction against the girl who had made her own heart throb is unmistakably that of a jilted lover and not of a friend. How could it be that the foolish adolescent girl she had left behind, so lacking in imagination, should have discovered the lyrical beauty of sentiment and desire? Thérèse knew only too well how incapable of responding to the fervent longing of the heart, how indifferent to the dashed hopes of those who live in helpless wait Anne had been: "How could this song of songs have burst from the dry little heart she had known? — for it *was* dry, as she knew only too well ..." (29). How else could she have known, if not through the impassiveness that had made her suffer, Anne's irresponsiveness to her tacit entreaties, the casual and repeated "Oh no — not every day" given in answer to her anxious question, "coming tomorrow?" A passion such as Thérèse nourished relies for continuity on ignorance. She must never acknowledge the nature of her desires in a world that would find them inadmissible. The key to their being rests on the secrecy that shrouds them from everybody and makes them seemingly impervious to her own investigating efforts. If ever they were allowed to the surface those desires would be condemned to perish in shame. Her anguish would have a name, her yearnings an aim. But Thérèse

---

[14] Hopkins gives "sty" instead of "trough." The original reads, "C'était moi l'auge."

comes here quite close to recognizing the character of her trepidation in the hot summer afternoons at Argelouse, of the wretchedness that always seized her when Anne went away.

What follows is startling only if one refuses to see in Thérèse a would-be lover rather than a friend. She herself does not even try to explain an act performed as an ancient ritual and aiming at bending fate to will: "Two years ago, in the hotel bedroom" she reflects, "I took the pin, and I pierced the photograph of that young man just where the heart should be — not in a fit of temper, but quite calmly, as though I were doing a perfectly ordinary thing" (30-31). The fact is that that kind of black magic performed with determination has from time immemorial been a last recourse from shattered hopes and unrequited passions. In that context, it is indeed "a perfectly ordinary thing" that Thérèse should yield to superstition in her bid for vengeance. She turns against the rival who had known how to inspire fiery emotions and desire in the cool adolescent she had left behind. Everything in herself revolts against that act of betrayal. Her teeth clenched, she "was surprised at her own appearance in the glass" (30). The presence of Bernard now becomes intolerable: "She felt no hatred for him, but simply a wild desire to be alone with her pain, to discover where it was that the blow had struck her!" (31). The language is quite explicit here. Thérèse lives the tragedy of a woman condemned to give vent neither to love nor to pain. Where was the hurt, she asks herself ? Does she also wonder what the hurt was? Her questions seek no answers at any rate, except that she must have solitude, to dress her wounds and contemplate undisturbed the extent of her misery.

"I could have wished, Thérèse, for sorrow to have turned your heart to God," Mauriac says in his brief foreword. But creations have a way of voicing their own truth and of asserting their own inner laws, heedless of all preconceived ideas. The author, no doubt, intended the slow germination of a conscience and the coming to grips with her evil deed or his heroine. Yet Thérèse remains to the end the free spirit initially delineated in the story, unconcerned with her soul and the dimensions of evil. Her redemption would have exacted "a cry of sacrilege" from the best intentioned of readers, the author concedes. I suggest that the reason for it is that Thérèse's depravity was not in the temptation of murder as such, and the author indirectly alludes to that. Her rebellion, in fact, probably "commanded her creator's not altogether unconscious sympathy," as O'Donnell points out.[15] Mauriac was all too aware of the wearing down of dreams and the enslaving tyranny exercised relentlessly within a home in the name of kinship and love. Murder was not the cause of Thérèse's dilemma but its result. It was the "necessary" step she had to take in order to reassert her right to her own wilderness and to the nonconformity of her desires. But she appears so caught behind "the living bars" of family life that readers may fall into the trap of believing that it was only against them that she chafed. The author manipulates us into assuming that Thérèse's unconscious if violent rebellion was against the mounting and stifling monotony and the empty rituals within the entrapping walls of her country house. But she had not been in the dark before, and her revolt had started long before those walls began to close about her. It was during her honeymoon, when she had not yet lived in the La Trave household but had already received the jolt of Anne's betrayal, that she looked dispassionately at the "country-bred fellow" she had married and yearned, with a mind all too clear:

> If only she had not got to make such an effort to eat her lunch and smile, to compose her features and to keep her eyes from blazing. If only she could fix her mind freely upon the mysterious despair which seemed to have seized upon her. (31)

The English translation is faithful to the original. Thérèse talks quite literally of the mysterious despair ("désespoir mystérieux") that had got hold of her, as her mind went over the fiery words in Anne's letters. Bernard is no longer merely the male who had violated the sanctity of her body, he is the intruder into the passionate world of her feelings and emotions. The only way she finds of converting him into a bearable presence is to make of him a sounding board for a name she needs to mention: "she had to talk about Anne" (32). Like those of all lovers, Thérèse's words, too, converge to the object of her desires. She needed to evoke the only name and face that had for so long filled the realm of her reveries.

The crime of Mauriac's heroine is presented like a living organism with a volition of its own, a germ that, once implanted, matures irrespective of will or consciousness. It does not become evident until the night of the forest fire, when Thérèse watches, mute and fascinated, Bernard taking, unaware, a second dose of his Fowler prescription. But murder was by then within her, an unrecognized yet germinating

[15] *Op. cit.*, p. 18.

embryo. Its stirring was merely a confirmation of the life that had already been infused in it. If one could trace that life at its inception one would have to go back to the far away days of Thérèse's honeymoon. There was first the revulsion inspired by the cumbersome body that shared her bed and which she forcefully pushed away as it sought her warmth during sleep. And then there was the prospect of squalor and emptiness, as the loss of the only love she had ever nourished took for her the shape of a "mysterious despair." All that followed the terrible moment of recognition that happiness now lay forever beyond the boundaries of the possible for her, is a manifestation of that awareness. Without hope there could only be destruction for a nature without docility Lacking the resignation of the meek, Thérèse could only strike back with the weapons at her disposal: her charm and her intelligence at the service now of vengeance and her thirst for freedom.

Nelly Cormeau whose study is somewhat too deferential to Mauriac and to what is perhaps his technique of deception (to what I see as the author's effort to depict seething and passionate natures under the guise of religious innuendoes) refers nevertheless to Thérèse as a creature branded by a terrible passion and an ineluctable fate.[16] I have chosen to call Thérèse's passion by its name, and to answer her ill-fated search with words and thoughts shaped in her own mind, dictated by her emotions, and yet left unacknowledged. She goes meticulously over the events that followed her return to Argelouse after the honeymoon, her meetings with Azévédo and her cruel duplicity against the girl she had so intensely wanted close to her. But she knows now that she could not allow Anne to realize a dream from which she was herself excluded. As for the arsenic she poured drop by drop into the glass of the man who was her avowed master, that was an act similar in its nature to the one of pushing him away from her nuptial bed. Her vengeance, however, was not directed against that man, for whom she had little consideration but hardly any animosity. Had she been able to isolate herself from his presence, from his touch above all, he would have played a negligible role in her life. But Anne and the desire, which that blond adolescent had unconsciously culled from her heart, had ineluctably shaped her existence and condemned it to a frightening solitude. If Mauriac leaves Thérèse at the end on a Parisian sidewalk deprived of redemption, it is because no redemption is possible from the imperatives of nature and the assertive demands of the heart.

[16] Nelly Cormeau, *L'Art de François Mauriac* (Grasset, 1951), pp. 307-08, 311.

Argile and the Poetry of Claude Esteban: An Introduction

ROBERT W. GREENE

Ever since the *belle époque* (1885-1914), and even before, poetry in France has often shown its freshest, most innovative face, as well as its most polemical side, in the pages of "little" magazines. One has only to think of the crucial role played by such publications during the dada-surrealist era to be reminded of their special contribution to the evolution of the genre. Moreover, the tradition that had Tzara, Breton *et al.* displaying their work and presenting their theories first in what the French call *revues éphémères* has remained intensely vital down to the present day. Over the last two decades, for example, little magazines have provided both a forum for what was new in poetry and an invaluable refuge for the endangered species that poetry was rapidly becoming.

Poetry's always precarious situation deteriorated sharply in the mid-1960s when the two old and distinguished outlets for it, *Cahiers du sud* and *Mercure de France*, disappeared from the scene. Shortly after the demise of these periodicals, poetry suffered yet another setback when in 1966 the sculptor-painter Alberto Giacometti died. By the time of his death, the Swiss artist's work had elevated him to the status of patron saint and rallying point for a cluster of important younger French poets, including, most notably, Yves Bonnefoy, André du Bouchet, and Jacques Dupin. Partly in response to these losses, in the spring of 1967 the aforementioned poets, together with several other writers, founded, with the financial backing of the Fondation

188

Maeght, a review named, self-consciously enough, *L'Ephémère*. *L'Ephémère* was dedicated to the memory of Giacometti and to the preservation of the approach to creative endeavor that he embodied for these poets.

As their various writings on Giacometti show, Bonnefoy, Du Bouchet, and Dupin were drawn to the artist because of his uncanny ability to involve destruction itself in the act of creation.[1] What also evidently attracted them to Giacometti was, in the face of life's absurdity, "son intransigeance dans la recherche de l'absolu."[2] In one way or another, the contradictory elements perceived by these poets in Giacometti's oeuvre—the incorporation of death and destruction in birth and creation, the assumption that art is a perpetually thwarted yet continually renewed quest for some absolute—inform their respective and otherwise quite disparate bodies of poetry. Furthermore, because Bonnefoy, Du Bouchet, and Dupin published far more texts apiece in *L'Ephémère* than anyone else, the review in a sense acquired its identity from their many contributions to it during the five years of its life, 1967-1972. After 1972, the spirit of *L'Ephémère*, as epitomized by these three poets, would live on in the pages of another review to be sponsored by Maeght, *Argile*, a review, however, that would be directed by a single individual instead of a committee and that would, consequently, exhibit an even greater unity of purpose than its predecessor.

Argile, a deluxe, large-format review of poetry, essays, and graphics launched in December 1973, ceased publication in the spring of 1981 with the appearance of the double issue nos. 23-24. Throughout the seven-plus years of its existence, *Argile* was edited by the poet, art critic, and translator Claude Esteban, who was also a former contributor to *L'Ephémère*. The review's—and Esteban's—conception of poetry was set forth in a position statement tipped into its inaugural number:

---

[1] See, for example, Jacques Dupin, *Alberto Giacometti* (Maeght, 1966); André du Bouchet, *Qui n'est pas tourné vers nous* (Mercure de France, 1972); and Yves Bonnefoy, "L'Etranger de Giacometti," first published in *L'Ephémère*, no. 1 (printemps 1967) and reprinted most recently in *L'Improbable et autres essais* (Mercure de France, 1980), pp. 315-28. It should also be noted that Bonnefoy is currently completing a book-length study of Giacometti.

[2] Jean-Paul Sartre, *Situations*, III (Gallimard, 1949), 293.

Entre les rhétoriques anguleuses et l'éperon intraitable des idéologies, est-il place, aujourd'hui surtout, pour le poème? Opiniâtres ou naïfs, nous le croyons encore, donnant pouvoir aux mots de convoquer l'obscur, d'inventer au-dedans comme un souffle qui les traverse. Et telle présence soudain tangible, dans l'étoilement des idiomes et la diaspora des contrées, vient confirmer, s'il était nécessaire, les raisons secrètes du coeur.

Affronter l'étendu, l'erreur, la précarité de l'échange, n'est point, tant s'en faut, s'y résoudre. Quelques chemins, ici et là frayés, attestent l'espoir d'une concordance. Stèles superbes ou signes à demi rompus sont là, moins pour nous guider que pour exiger derechef une reconnaissance, un visage. A nous de les accueillir, à nous de tenter, une fois de plus, parmi les branches aveugles du multiple, l'orientation et la voie.

Ici, sans autre lieu que la terre vacante, la terre intacte sous nos pas, et *dans l'incertitude où nous sommes* — disons-le avec Reverdy — *de vivre si près du ciel sans jamais pouvoir le toucher.*

Diffident, if not beleaguered in its tone, lush, almost baroque in its style, Esteban's declaration nonetheless signaled to *Argile*'s readers that it intended to continue the struggle in which *L'Ephémère* had been engaged. It announced in effect that, for *Argile*, poetry was still, however outmoded or naive this stance might now seem, first and foremost a quest, a search for the real, for truth, for communion, for something at once within and beyond the here and now. In striking contrast to the semantic materialism of, say, writers associated with the review *Tel Quel*, *Argile*, following the lead of *L'Ephémère* (and before it of *Mercure de France*), would evidently carry the standard of what could be called a modified or chastened transcendentalism. It would reflect the conviction that poetic activity is justified only when it acknowledges as its *raison d'être* the desire for contact, however fleeting, with an ineffable presence that somehow both inheres in and transcends its instrument, its words.

While editing *Argile*, Esteban also published a number of books, the most important of which, without question, was *Terres, travaux du coeur*, a volume containing his collected poetry up to that time. Almost simultaneously, he brought out a group of essays in poetic theory entitled *Un Lieu hors de tout lieu*.[3] Between them, these two works constitute a kind of "defense and illustration" not only of their author's

---

[3] Claude Esteban, *Terres, travaux du coeur* (Flammarion, 1979), *Un Lieu hors de tout lieu* (Editions Galilée, 1979).

oeuvre but also of that current in twentieth-century French poetry that *Argile* in particular fostered during the 1970s.

Esteban's theoretical collection, supple in its articulation, laced with fine distinctions and discriminations, punctuated by tactfully phrased disclaimers, propounds nevertheless an unambiguous if highly nuanced thesis. The general orientation of Esteban's rather complex thought is perhaps most clearly indicated in his preference for Rimbaud over Mallarmé or, more precisely, his preference for a certain Rimbaud over a particular aspect of Mallarmé's legacy. The following celebrated passage from Rimbaud's "Adieu," quoted (at least in part) in both the first and last of the five chapter-essays that make up *Un Lieu hors de tout lieu,* serves to frame Esteban's theory:

> Moi! moi qui me suis dit mage ou ange, dispensé de toute morale, je suis rendu au sol, avec un devoir à chercher, et la réalité rugueuse à étreindre! Paysan![4]

In modern times, Rimbaud especially exemplifies the poet's need to embrace rugged reality, shows the way to what Esteban repeatedly refers to as "l'immédiat." Poetry, which for Esteban is "à la fois, métaphysique et trans-linguistique" (p. 134), creates that privileged place where meaning can perhaps arise. It forges connections among individuals who would otherwise remain discrete subjectivities, and between these separate selves and the world. Poetry answers, neutralizes all diasporas of the spirit and is therefore profoundly religious in character; it is an act that binds together, that reclaims the alienated and the lost. It does so by a movement of return, a "retour amont," to borrow (after Esteban himself, p. 110) René Char's memorable phrase. Poetry thus becomes "le lieu d'un ressourcement spirituel, corps et esprit brassés ensemble, à travers et par le truchement des mots" (p. 110).

But do words in poetry function essentially in relationship to one another (à la Mallarmé), within a self-enclosing set of *mises en abyme* (à la Francis Ponge)? Not for Esteban, who maintains that "la parole de poésie ne dialogue pas avec soi seule, mais avec ce qui dans les mots garde mémoire d'un passé profond, d'une histoire ancestrale et coexistentielle à une terre" (p. 108). While he admires Mallarmé for

---

[4] Arthur Rimbaud, *Oeuvres complètes,* ed. Rolland de Renéville and Jules Mouquet (Pléiade, 1954), p. 243.

having launched "une conduite de poésie comme vouée à la captation verbale des essences" (p. 55), he regrets that this development has led to "la transparence, jusqu'à la pureté comme adamantine des vers. Apesanteur astral" (p. 56). Now if poetry is to survive at all, according to Esteban, it must "renoncer... au vertige mallarméen, à cet appel... de la transparence, pour s'immerger derechef dans la houle opaque de l'élémentaire" (p. 63).

More completely than anyone else, including Rimbaud, Virgil, guide to Dante, reflects the attitude that Esteban considers appropriate for the poet, the posture of reaching down into "the opaque groundswell of the elemental." He finds in the *Georgics* the seminal image of his own poetic theory, the evocation in Virgil's work of the peasant who, laboring at some future time, turning over his field with his ploughshare, "fait surgir hors du sol, à l'échancrure du sillon, les ossements, les armes, les cuirasses de guerriers morts entremêlés" (p. 28). Virgil's ploughman no longer remembers either the combattants or their causes, but what he has uncovered "lui disent la continuité d'une histoire—et que le blé doit renaître d'une terre où les vivants ont pesé et que les morts nourrissent encore de leur poudre" (p. 29). Virgil's lesson for Esteban is that words and soil, interpenetrating, beckon to us through the accumulated layers of the past. Is the French poet, then, advocating a basically Cratylic position, the belief that words, reaching back beyond history, actually express the essence of things, instead of being simply linked to things by custom and convention? I think not, since Esteban is at pains to take his distance from any myth of origins, of pristine meanings for words; he distinguishes between "limon primitif" (primordial slime) and the "sol" or "terroir" or "argile" that real men living in and through real time, endowed with nature and creating cultures, accrue and transmit down through the ages. For Esteban, as for Virgil (according to Esteban), the Latin formula applies: *homo homini humus.* "L'homme est la terre de l'homme, le lieu de son enracinement et de sa finitude, le seul horizon réel qui mérite d'être exalté" (p. 32). Thus it is not Plato's dialogue but the story of Antaeus that enjoins Esteban's poet — always touch mother earth. Hold fast to it for strength, for sustenance, and for survival.

Esteban believes that words have a materiality that is rooted, quite literally, in history (p. 108). But he stops short of the semantic materialism of Ponge, for example, seeing a "Moi profond" (p. 126), a controlling Subject, at the center of poetry. As if to underscore his differences with Ponge, he rejects Ponge's most cherished idol, Lucretius, in favor of Virgil (p. 24). Also, poetic composition, virtually an end in itself for Ponge, is for Esteban merely a means (p. 138); it is the search for the immediate through the mediating powers of language (p. 140). While Esteban concedes that poetry is in some sense an adventure unfolding within the confines of the poet's mother tongue, thereby agreeing with Ponge, unlike Ponge, he also sees poetry as linked indissolubly "au poète singulier... à une personne autre que verbale" (p. 141), to an individual, moreover, at once corporeal and spiritual, in whom others can recognize themselves. Parodying Ponge's well-known phrase ("le parti pris des choses"), Esteban characterizes his own stance as a "parti pris de la présence" (p. 141).

Near the end of *Un Lieu hors de tout lieu*, in terms echoing the title of his collected poetry, Esteban speaks of the restoration, the reconciliation that poetry can perhaps afford: "Nous demandons à la poésie... qu'elle restaure ce 'lieu commun'... où terres et travaux du coeur, réalité naturelle et paysage humain, bougent et s'émeuvent ensemble" (p. 136). Here, possibly, in this "lieu commun," this common place at once linguistic and trans-verbal, earth and words, self and other, person and universe can achieve the harmony of co-presence.

Terres, travaux du coeur is divided into three main sections which are entitled "La Saison dévastée (1967-71)," "Dans le vide qui vient (1972-75)," and "Dieu transparent (1976-78)." The second of these poetic sequences, "Dans le vide qui vient," which first appeared in 1976 as the sixth volume in Maeght's "Collection Argile," illustrates with particular vividness the sway that Virgil's *Georgics* holds over the French poet. One poem within this sequence, untitled, as are nearly all of Esteban's poems, has as its epigraph, a line from the *Georgics*: "Grandiaque effosis mirabitur ossa sepulcris" ("And the graves having been dug up, he will marvel at the great bones"). The Latin epigraph is, then, in effect, glossed in Esteban's poem. (It will be noted that the general outlines of the scene hauntingly if fragmentarily evoked in the poem also appear in *Un Lieu hors de tout lieu*):

(1) Côte à côte, jadis, dans le déclin des astres.

(2) Voici qu'un homme
(3) les découvre au retour de son champ

(4) vides
(5) et l'histoire sur eux comme une
(6) mousse grise.

(7)   La pluie, les vieux labours
(8)   ont confondue leurs plaies.

(9)   Etait-ce un même orgueil qui cherchait le silence—

(10)   Des armes se redressent
(11)   butent
(12)   contre le fer

(13)   qu'une rouille retient, aride, loin des astres. (p. 121)

Esteban's poem fleshes out Virgil's line via an interlocking series of binary oppositions. Also, interposed between Virgil and Esteban, and woven into the fabric of the text, is a stanza from Théophile Gautier's "L'Art," perhaps the best-known celebration of the sempiternal powers of art in all of French literature: "Et la médaille austère / Que trouve un laboureur / Sous terre / Révèle un empereur." But the Latin proverb *ars longa, vita brevis*, which in an important sense motivated, inspired Gautier's "L'Art," plays virtually no germinal role in Esteban's poem. Rather, the cliché that generates it is another, equally familiar but quite different antithetical stereotype, the collocation of swords and ploughshares, of swords beaten into ploughshares, that Biblical polarity-veering-toward-identity. Ethical and perhaps spiritual matters are at issue here, not esthetic or, even less, estheticist concerns. Undoubtedly, Gautier and the whole art-for-art's sake ethos are invoked in "Côte à côte," but only so as to be dismissed, only so as to set off the didactic intention that Esteban's text shares with the *Georgics*.

The specific "lesson" that Esteban expounds in "Côte à côte" involves a humanist continuum. The poem's thirteen lines and line-fragments glorify a *hic et nunc* attitude in defiance of eternity's silence. Past and present join in an ongoing dialectic to confront the endless aridity of the stars. The first and last lines, 1 and 13, perfect alexandrines with identical endings ("des astres"), formally mark the poem's open and close. By homophony with "désastre," thus on a subliminal level only, the "echo" ending also calls attention to the twin voids between which human existence is suspended, thereby valorizing still further whatever it is that continues, that survives down through the ages.

The twelve-syllable line, complete with proper caesura, furnishes the poem's basic rhythmic structure, shaping not only the opening and the close of the poem but also line 9 and, when combined, lines

5 and 6, lines 7 and 8, and lines 10, 11, and 12. Carried along on this traditional, consecrated pulsation is a series of antitheses which, transformed into binary oppositions, collectively express the spirit, the breath that binds men together across the centuries. On the strictly antithetical plane, agriculture is contrasted with war, the farmer is contrasted with the soldier, the ploughshare with the sword, friends with enemies, verdancy with greyness, moisture with aridity, fullness with emptiness, fecundity with barrenness, life with death.

On another level, however, parallelism or similarity counters difference and contrast. The poem, as has been noted, ends as it begins with the pharase "des astres," even if the stars' involvement in human destiny, implicit in line 1, has given way, in line 13, to a distancing, even a denial of that influence. Also, the long-dead adversaries are first encountered side by side, as if in life they had been lovers or at least allies rather than enemies. This notion, moreover, is reinforced by lines 7 and 8: "La pluie, les vieux labours / ont confondu leurs plaies," as well as by lines 5 and 6: "et l'histoire sur eux comme une / mousse grise" and line 9: "Etait-ce un même orgueil qui cherchait le silence — ." A more fundamental paradox characterizes lines 10 through 13, where swords, resurrected, strike against the ploughshare which, caught in ancient rust, is held aloof from any cosmic connection. The engagement, the exchange between different men in different conditions of life at different historical moments, has been made; the continuous contact of real existences has been reestablished through the concentration of qualitatively and temporally disparate human activities in one and the same earthly place. Here, perhaps, we have reached that "place outside every place" of which Esteban has spoken. A real field located somewhere in Italy? Yes and no. Rather, it is the evocation or, more precisely, the excavation of *that* field in *this* field of words, in this place of presence or, at least, of possibility.

As several aspects of my reading of "Côte à côte" might suggest, Yves Bonnefoy is quite probably Esteban's most powerful living mentor. Like his elder, for example, the author of *Terres, travaux du coeur* is obsessed by dreams of what Bonnefoy has often called "le vrai lieu," or, to use Esteban's own words, "un lieu hors de tout lieu," the site of being's threshold. For Bonnefoy, as for Esteban, poetry represents the promise of a kind of utopia where the immediate and the inaccessible meet. Significantly, Esteban has entitled his study of Bonnefoy's art criticism "L'immédiat et l'inaccessible." This essay, the longest and most ambitious in a collection bearing its name, tells us as much, perhaps, about its author as it does about its subject. Reflecting upon Bonnefoy's magisterial study of early baroque art, *Rome 1630: L'Horizon du premier baroque*,[5] Esteban, like Bonnefoy, is drawn especially to Bernini, sculptor-architect of the magnificent baldaquin in St. Peter's basilica. For Bonnefoy, according to Esteban, Bernini represents "comme la réconciliation chaleureuse de l'immédiat et de l'inaccessible";[6] in the Italian artist's masterpiece, the permanent and the universal dwell in the contingent and the particular, and time and history become vehicles of transcendance. Such paradoxical notions, which are central to Bonnefoy's appreciation of Bernini, are completely compatible with Esteban's esthetic outlook and poetic practice.

Esteban's final poetic sequence in *Terres, travaux du coeur*, "Dieu transparent" (sections of which first appeared in *Argile*, nos. 9-10, 13-14, and 18), makes clearer than ever before another enduring filiation, his belief, along with Heidegger, that "poetry is the establishing of being by means of the word."[7] Also, as a group, "Dieu transparent" seems more cohesive, more unified than Esteban's earlier sequences. The litany-like repetition of the phrase "Dieu transparent" and its variants ("Dieu traversé," "Dieu dénudé," "Dieu dépouillé," "Dieu terrassé," "Dieu dévasté") tends to draw the individual poems of the group into a whole. The sporadic recurrence of a particular network of images performs a similar unifying function; trees, their sap and pith, and peatbogs, interact to suggest the slow, incremental processes of growth in and from the earth. Also, we are plainly in a post-credal age in "Dieu transparent" — God is transparent because He has vanished. The need or the thirst for God, however, has not disappeared, nor has the sense, fragile though it may be, that "la flamme de l'unique... traverse le multiple et / le rassemble" (p. 225). Something special, almost sacred, rises up through the spiral of history, the accumulating strata of earth and words, through the ever-widening circles of aging tree trunks, to us. It is a presence as elusive and yet as vital as breath itself. Coming forward in time from what was uttered long ago, it gathers up the manifold and the concrete, and is plenitude to its vacant surroundings:

[5] Yves Bonnefoy, *Rome 1630: L'Horizon du premier baroque* (Flammarion, 1970).
[6] Claude Esteban, *L'Immédiat et l'inaccessible* (Editions Galilée, 1978), p. 184.
[7] Martin Heidegger, "Hölderlin and the Essence of Poetry," tr. Douglas Scott, in *Existence and Being* (Chicago: Henry Regnery, 1970), p. 281.

......
Ce qui fut dit
traverse le multiple et
le rassemble.

    Sans rompre la mesure,
sans altérer ce que les heures
ont bâti.

    Pacte visible.

Avec le vide à ses côtés, comme témoin. (p. 225)

It is the thirst for the divine which, turning back on itself, commands, in spite of the void, Rise, Transcend:

    Mais tu n'existes pas. Des mots
plus grands que nous

ont fait ton corps, ton âme transparente. Pour
nous laisser plus seuls

avec ce vide dans la voix.
......

    Pourtant le nom demeure
qui t'invente. L'éclair qui te convoque. Cette
soif.

    Eprouve-les. Sois le doute et l'échec. Sois
la parole insuffisante.

Traverse tout ce vide — et monte
par-delà. (p. 232)

Like Bonnefoy's, Esteban's climb toward the absolute bespeaks not nostalgia for perfection, for some lost paradise, but rather the lucid embrace of multiplicity and imperfection, of Rimbaud's "réalité rugueuse." Paraphrasing the title of Bonnefoy's poem "L'Imperfection est la cime," Esteban concludes his collected poetry with the line "Tout l'imparfait s'évade vers la cime" (p. 262).[8] For Esteban, the entire category of the imperfect flies toward the summit. Just so, humans affirm their solidarity, their continuity across time and space, by vaulting beyond themselves in a "pacte visible" that fuses the opaque here and now with a transparent god.

In "Traduire," an essay on translation that Esteban published in *Argile* (no. 22 [printemps 1980], pp. 72-91), the poet reprises a no-

[8] See Yves Bonnefoy, *Poèmes* (Mercure de France, 1978), p. 117.

tion that implicitly structures much of his practice in *Terres, travaux du coeur*, the belief that words come to the poet's hand laden with individual histories which the poet must assume completely if he is to function as a poet (pp. 87-88) Elsewhere in "Traduire," Esteban draws a distinction between the two divergent conceptions of poetic activity he sees operating today, between poetry as "une expérimentation extrême du langage, ainsi que certaines écoles néo-positivistes s'attachent à le démontrer" and poetry as "une aventure d'absolu à travers les mots d'une langue" (p. 79). From this essay, as indeed from his writings as a whole, it is clear that Esteban subscribes to the latter conception of poetry.

That poetry for Esteban consists in such an adventure is made abundantly clear in "Conjoncture du corps et du jardin," a sequence of twenty-one brief, untitled but numbered prose poems that he published in the final issue of *Argile* (nos. 23-24 [printemps 1981], pp. 207-17). As the first text in the series shows, the poet juxtaposes traditional opposites here — flesh and spirit, self and other, sunlight and dewdrop (hence, fire and water), sleep and wakefulness, stillness and movement, dream and realization:

> Dès l'aube, je descends. Je m'allonge contre un caillou. Je lèche le crachat des feuilles. Qui se réveille? Est-ce mon corps ou moi? Rien n'est sûr. Un miracle peut durer longtemps, s'il respire. Je progresse, les yeux mi-clos. Dédales de mon désir. Dans la toile d'une arraignée je trouve un soleil qui tremble.

It is almost as if Esteban begins "Conjoncture du corps et du jardin" where Yeats ends "The Circus Animals' Desertion." The figure of the poet in the garden, still somnolent at dawn, reclining on the pebble path, licking the foliage's dew or sap, advancing through the murk of his desire until he finds a shimmering sun in the spider's web, recalls Yeats's magnificent close: "I must lie down where all the ladders start / In the foul rag-and-bone shop of the heart."[9] Miracles of art, ladders to the infinite, "Monuments of unageing intellect," must arise from the secure purchase of things earthly, the sweaty here and now, in order to endure. As Esteban observes in the second text of the series, "il faudrait, pour surgir, faire sienne un peu de la salive des arbres." Thus, the imposing silhouette of Antaeus, that giant who

---

[9] W.B. Yeats, *The Collected Poems* (London: Macmillan, 1963), p. 399. It seems pertinent to recall here that *Argile*, no. 1 (hiver 1973) contains no fewer than eleven poems by Yeats, translated by Yves Bonnefoy (see pp. 64-93).

draws strength upward into his towering torso via feet planted squarely on the ground, may once again be glimpsed presiding over Esteban's poetic universe.

The title of the sequence, specifically the word "conjoncture," suggests that the meeting between the poet's corporeal being and the garden is not simply a *rencontre*, an encounter without issue. Rather, the key word's connotative dimension implies that important consequences will follow. The semantic and orthographic similarity of "conjoncture" and "conjonction," moreover, indicates that the meeting may have cosmic repercussions, inasmuch as two celestial bodies crossing paths, conjoining, in the same "house" of the zodiac, properly interpreted, constitute a classic sign, if not determinant, of individual destiny. On the other hand, the absence of any personalizing term in the title, such as the possessive adjective "mon" before either "corps" or "jardin," leads us to suspect that the destiny to be enacted in this series of poems will take place not on the individual but on the universal plane. From the outset, the spare, impersonal style of the prose fuels our suspicions in this regard. "Conjoncture du corps et du jardin" will thus have little of the confessional mode about it.

The twenty-one short prose texts form a meandering meditation on life, death, love, the transcendent mystery of the self and the distinct but somehow interchangeable activities of the body and the garden. They speak of words and things and of the problematic relationships linking them. They speak also of new beginnings, of passages from one state to another, of limits respected and transgressed, of thresholds crossed, with always the fleshly and the vegetal, the body and the garden, interpenetrating: "Tout est jardin" (vi); "Tout cet arbre enfin moi" (x); "Ce jardin est mon corps aussi" (xx). The garden is at once sexualized (ix) and asexual (xiv). The poet becomes the spokesman of the dead, perhaps of death itself: "Je suis le seul qui veille sur les morts... Je les couche avec moi parmi les ronces. Je suis celui qui donne au rien le pouvoir de poursuivre encore" (xviii). Death, moreover, a chill hunk of winter, lies at the very heart of summer, hence of life, and the garden becomes the body's grave site (xix). (Following Bonnefoy and Giacometti, Esteban evidently treats death as the *sine qua non* of life.)[10] In the end, the garden has more in com-

---

[10] See, for example, in the case of Bonnefoy, text v of *Anti-Platon* where the poet speaks of "indispensable mort" (*Poèmes*, p. 15). As for Giacometti, the "indispensability" of death is visible in nearly all of his works, but perhaps especially in those pieces of sculpture entitled "L'Homme qui marche" and "L'Homme qui tombe."

mon with a cemetery than it has with some lost Eden or with nature construed as a mirror of the poet's soul: no conventional metaphor compromises the death-haunted yet vibrant strangeness and particularity it reacquires in Esteban's hands.

Moving in and out of phase with his body, the garden is explored by the poet in all its inalienable alterity. Intersecting again and again, body and garden effect an exchange that unleashes, for poet and reader alike, the experience of presence, "the sense of mystic unity with... otherness," to borrow G.D. Martin's apt gloss of the notion of *présence* at work in Yves Bonnefoy.[11] For Esteban, too, such an experience, such an exchange between self and other, however brief and imperfect, is all-enabling. Through it alone, for example, does love, that imprisonment-cum-liberation, that greatest of death's redeemers, that utter transformation, come to pass:

> Je t'aime depuis toujours. Je t'emprisonne dans une image. Je te rends aux chemins, toi qui mourais sur chaque fleur. Délaisse nos saisons. Altère le savoir des signes. L'air est sublime. Le ciel monte. Nous marcherons comme si dieu dormait. (xxi)

This rising close to "Conjoncture du corps et du jardin" simply but stunningly celebrates the miracle of "All changed, changed utterly." We await with eagerness the fruits of that sea-change in Claude Esteban's oeuvre after *Argile*.

---

[11] G.D. Martin, "Bonnefoy's Shakespeare Translations," *World Literature Today*, 53 (Summer 1979), 488.

Rhetoric, Reference, and Mode

LITERATURE AND SINCERITY · JEAN-PAUL SARTRE

Rhetoric, Truth and Power: Lanson's Solution

MICHEL BEAUJOUR

I should like to evoke one minor episode in the ancient and endless struggle between philosophy and sophistry, science and rhetoric, truth and plausibility. This conflict in which all intellectuals are active participants, whether they realize it or not, revolves around two contradictory interpretations of what the Greeks conveniently but confusingly called *logos*. As we know, Classical and Renaissance Latin writers had a choice between at least two translations which were etymologically related and almost homonymous, but quite divergent in meaning: *ratio* and *oratio*. Translating these two terms into modern English or French turns out to be rather tricky. The first term suggests cold, strict, and methodical procedures, while the second denotes the seductiveness of eloquence, the power of words, all the wiles of discourse or, perhaps more pertinently, *ratio* evokes a deep structure of universal and impersonal arguments, while *oratio* refers to the local, individualized surface of an actual discourse uttered in contingent circumstances. If this is so, then we can easily understand why *oratio* should appear unworthy and even expendable within an *episteme* or *ideology* placing the findings of scientific method at the top of its value system. Such was the case — to simplify matters considerably — within the ideology of the French intellectual establishment at the end of the nineteenth century.

The historical episode I want to evoke is quite local in context, but the participants thought, of course, that they were shaping the future of mankind, as in a way they were. The episode revolves — as things

often do in French education and intellectual life—around a ministerial
decree to replace the teaching of rhetoric in the *lycées* with that of literary
history. The ideological stakes were high, and perhaps worth thinking about (especially here and now, in an American context, where
the teaching of literature is increasingly replaced with that of elementary rhetoric in the guise of writing courses, and where the teaching
of so-called creative writing is not considered a laughable oddity).

In any case, Jules Simon's ministerial circular of 1872 was a first
official attempt to put an end to the teaching of rhetoric in French
lycées (Larousse ironically states that Simon wrote "eloquent books
of ethics": in short, he was a rhetor in his own right). The cultural
implications of Simon's decision were many and wide ranging:

1. It condemned the ancient rationale of humanistic studies, according to which young people read and studied canonical authors
in order to imitate them in their own writings.

From now on, it would be enough to understand and appreciate
literature. Imitation was neither expected nor encouraged. The
ideology of "originality" went hand in hand with the idea that there
are better things for an adolescent to do than imitate Cicero, or even
La Bruyère. "Creative Writing" was to become a specialized, marginal,
and extracurricular activity.

2. The epistemological status of the literary text and its commentary changed radically. The texts became objects of study, like natural
phenomena. Students learned to write *about* literature, and they acquired the rudiments of a "science" of literature called *literary history*.
The seriousness of literary studies, their truth value, resided in that
science, rather than in the texts themselves, which expressed mere
opinions.

3. A new manner of dealing with literary texts within the
pedagogical context was introduced into the curriculum. That was
the famed *explication de textes* otherwise known as *explication française*.
Textual commentaries had hitherto drawn attention to rhetorical
features, which *could* be imitated, and to moral examples, which also
could be imitated by the pupils.

According to its exponents, Ferdinand Brunot and Gustave Lanson, *explication* was to have nothing to do with literary criticism and
imitation. It was to be a strictly grammatical and philological commentary, an oral *translation or rendering* of an authoritative text, a search
for the *proper* or *literal* sense of the text. The commentary was expected
to eschew all oratorical effects, and avoid imitating the style, diction,

figures of the text being commented upon. In short, the teacher and pupil were to avoid any illusion that explication was a "creative" genre. It was to be a scientific classroom exercise, on the same order as laboratory experiments in the natural sciences.

As a result of this emphasis, literary *oratio* (style, discourse, persuasion) was turned into a scientific object. The language of explication (and also of literary history, presumably) was expected to achieve *a zero degree* of rhetoric, and to become as transparent and neutral as the referential language of natural scientists.

Thus the literary curriculum of the French lycée in the third Republic strictly excluded imitations and literary self-expression. *Ratio* was to reign in the domain of *oratio*: this set the stage for a very ambiguous and potentially absurd situation.

One might note in passing that quite a different situation obtained in the pedagogy of *philosophy*, which crowned the secondary school curriculum: the young student of speculative philosophy was expected to try his own hand at doing speculative philosophy. In this process, many of the traditional rhetorical *topoi* of invention would surface, so that philosophical essays were in effect thoroughly rhetorical and commonplace. The philosophy class was the only one where the student was allowed to imitate the texts he had just read and wax eloquent, under the guise of philosophizing. A very Platonic crossover, so to speak. In its efforts to preserve truth from the pitfalls of literary *oratio*, the French educational system had turned philosophy into a substitute for *belles-lettres*. The effects are still felt in French philosophy.

This situation is nevertheless a clear sign of the relative status accorded to literature and philosophy in the late nineteenth-century French value system. Philosophy had inherent seriousness, because it dealt with the True and the Good, and it saw itself as a *rationale* for the *positive sciences*. Philosophy was indeed *ratio*. On the other hand literature was not inherently trustworthy or truthful: it expressed opinions, it displayed insights but also the frailty of individual minds left to themselves without the succor and grace cf scientific methods. It was desirable, then, to preserve from its contamination those young minds which might yet be saved by the lights of science, progress and positive philosophy. The forces of darkness, alas, attract the best writers, and literature was too often a vehicle for unscientific, or Roman Catholic and royalist ideas.

By the last third of the nineteenth century, the struggle between *ratio* and *oratio* had become, with the establishment of the republican doctrine, a public ideological and political issue in France. Suppression of rhetoric was part and parcel of the struggle against the aristocratic ethos and Christian beliefs. In a narrower, pedagogical sense, it was an attempt to eradicate the influence of the Jesuits, who had hitherto dominated French élite education, and were now barred from teaching in France.

The ideologues of the third Republic were motivated by a powerful urge, which Michel Foucault has called a *Will to Truth* in his effort to reveal the resemblances between this urge and the Nietzschean *Will to Power*. In Foucault's words, this urge can be seen as a "prodigious machinery geared to *excluding*": gushing out, rejecting all that was not consonant with the will's own definition of the Truth. Attempts to challenge the powerful definition of the Truth and the basis upon which it excluded competing definitions, were termed ridiculous, dangerous or *insane*. A frantic insistence on *ratio* against *oratio* led to the establishment of a totalitarian enlightenment.

This *will to truth* was bound up, at least in France, with a will to power which the defeat of 1871 had exacerbated. The will to truth, the will to power and the desire for revenge against Germany were tightly interconnected, so that *oratio* and rhetoric could be indicted for lukewarm patriotism and even treasonable divisiveness. On the other hand, historical science (the social sciences, including literary history, were fundamentally historical) could transcend all special interests, provided it truly followed the scientific method. Lanson could therefore write in his great article of 1910, which summarized the work and hopes of the past decades:

> Literary history unites... it thus becomes a means of bringing together compatriots who are divided and opposed on all other scores... we do not work only for *truth* and *mankind*: we work for the *fatherland* (la patrie).[1]

Other literary disciplines, such as criticism, were dangerously argumentative and emotional; they were steeped in *opinion*, and too visibly shaped by their rhetorical matrix. Thus Lanson: "[Literary] criticism, whether it be dogmatic, freewheeling or passionate, is divisive: literary history draws us together, as does science, from which it derives its inspiration" (p. 56). The facts and so-called laws of literary history (= the science of literature) were not understood to be the

[1] Gustave Lanson, "La Méthode de l'histoire littéraire" (1910), in his *Essais de méthode, de critique et d'histoire littéraire*, ed. Henri Peyre (Hachette, 1965), p. 56.

ever challengeable products of a dialectical conflict between competing models. On the contrary, they were the result of an unfolding of the truth which commanded the unstinting assent of all rational and *competent* men of goodwill. Thus literary history, as *scientific ratio* and historical *logos*, was unitary, centripetal and it admitted of no alternative models or laws. As *reason* and *truth*, it was potentially acceptable to all mankind. Literary history was radically contrasted with the rhetorical disciplines, based on the recognition of conflicting points of view and interests, the need to play with desires and passions, to cultivate cultural axiologies, to arbitrate between irreconcilable positions, and to dissolve differences within wider commonplaces. In point of fact, literary history (history in general) was the ultimate rhetorical ploy of the nineteenth century, since it attempted to establish a new set of commonplaces, based on the national interest, and transcending all differences of opinion for the benefit of the Fatherland. The paradigm of this monological but capacious and relatively humane historiography is to be found, of course, in Lavisse's *Histoire de France* and especially in the admirable rhetorical machinery of his elementary textbooks. Whether such massive ideological undertaking ought to be called science is a moot point. The solution depends as much on the position of the beholder as it does on our own definition of what constitutes the scientificity of the social sciences in general.

Lanson was seemingly unaware of any conflict of interest between a claim of universal scientific validity for his literary history, and the fairly obvious fact that this historiography was a war-machine against virtual enemies, as well as the embodiment of a nationalist ideology. Evidently, the main purpose of the ban on rhetoric, and the claim of a scientific status for patriotic historiography, was to patch up the ideological differences that plagued France in the late nineteenth century and made it incapable of tapping its energies for the national struggle. Rhetoric obviously pitted the agnostics against the Catholics, the Dreyfusards against the anti-Dreyfusards, the royalists against the Republicans, the conservatives against the socialists etc... History reminded the various parties of the fact they shared a common destiny, perhaps even a common mission, and attempted to channel their animosity against the outside. In short, rhetoric, polemics and eristics were licit only in the struggle between nations with conflicting histories; rhetoric was to deal with the commonplaces of civilization vs. barbarism. Compatriots, on the other hand, were to contribute arguments against the enemy, in the guise of building a scientific history. This vast ideological undertaking would eventually pay off with the national unity displayed by the French people during the first World War.

If Lanson's condemnation of rhetoric was predicated on monolithic Jacobinism and Republican patriotism, it was also motivated by genuine democratic feelings. The teaching of rhetoric, inherited from an aristocratic pedagogy, prepared young men for lives of hereditary power, conspicuous display, and useless leisure. Far from being reminiscent of Athenian democracy and the Roman republic, school rhetoric reminded Lanson of the inequities of the Ancien Régime:

> Our classical education [he wrote] brings more evil than good to all those who are *not* destined to become writers of light comedy, novelists, poets, reviewers or journalists, or simply gentlemen of leisure: the vast majority, to be sure, belong to this category. It is evil, not because it teaches Greek and Latin but because it is dominated too exclusively by "literary" studies which are concerned only with the bold play of ideas, or the beauty of their form.[2]

Lanson here was echoing August Comte, who in the 1830s had already laid down the following pedagogical principles in his famous *Course of Positive Philosophy*:

> ...enlightened minds unanimously acknowledge the need to replace our European education, still essentially theological, metaphysical and literary, with a *positive* education, in conformity with the spirit of our own epoch, and adapted to the needs of modern civilization.[3]

Democracy, science and technology would supersede the aristocratic estheticism of the past. However, Lanson's basic positivism was also tempered with Ernest Renan's ambiguities and nostalgias — Lanson had heeded Renan's *caveat* against Comte's radical critique of the historical disciplines and the social sciences. The past somehow had to be preserved. A firm believer in the "scientific method," Renan wished nonetheless to preserve poetry, ethics, religion, and mythology, which were perhaps as necessary to mankind as the Truth itself. These beliefs were an odd synthesis of Chateaubriand and Auguste Comte. Above all, Renan was an admirably gifted writer, who had enough integrity not to condemn theoretically his own literary practice. Then

---

[2] *Ibid.*, p. 57.
[3] Auguste Comte, *Cours de philosophie positive* (1830-1842), Première Leçon.

again he had deeply benefited from the kind of rhetorical education which the Third Republic undertook to eliminate. According to Renan, "positive science" and the "idea of a critical search for the truth" had been quite alien to the aristocratic school where he had been a scholarship pupil around 1840. There, *success* had been measured strictly in terms of wit, eloquence, talent, and literary ability. Other pursuits were scorned by the pupils, science unknown: mathematics "seemed to them quite a base sort of work in contrast with the literary exercises which were presented to them as the ultimate goal of the human mind." Quick wit and eloquent dialectics were not tantamount to solid, orginal thinking, however. On the contrary, the bright little rhetors of Saint-Nicolas, relied heavily on the commonplaces and humanistic verisimilitude. In short they were being admirably prepared for their future aristocratic careers of the pulpit, the courtroom, and the embassy. They were not at all trained to make scientific discoveries or to revolutionize philology and historiography. And as the *Truth* came to be defined in terms of *science*, this training had become anachronistic. It preserved into the nineteenth century the values and modes of reasoning of the Ancient aristocrats, which had been restored by Renaissance humanists:

> Verisimilitudes which commonsense appreciated, connections confirmed only by the most general logic, a boldness of invention which gloried more in creation than in verification, a beauty of composition and expression which accredited ideas more powerfully than intrinsic rightness, an irrestible and unconscious faith in subjective feelings, a higher regard for cleverness than for precision, a greater urge to persuade others than to assure oneself patiently of the truth: this is the art of thinking and proving which was found, admired, in the writings of the Greeks and the Romans, and borrowed from them...[4]

This is Lanson's own description of rhetorical invention, and I must say it is an admirable description, despite its pejorative bias. The rationale of Lanson's critique is clear enough: rhetorical invention is *commonsensical* (in a negative sense of the word) and *tautological*. This of course is something that had been said at length by Francis Bacon long before him. Rhetorical invention was alien to science and progress, it could only rehash and rephrase. The unknown and the im-

[4] Gustave Lanson, "Contre la rhétorique et les mauvaises humanités," in his *Essais de méthode, de critique et d'histoire littéraire*, p. 58.

probable were quite beyond its reach. The incredible but true had no place among its plausible commonplaces. And it was therefore wrong to teach this mode of reasoning to young people who would be responsible for the shaping of future and unpredictable knowledge.

Rhetorical invention is *memory*, it is oriented toward the past, it is incapable of conceiving a future different from the past and the present. The question facing Lanson and his contemporaries, then, was: Can rhetoric be turned around? Can it be made to generate the future? This question was tantamount to asking whether literature had a future, at least within the pedagogical system. Lanson was certainly not deceived into thinking that literature could easily be reconciled with the "scientific method," although he did believe one could speak scientifically about literature by doing literary history. Concerning the future of literary invention, however, Lanson's answer was more subtle, and more puzzling: he attempted to uphold concurrently the mutually exclusive demands of *science* and *rhetoric*, while avoiding the dissociation of sensibility which was an easy way out of this dilemma. He avoided (perhaps wrongly) assertions that the truth of science, and those of myth, religion and poetry although they are of a different nature, somehow converge in the human psyche, or in the cosmos.

What Lanson did intimate is bolder and stranger: he turned rhetorical and poetic imagination, the invention of literature, into a *science-fiction*. Let us see how he negotiated this remarkable reversal:

> When Science, having completed its demonstrations, or being powerless to stretch them further, calls upon imagination in order to translate its abstract formulas into concrete terms, or in order to anticipate the realization of its findings in their ideal fullness, then indeed, it becomes literature and poetry.[5]

Here, as we see, literature is a metamorphosis of science: when science reaches the ultimate limits of its formal language, its "formulas," it turns into literature. Conversely literature feeds on the fringes of science, on its *aura*. Thus: "One might say that each science belongs to literature precisely by what remains uncertain and unknown in it" (p. 119). Or, in a less attractive fashion, literature can be seen as a recycling of science's leftovers; this proposition can be turned around: literature is the future of science: "Science is not precisely the material of literature, but it supplies literature with its material,

---

[5] Gustave Lanson, "La Littérature et la science" (1895), in his *Essais de méthode*, p. 119.

which is all that science does not use or does not reach" (p. 122). At this point, of course, one is reminded of the fact that Lanson belonged to a generation following that of Jules Verne: a contemporary of Renan, Lanson was ten years older than H.G. Wells.

The fluctuating border between scientific truth and rhetorical invention (or imagination) and the turning of science into literature as it reaches the extreme limit of its light beam calls for a literature which is at once vision and darkness. Something like the old metaphysics. At any rate, we see how reluctant Lanson was to let go of mythopeia and poetic invention, how eager he still was to consider *oratio* a continuation of *ratio;* yet he also knew *science* to be radically different from *imagination*, and better in a sense, although less fascinating. The prophetic mission entrusted to poetic invention (reminiscent as it is of Lucretius and Ronsard's hymns, not to mention Hugo's epics) was but a holding action, perhaps a nostalgia couched in the form of a prophecy, as so often is the case.

What Lanson did not, and could not see, filled as he was with admiration and envy for the progress of science, is that much of what passed for science, in his time (in any time) was in fact poor literature. This certainly is true of the social and psychological sciences of his time. Yet consider his views on psychology:

> Psychology is and will remain the proper and inalienable domain of the novelists and the poets. All is uncertain, all is possible in it. My apologies to the philosophers! I do not mean *their* psychology. This psychology, built by the likes of Descartes, Condillac, Taine, Ribot and others in our own country, this psychology is a science, for it deals only with generality, with general definitions and laws.[6]

It has become easy for us to see such a passage as the epistemological nonsense it really is. We may not have become much wiser, but we do know that no general discourse is more intimately interwoven with rhetoric than speculative psychology, and especially Descartes's book on the *Passions of the Soul*. It would be easy to show that Taine's and Ribot's psychological discourses were generated dialectically out of a fund of commonplaces: their writings are more abstract and more general versions of the psychology found in the novels, essays, and poems of their contemporaries. As the scientific credentials of such discourses have fallen to dust, we are enabled to grasp what socio-cultural interests they did serve. We can also perceive their specific

[6] *Ibid.*, p. 121.

function within the vast array of persuasive and cautionary discourses which were once thought to be scientific, philosophical, and objective. Much that has been uncovered by the various archeologies of knowledge and deconstructive strategies points to one conclusion: what then passed for science (especially among the softer disciplines) can now be ascribed to the ideology of power in the nineteenth century.

I suspect that Lanson came close to suspecting as much, although his religious respect for the scientific method kept him from lapsing into scepticism and antipositivism. He wanted to preserve an epistemological gulf between *ratio* and *oratio*, the statement of *general laws* and *special pleading*. I also sense that Lanson feared that the social sciences and the old rhetorical apparatus secretly were communicating vessels.

Another great foe of rhetoric suspected as much. This is what Benedetto Croce (an exact contemporary of Lanson) had to say in his *Esthetics* about the collusion of rhetoric and science:

> Some, while admitting the aesthetic non-existence of rhetorical categories, yet make a reservation as to their utility and the service they are supposed to render, especially in schools of literature. We confess that we fail to understand how error and confusion can educate the mind to logical distinctions, or aid the teaching of science (i.e., the science of literature) which they disturb and obscure. Perhaps what is meant is that such distinctions, as empirical classes, can aid memory and learning, as was admitted above for literary and artistic kinds. To this there is no objection. There is certainly another purpose for which the rhetorical categories should continue to appear in schools: to be criticized there. The errors of the past must not be forgotten and no more said, and truths cannot be kept alive save by making them combat errors. Unless an account of the rhetorical categories be given, accompanied by criticism of them, there is a risk of their springing up again, and it may be said that they are already springing up among certain philologists as the latest *psychological* discoveries.[7]

I am not sure that Croce was alluding here to the rhetorical orientation of Freudian psychoanalysis, which presented itself nonetheless as a science of the unconscious. But he certainly had something like it in mind. At any rate, the modern return to *metaphor* and *metonymy*, the linguistic model of the unconscious, has given rhetoric a new lease on life. Discredited as a pedagogy of logical distinctions, as Croce

---

[7] Benedetto Croce, *Aesthetic as Science of Expression and General Linguistic*, tr. D. Ainslie (1909; rpt. Boston: Nonpareil Books, 1978), p. 72.

rightly says, it has revenged itself by challenging the very basis and rationale for logical distinctions in the mind, and within our culture. It has become a weapon, in the hands of the Freudians (and the Nietzscheans, one might add) against the certainties of nineteenth-century scientific truths. It uncovers the networks of power at play in the cool assertions of positivism. And it has provided the neo-rhetoricians with a deconstructive power which a Lanson and a Croce could not have anticipated. As a result, at least in the sciences of man, the old positivist question of truth as adequation has receded before the analysis of semiotic systems, and their manipulation: *who* imposes *what* on *whom*. As the overarching claims of a unique *ratio* are fading, we become increasingly aware of the web of *oratio* with its conflicting strands and its unsettled dialectic. But this, presumably, is another form of wishful thinking.

Seeing and Believing in Dante and Beckett

NEAL OXENHANDLER

> ...all I want to do is sit on my ass and fart and read Dante[1]

The term "Modernism" refers to a vast congery of changes of aesthetic form and sensibility which can be localized in the last years of the nineteenth century and the first half of the twentieth, ending approximately with World War II and the beginning of what we now call "Postmodernism." Certain works serve as touchstones for Modernism — the *oeuvres* of Joyce, Mann, Proust; Picasso's painting; the music of Schoenberg and Stravinsky; and those highly idiosyncratic works which characterize micromodernist movements such as Surrealism.

Definitions of literary movements are at best approximations but they serve a useful heuristic function. They allow us to perform acts of grouping and classification which are essential to any historical understanding of literary change. They draw attention to various levels of continuity, various incidents of disjuncture.

Such classifications cannot in themselves produce judgments about literary change; they cannot specify the relation of Modernism to the past nor tell us what lies beyond Postmodernism and its apparent break with the tradition. Rather than attack such huge questions in the space of an article, I have brought together two writers, Dante and Beckett, within whose confluence these questions (and possible answers) are implicit. Since we are within Postmodernism it is too early to grasp it as a whole; however, the opposing tendencies listed in *Figure 1* suggest the axis of change through Modernism to the Postmodern:

---

[1] Walter Lowenfels, "Extracts from *My Many Lives: The Paris Years, 1926-1934*," *The Expatriate Review* (Winter/Spring 1972), p. 13

THE "OLD"	THE "NEW"
I. *Formal questions*	
Controlled form	Random form, Open form
Organicity, continuity	Disjunctiveness, juxtaposition
Composed	Improvised
Logical, causal, sequential connections	Absurdity, incoherence, irrelevance
II. *Genetic questions*	
Language as means	Language as end
Personal art	Impersonal, objective art
Rational composition	Delirium, trance
Fullness of language	Emptiness of language
The piano, the violin	The tape-recorder, the synthesizer
Poetry as the writer's soul	Poetry as the writer's situation
III. *Content and function questions*	
Art as meaningful Content	Art as trivial Preoccupation with formal arrangements
Art that makes The beautiful	Art that destroys The banal, the quotidien, the ugly, the horrible
Art as transcendence ("Anywhere out of this world," Baudelaire)	Pop and collage art, things of this world
Poetry of consciousness	*Chosisme*, poetry of things
Poetry of freedom	Poetry of anarchy, disorder
	From engaged art to nonart
Pure art (as in Mallarmé)	Isolation, dehumanization
Communality	The automat (man as thing, as
The person (man as spirit)	pawn, as victim, acted upon, atom in the mass)
IV. *Questions about the reader or audience*	
Emotional response (catharsis, pleasure, pity and fear, identification)	Distancing, alienation, theater of cruelty, assault
Aesthetic distance	Reader/audience participation, involvement
Submission to, acceptance of the work	Confrontation, challenging of the work

Figure 1

Viewing this historical shift as a function of the tendencies listed above it becomes clear that Postmodernism differs from Modernism primarily in the degree to which these impulses are pursued. In general the Postmodern represents an absolutizing of an impulse. which, in the works of the Modernists, had been curbed by a contrary impulse. Seen in this way it becomes clear that Modernism was far more conservative than we normally believe it to be. The energy which animated it was not something new but rather inherited from the late Middle Ages and the reformulation of the Aristotelian theory of Beauty by Thomas Aquinas. Like the *Commedia* of Dante, Modernist works are dominated by the goals of achieving Beauty and its correlative, Truth. These, by oftimes radical strategies, remain the goals of Modernism as they were also the goals of the long tradition of representationalism that stemmed from Aquinas. Modernism differs from this Classical aesthetic in its degree of experimentation and its stress against such principles as unity, coherence, balance, etc., which had always been understood to be necessary for the production of Beauty. In my view Modernism never wholly breaks with this Classical aesthetic. It is only after the great watershed of the *entre-deux-guerres* and the upheaval of World War II that the final disjunction occurs. The War represents the boundary which bars Modernism from the second half of the century. Existentialism, popularized after the War, stands as an impulse more ideological than aesthetic in character; and with the playing out of the attempt to revive humanist values on a new basis by Sartre and Camus the resulting aesthetic vacuum was filled by initiatives such as the French *nouveau roman* which rejected the signified in favor of the signifier and thus provided a body of proof texts for the Structuralist obsession with language with which it was in symbiosis.

Yet even in Postmodernism the link with the past is not wholly broken. Continuity remains essential to the Postmodern to the degree that it is an art of reaction, dependent on a system of reflexes conditioned by works of the tradition. This surely is clear in the Dante/Beckett relationship; we read Beckett ironically, against a background of expectations formed by knowledge of Dante and other writers of the Classical canon. If there were nothing more than this to the Dante/Beckett relationship (taken here as a paradigm for Postmodern continuity) then we could view Postmodernism as a form of radical rejection of the past. Yet there is more, very much more in Beckett's indebtedness to Dante. Before further exploration of this specific case of intertextual continuity, more needs to be said on several topics, notably the treatment of referentiality along the axis of evolution.

We can date the seeding of Modernism to the advent of Cartesianism.[2] Descartes's splitting of the subject/object relation into a dyad marks a break with the realist metaphysics of the Middle Ages. By positing the self prior to the world Descartes introduced more than a mere logical split. If self and world are not given simultaneously in a single act of thought, they will remain forever sundered. You cannot recuperate the world as an afterthought. This is the message of Edmund Husserl with his axiom that thought is always thought of some thing. Which is not to say that Husserl by his view of intentionality led us back to the fusional metaphysics of the Middle Ages. What he did rather was make it possible to view that metaphysics from a modern perspective and hence to appreciate anew the seamless vision of that period and of the Renaissance. Dante's *Commedia* is exemplary in this respect. There is no epistemological doubt in the *Commedia*. Poised on his vantage point between past and future, between history and eschatology, Dante sees all in one immense fusional gaze of which the various formalist and aesthetic unities of his work are the sign.

The issues I am discussing here converge in the notion of seeing, a recurrent *topos* in the *Commedia*. Dante's poem is powerfully visual: he travels through the here-after as spectator of the fate of others. In canto II of the *Inferno* he questions Vergil's incitement to go into the eternal world since he is neither Aeneas who visited hell nor Paul who was rapt in heaven. Once reassured by Vergil, Dante, though unworthy, is determined to report accurately the things seen. The issue of authority is important; he must over and over again guarantee the truth of his vision. This phatic guarantee of the truth of discourse about things seen is a hallmark of the medieval mentality and of that faith in the noumenal whose erosion begins with Descartes.

---

[2] Beckett's use of Descartes has been demonstrated by Kenner and other critics. Along with the splitting of mind from world comes a concomitant splitting of mind from body, amusingly conveyed by the image of the bicycle rider. Beckett's instrumentalist view of the referent influences not only his concept of history but also contributes to that weakening of the self-concept which is a familiar aspect of his work.

Beckett's *comment c'est*, published in 1961,[3] is the most Dantesque of all his works. Divided into three parts, it is written in short prose passages which typographically recall Dante's *terza rima*. Beckett's narrator too insists on the veracity of his vision:

> instants passés vieux songes qui reviennent ou frais comme ceux qui passent ou chose chose toujours et souvenirs je les dis comme je les entends les murmure dans la boue (p. 9)

> past moments old dreams back again or fresh like those that pass or things things always and memories I say them as I hear them murmur them in the mud (p. 7)

Dante insists on the veracity of his report on the visible but Beckett is turned inward. Though he uses the word "entendre" (which he translates as "to hear") it signifies its second meaning, "to understand," as much as its first; what he hears and murmurs back into the mud is the suspiration of memories and old dreams. Dante's seeing is turned outward toward the world. Thomism, the basis for Dante's epistemology, postulates a "visible species," i.e., a figment which locks the knowing subject to its object. Beckett's internal murmur signals an immanent process, only indirectly linked to the world of things. The difference between Dante's realism and Beckett's phenomenalism is in the index of faith in mundaneity, that faith which informs our perception of the world. Never strong in Beckett even in the early fiction this faith in the reliability of knowledge became progressively weaker as Beckett's style of thought evolved.

Most commentaries on Beckett focus inevitably on his language, his saying; but neither thematic nor formal analysis can take us back to that preverbal stratum of consciousness where language originates in a silent hearing. Recent scholarship has studied the parallels between Beckett and Geulincx or Mauthner, helping to situate him in a long tradition of nihilists and nominalists; yet the nonverbal hearing at issue here remains obscure because it is something other than language and cannot be probed except indirectly, through analogy and metaphor. As a literary process, affective as much as cognitive, it resists any frontal attack.

In respect to hearing a more fruitful parallel than that with Geulincx or Mauthner would be that with Proust. Over and over Proust for-

---

[3] Samuel Beckett, *comment c'est* (Minuit, 1961). Beckett's translation entitled *how it is* was published in 1964 by Grove Press. References are to these editions.

mulates the paradox of phenomenality: "When I saw an external object, my consciousness that I was seeing it would remain between me and it, enclosing it in a slender, incorporeal outline which prevented me from ever coming directly in contact with the material form..." Or again "We imagine always when we speak that it is our own ears, our own mind that are listening. My words would have come to her only in a distorted form, as though they had to pass through the moving curtain of a waterfall before they reached my friend, unrecognisable, giving a foolish sound, having no longer any kind of meaning."[4]

Beckett's scepticism about the referent and his constant inner focus on the nonverbal reverses our conventional view of Postmodernism. It is perhaps a historical accident that Poststructuralist criticism has provided our best analyses of contemporary writing. In any event, the tendency of that criticsm has been to give priority to language over any kind of psychic process. Concern with non-verbal psychism is usually dismissed as mysticism. Yet Beckett has made clear his order of priorities. He told an interviewer, "I conceived *Molloy* and what followed the day I became aware of my stupidity. Then I began to write the things I feel,"[5] This is surely not obscurantism on his part. Rather it is Beckett's recognition of what has been the originary concern of every major artist — emotion.

Beckett's evolution seems determined by a guiding principle, undoubtedly that "feeling" to which he refers; yet criticism has been singularly impotent to deal with this issue. The problem of course lies in our inability to go behind the verbal to that primordial psychic process where the work originates. We must use various indirect tactics to reach the nonverbal. In what follows I would like to do this through a comparison with Dante, a model present either explicitly or implicitly in everything Beckett has ever written.

Beckett's long involvement with Dante parallels that poet's similar involvement with Vergil, though Beckett never abandoned his mentor as Dante did at the gates of heaven; or perhaps will do should he ever reach that place.

The most explicit borrowings from Dante occur in Beckett's first published book, *More Pricks than Kicks* (1939),[6] itself a reworking of

---

[4] *Remembrance of Things Past*, tr. C.K. Scott Moncrief (New York: Random House, 1934).

[5] Quoted by Ruby Cohn, *Back to Beckett* (Princeton: Princeton University Press, 1973), p. 119.

[6] Samuel Beckett, *More Pricks than Kicks* (London: Calder and Boyars, 1970).

the long unpublished *Dream of Fair to Middling Women*. As in the poems, there are numerous borrowings of images and turns of phrase, drawn mostly from the *Inferno* where Dante's account of suffering and horror is used ironically by Beckett to underscore his vision of modern life.[7] This use of the great ancestor is in keeping with Modernist uses of the past, e.g., by Joyce and Eliot, both longtime frequenters of Dante.

This way of using Dantesque intertexts is metaphorical in that it quotes the intertexts as similar but different from the presentation of contemporary scenes. Belacqua Shuah, the hero of *More Pricks Than Kicks*, rushes frantically about the streets of Dublin yet remains depressed and and mentally slothful, like his Dantesque counterpart in canto IV of the *Purgatorio*. His similarity with Dante's Belacqua is given by his name more than any specific trait; the difference is a matter of several centuries and several hundred miles. Belacqua Shuah sees his world clearly enough, drawing it in a chiseled manner that recalls the early Joyce. The search for that hearing to the second power has scarcely begun. Over the years that followed and during the lengthy process of maturation the focus of the work changed even though the presence of Dante remained constant.

Dante's realism is in no sense mitigated by the use of fantasy nor by his writing in the allegorical mode. The contrary is true. Because it presents itself as work of literature rather than some kind of ersatz reality, the *Commedia* mediates a hierarchical view of reality guaranteed by its own internal coherence. It presents mimetically grounded characters whose reference to Being will not be put in doubt until the trumpet of the Last Judgment. Dante's poetic world is related to Being both as metaphor and metonymy: his characters are born out of experience, linked by their closeness within the experiential order; they are not only products of history but emblems of what is yet to come.

comment c'est introduces us into a realm similar to the *Inferno*. The narrator, Bom, drags himself through the mud, muttering his endless parody of prayer:

---

[7] The best analysis of Beckett's references to Dante is by John Fletcher, *Samuel Beckett's Art* (New York: Barnes and Noble, 1967), pp. 106-21. Fletcher shows the pervasiveness of the *Commedia* in inspiring both themes and language in Beckett's early writings.

cette voix quaqua puis en moi quand ça cesse de haleter troisième partie après Pim pas avant pas avec j'ai voyagé trouvé Pim perdu Pim c'est
fini je suis dans la troisième partie après Pim comment c'était comment
c'est je le dis comme je l'entends dans l'ordre plus ou moins des bribes
dans la boue ma vie la murmure à la boue (p. 30)

this voice once quaqua then in me when the panting stops part three
after Pim not before not with I have journeyed found Pim lost Pim
it is over I am in part three after Pim how it was how it is I say it as
I hear it natural order more or less bits and scraps in the mud my life
murmur it to the mud (p. 20)

Little differentiation here — the book's beginning is not much different
from its end. Far removed from the *Commedia* where every canto clues
us to Dante's location on his ascent, *comment c'est* recalls Proust's novel
where one hears the same voice and the same argument wherever
one picks it up. What one encounters here is an integrated and pur-
poseful attempt to reconstruct the nonverbal order of experience. This
attempt takes place in response to vague imperatives, remnants of
a formerly integrated psychism. These imperatives are (in order of
importance) emotional, logical, and aesthetic.

Indications of logical order are given by the spatial and temporal
coordinates: after a voyage, in the mud; before with and after Pim.
The emotional imperative, the ultimate motive of textual production,
is both positive (relation to the other) and negative (alienation from
own voice). The aesthetic order is given in the pacing of the work
against breath units; in the careful reduction of concreteness and
specificity; in the building of complex networks of echoes and associations.

Beckett's relation to Dante in the early works, I have said, is
metaphoric; in the later works, however, that relation changes. It
becomes instead chiasmic, involving a crossing of the original position. In making this crossing Beckett's status as a Postmodern also
changes, as I hope to illustrate.

In the following passage from *comment c'est* Beckett makes a complex use of Dante, one fundamentally different from any that had come
before. We see Bom, the narrator, kneeling bare-assed on a trash heap,
holding a banner between his teeth:

encore moi toujours et partout dans la lumière âge indéterminé vu de
dos à genoux les fesses en l'air au sommet d'un tas d'ordures vêtu d'un

sac au fond crevé pour le passage de la tête entre les dents la hampe horizontale d'un vaste vexille où je lis

en ta clémence de temps à autre qu'ils dorment les grands damnés ici des mots illisible dans les plis puis rêver peut-être du bon temps que leur valurent leurs errements pendant ce temps les démons se reposeront dix secondes quinze secondes (p. 56)

me again always everywhere in the light age unknown seen from behind on my knees arse bare on the summit of a muckheap clad in a sack bottom burst to let the head through holding in my mouth the horizontal staff of a vast banner on which I read

in thy clemency now and then let the great damned sleep here something illegible in the folds then dream perhaps of the good time their naughtiness procured them what time the demons may rest ten seconds fifteen seconds (p. 36)

A reference to Dante is signalled by the unusual word, *vexille*, used by Dante in *Inferno* XXXIV, where the appearance of Satan is announced by a slightly modified line from the Easter hymn "The royal banners forward go." Dante has changed the line to read "Vexilla regis prodeunt inferni" ("The banners of hell go forth").

Bom's call for compassion toward "the great damned" does not merely echo the treatment of compassion in the *Inferno*; rather it goes *against* Dante. We recall that, although Dante had swooned from pity in canto v upon hearing the story of Paolo and Francesca, by the end of the *Inferno*, when in canto XXXIII he hears the tragic tale of Ugolino, he weeps no tears, having by this time learned that compassion for the damned is inappropriate.

A thematic gainsaying of Dante by Beckett would not in itself be startling. The issue seems of more importance, however, if we introduce the referential notion into the chiasmic relation. I have suggested that Dante, writing allegory, is the realist; Beckett, in the early works, writes the kind of lyrical realism found in Joyce's *Portrait of the Artist*, a style based on perceptual experience. Yet from the very start, Beckett tended to irrealize the referent in his shift toward a kind of suspended phenomenalism or what I have also called an immanent style of writing.

For Dante seeing involves a contextualization of the image within a framework of belief. Seeing and believing reenforce each other in a constantly changing relationship that extends throughout the hierarchy of Being. Seeing and believing coincide in Dante's "new style," to which he gave new dignity through its use for matters formerly held too serious to be treated in vernacular verse forms. Beckett, heritor of a concept of the poet that begins with Dante, also portrays a pilgrim moving between heaven and earth:

> rêve viens d'un ciel d'une terre d'un sous-sol où je sois inconcevable aïe aucun son dans le cul un pal ardent ce jour-là nous ne priâmes pas plus avant... (p. 57)

> dream come of a sky an earth an under-earth where I am inconceivable aah no sound in the rectum a redhot spike that day we prayed no further... (p. 37)

The final line, equating as it does prayer and sodomy, is more than an ironic echo of Francesca's last words to Dante ("That day we read no further"); rather the line implies a third term, poetry: "All poetry, as discriminated from the various paradigms of prosody, is prayer."[8] The implication of a sacral function to poetry is doubtless ironic; yet it provides an index to the belief value of poetry for Beckett, one in fact that places it *within* the great tradition rather than without.

If Beckett's work, more than that of any great contemporary, is situated at the juncture point of the Modern and the Postmodern, we should not be surprised to find that none of the tendencies listed in *Figure 1* is pursued to the end. Despite the tendency to disjuncture and open form, Beckett remains a formalist. Despite the dilution of the self/world bond he has abolished neither object nor subject. Molecules of the one pass through a membrane to the other. His familiar intertexts appear in shifting relationships, as I have suggested in respect to the *Commedia*. Yet another intertext, conspicuous by its absence in *comment c'est*, comes to mind: "Blessed are those who have not seen and yet believe" (John 20: 26).

---

[8] The statement was attributed to Beckett by George McGreevy in the July-September 1934 issue of *Dublin Magazine*. The reference is given by Deirdre Bair, *Samuel Beckett: A Biography* (New York and London: Harcourt Brace Jovanovich, 1978), p. 181.

Grammatical Insincerity and Samuel Beckett's Non-Expressionism: Space, Subjectivity, and Time in *The Unnamable*

EDOUARD MOROT-SIR

Samuel Beckett is not a philosopher; he never pretended to be taken for one. Nor is he a writer who wraps up philosophical ideas in literary clothes, be they poetic, dramatic, or narrative. Allegory and symbols are not his way of referring either to himself or to somebody else. He is not an artist who likes to test himself with different instruments, i.e., with varied linguistic possibilities in the accepted genres, as most of the writers of the twentieth century have done. He is fundamentally a poet who looks for the unique and rare meeting where words become at the same time music, meaning, and reference. However, Beckett the poet has always been repressed, wounded, not only, as poets usually like to be, by life, but by language itself: thus, in his works, an obsessive and sarcastic scepticism an obstinate, desperate will not to be seduced by the poetic gift or by any other gift in the manipulation of language, an anguishing quest for an impossible *linguistic sincerity*. That tension, which dramatizes Beckett's texts, from the first poems to the last ones (and I call "poem" any Beckettian text — novels and plays being nothing less than indirect and frustrated poetry), I propose to qualify it as *non-expressionism*. It implies an ethics, a logic, and an aesthetic in reverse. It destroys ideologies at the level of social or class justification, and their deeper sources. When Beckett says in *The Unnamable* "Overcome, that goes without saying, the fatal leaning toward expressiveness," he denounces grammar and syntax as well as rhetoric — the logical as well as the literary devices that have dominated literatures for centuries.[1] To be sincere, efficient — and it

---

[1] Samuel Beckett, *The Unnamable* (New York: Grove Press, 1958), p. 144. Hereafter abbreviated as *Un*; all page numbers within parentheses refer to this publication unless otherwise indicated.

should be more than a pious wish or a dramatic presentation which denies itself by its very success — non-expressionism needs to become a permanent, trying fight against the traditional rhetoric ornaments, surely; but, more seriously, against the universal functions of linguistic referentiality, which are *description, naming*, especially pronominal naming, and *narration*. My enumeration follows the order suggested by Beckett at the beginning of *The Unnamable*: "Where now? Who now? When now?"[2]

Willy-nilly the poet finds himself at the heart of the most difficult questions of modern philosophy. What is more philosophical indeed than the problems of Space, of the Self, of Time? Descartes and Locke, Hume, Kant, Schopenhauer, and many others, made of these interrogations the very center of their epistemologies. However, in spite of numerous references to philosophers, Samuel Beckett never relied on any kind of philosophical language. He has looked and still is looking for a poetic, non-expressionist solution for such theoretical aporias. For instance, the conclusion of the search made by *Un* reaches a recognized culmination for non-expression that was to be succeeded by thirty years of poetic experiments. Are the first sentences of one of the recent "experiences," *Company*, not a direct echo of *Un*? "A voice comes to one in the dark. Imagine."[3] In their double, constative and performative, assertive and exclamative, way, these words give an answer to the triple enigma of *Un*. Beckettian non-expressionism was thus dominated by the problematic of writing quartered into directions that lead to fights for three *rhetorical rights*: the *right of describing*, which corresponds to the philosophical discussions on the existence and essence of Space; the *right of the subject* or, more specifically, the

---

[2] It should be noted that the French text which came before the English translation inverts the second and third questions: "Où maintenant? Quand maintenant? Qui maintenant?" This difference between the French and English versions opens the way to infinite commentaries. If the interpretation suggested in my analysis is correct, the change in order for second and third questions means that in the French order chosen first, Beckett respected the usual philosophical order of critical philosophy since David Hume and Kant, whose epistemologies go from Space to Time, from Time to Subjectivity. Working on his translation from the French to English it is possible that Beckett became more aware of the problems of writing proper, hidden behind the three philosophical questions. This could be the reason why the English text goes from description to nomination, and finally to narration, i.e., from the possibility of finding a place to the possibility of designating a person and, from there, to the possibilities of telling stories, or, in other words, to the justification of writing.

[3] Samuel Beckett, *Company* (London: Calder, 1980).

right of using first person pronouns (it is well known that the subject-object relation has become, since Descartes, the modern problem of consciousness and the unconscious); finally, the *right of discursing*, that is, the double right to produce arguments and to tell stories: philosphers have transposed them into the complementary topics of reason and memory. As it appears in *Un*, the defense of those rights — a sort of chart of the writer — leads to the awareness of paradoxical values that ultimately defies any kind of writing and its legitimacy. I propose to call them the *non-expressionist values of Beckett's aesthetic of reference*: language refers to, with nothing with which to refer, and nothing to which to refer. These negative values are as follows: 1. The *unplaceable*, questioning the right of building up spatial relations and of describing; 2. The *unpronominable*, which shakes the confidence in the power of nominating and predicating; 3. The *unrelatable*, which negates any ordering of Time.

In modern philosophies, the problems of Space and Time have been discussed within the antinomy of Realism and Idealism so that any attempt to expression implies the existence of a reality to be expressed. Expressionism is thus necessarily connected with realism. Should we say in reverse that non-expressionism belongs to the idealist perspective? Considering the quasi-obsessive references Beckett made to certain forms of idealism, such as those of Descartes, Malebranche, Geulincx, Berkeley, Schopenhauer, one is tempted to agree. However, Beckett rejects idealism as well as realism for a very simple reason: he does not rely on philosophical reasoning, whatever it may be. It would be inappropriate to speak of the Beckettian idealism of Space and Time, or of his empirical or transcendental idealism of the Self. In consequence, I suggest we speak of a Beckettian *non-realism* as different from idealism: to reject realism as basic structure for semantics and aesthetics is no reason to fall into the trap of idealism!

Critics have rarely analyzed the properties of the Beckettian space except indirectly and partially, from a narratological perspective. In this essay, I can but suggest a few aspects in Beckett's processes of *linguistic spatialization*. For him, the theory and praxis[4] of space are not only related to its perception, but to its language and even more, in a matter of specific humor, to a special literary gift: "I who am

---

[4] Needless to say, my use of the word "praxis" has no Marxist connotations. It simply belongs to the theory of the speech-acts.

so good at describing places, walls, ceilings, floors, they are my special-
ty, doors, windows, what haven't I imagined in the way of windows
in the course of my career... nothing but the four surfaces, the six
surfaces..." (157). A few pages later, in almost the same style he boasts:
"I who am so good at topography" (160). These gifts should be connected with another gift that Beckett claims more than once, the gift
for logical constructions: logical order, spatial order have the same
semiotic origin and belong to very similar functions in the poetic
recreation of reality. Geometry and logic go together, but how?

Beckettian Space is not Euclidian-Kantian. It is not the classical
tridimensional frame with the straight line and the right angle as basic
forms, even if at times a Beckettian hero describes his disjointed walk
as a rectilinear path through zigzags. It is not a Newtonian container
within which objects are put in order and find their necessary coordinates. It is a *curved-and-hodological space*. It has a tendency to circularity,
closeness, and closing. I borrow from Sartre's *Being and Nothingness*
the concept of "hodological," which designates, as its etymology indicates, a space made of ways, roads, tracks, ditches, canals, which
permits movements; it is a sort of spatial praxis, which has very little
in common with the Promethean-Marxist praxis. It is also the place
marked by impotence and failure. Its dynamics concerns, not pro-
gressive movements and accelerations, but repetitions, circularities,
constant gyrations, seesaw motion, oscillations, coming and going,
in brief, a turning and spiraling way that aspires to neutralizing linear,
irreversible, and proversive movements, and desperately longs for a
standstill. Here are a few typical quotations: "I had already advanced
a good ten paces, if one may call them paces, not in a straight line
I need hardly say, but in a sharp curve which, if I continued to follow
it, seemed likely to restore me to my point of departure or to one
adjacent. I must have got embroiled in a kind of inverted spiral, I
mean one the coils of which, instead of widening more and more,
grew narrower and narrower and finally, given the kind of space in
which I was supposed to evolve, would come to an end for lack of
room" (39). "When I penetrate into that house, if I ever do, it will
be to go on turning, faster and faster, more and more convulsive,
like a constipated dog... until by virtue of a supreme spasm I am
catapulted in the opposite direction and gradually leave backwards..."
(46).

This curved space is also *globular*. "The space in which I was ma-
rooned being globular..." (40; in French: "l'espace où l'on m'avait foutu

étant globulaire"). "I was under the impression I spent my life in spirals round the earth. Wrong, it's on the island I wind my endless ways... When I come to the coast I turn back inland. And my course is not helicoidal, I got that wrong too, but a succession of irregular loops, now sharp and short as in the waltz, now of a parabolic sweep that embraces entire boglands, now between the two, somewhere or other, and invariably unpredictable in direction..." (54).

Hodological, curved, globular, the "unnamable" space is also more emptiness than fullness. More exactly, it is a bored-into space, a space made of holes. Beckett plays on the polysemy of "hole," meaning emptiness as well as open pit and abode, with a true need for it. "A hole in the earth, inhabited by Worm alone" (100). Holes are connected with gaps: "Gaps, there have always been gaps" (114); in French: "Des trous, il y en a toujours eu." Furthermore, holes take on a special importance for the human body and its openings: "For if they could make a small hole for the eye, then bigger ones for the arms, they can make one bigger still for the transit of Worm, from darkness to light" (98). Thus, the hole, as ultimate spatial expression in its ambivalence, is at the same time passage, place to hide and rest, unplaceability and void. This triple semantic perspective corresponds with the general linguistic situation. Actually, the objective, external space mirrors the characteristics of the universe of the words, which is prison, cage, vase, w.c., skull, etc. In brief, at these different levels, in the middle of objects or in the middle of words, the need for a place is a disguise for the need of void, the need for being and meaning a disguise for the appeal to nothingness and non-expressiveness.

The experience of space-nothingness as a hole takes on another value which is present in the Beckettian opus from the beginning to the most recent: the concept of *space-partition*. "In this way they'll bring him to the wall" (144; in French: "ils l'améneront jusqu'à la cloison"), "and even to the precise point where they have made other holes through which to pass their arms and seize him" (97-98). And let us read again this well-known text: "perhaps that's what I am, the thing that divides the world in two, on the one side the outside, on the other the inside, that can be as thin as foil, I'm neither one side nor the other, I'm in the middle, I'm the partition, I've two surfaces and no thickness, perhaps that is what I feel, myself vibrating, I'm the tympanum, on the one hand the mind, on the other the world, I don't belong to either" (134). The hole leads to the spatial experience of rupture, separation; it is a place between places, a no-place between inside and outside.

Space is finally a permanent fatality of division, a topographical impossibility.

Does such a situation refer to the Cartesian distinction between mind and space, soul and body? Yes, in a way, if we understand it as a distinction between inside and outside spaces, as a tension of simultaneous interior and exterior lives. However, Beckett never remains at this level of the individual experience of the spatial partition between soul and body. His Manichean cosmic sensibility transposes the problem of space into the problem of *light*.[5] At the same time, in the same locus, our human reality is division and confusion of light and darkness. Pure division is felt as inaccessible limit. Confusion or "mess" is our lot. It possesses a double quality, physical and moral: grey and mess, as the categories of confusion show the same semantic connotation: "These lights gleaming low afar, then rearing up in a blaze and sweeping down upon me, blinding, to devour me..." (88). "But this question of light deserves to be treated in a section apart" (95). "... it's a nice grey, of the kind recommended as going with everything, urinous [in French: *pisseux*] and warm" (103). "... light is to close your eyes, that's where he must go, where it's never dark, but here it's never dark either, it's they who make this grey, with their lamps" (108). "... Enough now about holes. The grey means nothing, the grey silence is not necessarily a mere lull, to be got through somehow, it may be final, or it may not. But the lamps unattended will not burn on forever, on the contrary they will go out, little by little, without attendants to charge them anew, and go silent, in the end,. Then it will be black... Worm will never know, let the silence be black or let it be grey, it can never be known, as long as it lasts, whether it is final, or whether it is a mere lull" (109-10). "But this grey, this light, if he could escape from this light, which makes him [Worm] suffer, is it not obvious it would make him suffer more and more, in whatever direction he went, since he is at the center..." (111). "it's he [the Devil] who showed me everything, here, in the dark, and how to speak, and what to say, and a little nature, and a few names, and the outside of men" (166-67). Now let us quote from *Pour finir encore*, just to underscore the continuity of Beckett's *spatial aisthesis*: "Pour finir encore crâne seul dans le noir lieu clos... S'y lève enfin

---

[5] See my study "Samuel Beckett and Cartesian Emblems" in *Samuel Beckett: The Art of Thetoric*, ed. E. Morot-Sir, H. Harper, and D. McMillan III (Chapel Hill: North Carolina Studies in the Romance Languages and Literatures, 1976).

soudain ou peu à peu et magique s'y maintient un jour de plomb. Toujours un peu moins noir jusqu'au gris final... sable gris à perte de vue sous un ciel même gris sans nuages."[6] "Poussière grise à perte de vue sous un ciel gris sans nuages et là soudain ou peu à peu où poussière seule possible cette blancheur à déchiffrer" (*ibid.*, p. 13). Space thus is dispersed into a grey dust which recalls the "subtle matter" of Cartesian physics. Only a voice remains in the dark: no object, no body is possible. And this is nothing less than eddying words. Beckett leads us from the visual to the verbal space, and the reverse, so that he checks any poetic attempt to a metaphorical sublimation à la Dante, from the physical hell to the spiritual and mystical heaven. Such is the way he pursues his methodical dissociation of the language of spatial references. His object-non-realism becomes subject-non-realism. By this expression I mean that the disintegration of space into linguistic grey and moral mess gives birth to the awareness of the impossibility of a subject, of an I, be it empirical, transcendental, or metaphysical, as the responsible source and warrant of writing. To complete its auto-destruction physics is converted into psycholinguistics: the unplaceable refers the writer to the right of nomination and grammatical subjectivity.

Such is the raison d'être of the passage from the first to the second interrogation-exclamation "Who now?" suggesting a sort of fall from "where" to "who." The problem of the subject is not lived and presented by Beckett in a philosophical way, as it is with Descartes, Hume, or Kant. Like space, where the problem of its essence and existence is identified with the possibility or, more exactly, the impossibility of description, Beckett does not try to find a theoretical answer to the question: What is the human self ? He faces the problem that the writer has to solve: How can I create persons, characters, and, finally, how can I use the pronominal deictics of the first and second persons? In traditional literary criticism, this is known as the problem of characterization, i.e., the right, for the author and his/her creations, to say "I" and "you." In *Un* Beckett, testing the spatial language, is also testing the psychological language, insofar as it has to be centered around persons. This is why *Un* appears to be an *extreme attempt to create human beings with words*, and it is the definite recognition of the failure of doing so. In the first passages of the book, the author discards

[6] Samuel Beckett, *Pour finir encore* (Minuit, 1976), pp. 9-10.

his former creations: "To tell the truth I believe they are all here, at least from Murphy on, I believe we are all here, but so far I have seen only Malone" (6). And a few pages later: "All these Murphys, Molloys and Malones do not fool me. They have made me waste my time, suffer for nothing, speak of them when, in order to stop speaking, I should have spoken of me and of me alone" (21). Earlier Beckett had already declared: "Method or no method, I shall have to banish them in the end, the beings, things, shapes, sounds and lights with which my haste to speak has encumbered this place" (15). Such is the difference between *Un* and the preceding novels which accepted the principle of characterization, i.e., the right to choose surrogates, spokesmen. With *Un* the effort in creating the "pseudo-couple" Mahood-Worm is directly conscious of the relation between the two characters and the scriptor.

There, we witness a methodical destruction of subjectivity. One after the other the traditional techniques called for in the constitution of selves, with the help of proper names and pronouns, fail. First, the *incorporation* of the self in the case of Mahood. It is clear that the name Mahood suggests that Beckett tried to create a person with a human nature (the essence of manhood). Mahood is unable to achieve this project. The author is condemned to produce a monster, an incomplete space in body form: the subject cannot get its *corps propre* ('body proper'), as phenomenologists would say, i.e., its personal incorporation. Physical deformations which are present from the beginning of Beckett's writings reach their final state in *Un*. Mahood is reduced to a trunk without limbs, an eye which does not see, and a mouth full of words which do not belong to it. The body is just "the old vase in which I shall have accomplished my vicissitudes" (58). Mahood has to be eliminated, not because he is a monster, but because he cannot give to the author-narrator a *subjective substance*. "I left it yesterday, Mahood's world, the street, the chophouse, the slaughter, the statue, and, through the railings, the sky like a slate-pencil... The stories of Mahood are ended. He has realized they could not be about me, he has given up" (80). Thus, there is no chance for a subject incarnating human nature, physically and mentally. There remains only one unique possibility: to go beyond species, biological or cultural.

Then, the scriptor, who still reserves the right to say "I" (in *Company* this right will be questioned), almost completely gives up the structures, however distorted and shaky they may be, of visual space. He concentrates on *audio-space*, this form being reduced to a non-localizable

place where sounds from an unknown origin are perceived. The only reality is made of *voices*. "The fact is all this business about voices
requires to be revised, corrected and then abandoned. Hearing nothing
I am none the less a prey to communications. And I speak of voices!
After all, why not, so long as one knows it's untrue" (67). Everything
becomes "a question of voices" (81). Such is the appearance of Worm.
"Now I seem to hear them say it is Worm's voice beginning, I pass
on the news, for what it is worth" (81). And this definitive remark:
"Worm, be Worm, you'll see, it's impossible... But it is solely a question of voices, no other image is appropriate" (83). From here we are
obsessively led to the opening sentence of *Company*; "A voice comes
to one in the dark."

Voices are words, words are voices; space reaches its limits of *desincarnation, décorporation*, and referential doubt. It is no longer a world
of things, but a world of words. More precisely, the world of things
was already made of words, but ignored it. Within words, the scriptor (will he deserve the name of author?) finds the same characteristics
as those of visual space: dominance of curves, and closeness, constant presence of holes, movement toward emptiness, seesaw between
light and darkness, a permanent confusion and semantic mess against
which he wages a losing fight. At least, it should be his duty, his fatality.
One understands now why the principle of characterization reveals
itself as impractical and artificial, source of psychological or sociological
illusion. Subjectivity and its interior, classic or romantic universe are
dissolved into a mist of words and meanings.

Below is a collage of quotations from *Un* that will illustrate the *fatal
referential transfer from space to language*, from things to meanings: Spatial
desincarnation is completed by the awareness that, if things are words,
the reverse is not true. The linguistic universe subtends spatial structures
and weakens them; then, the need for a place among things is changed
into the place of a meaning among meanings; and that is the need
of being a subject: Beckett explores Benveniste's principle of linguistic
subjectivity, and finally destroys it:

"I'll say what I am... I'll fix their jargon for them... First I'll say
what I'm not, that's how they taught me to proceed, then what I am"
(53). "... Two holes and me in the middle, slightly choked. Or a single
one, entrance and exist, where the words swarm and jostle like ants,
hasty, indifferent, bringing nothing, taking nothing away, too light
to leave a mark" (94). "... I'm in words, made of words, others' words,
what others, the place too, the air, the walls, the ceiling, all words,

the whole world is here with me, I'm the air, the walls, the walled-in one, everything yields, opens, ebbs, flows, like flakes, I'm all these flakes... I'm all these words, all these strangers, this dust of words" (139). "... like a caged beast born of caged beasts..." (139).

The relation between subject and words cannot be settled by the characters and their proper names. Mahood is no help in assuring subjectivity and through it, referentiality. Worm also is a proper name without possible qualifications; he is deeper than the Unconscious, Freudian, or Jungian! He is an un-name naming unnamability and silence. Then, in a parallel ordeal, Beckett tries the pronominal power, i.e., the personal deictics as a possible solution for the temporal "now" and the spatial "here." In *Un* the pronominal problematic is brought back to the basic tension between *I* and *they*, the right to say *I* as opposed to *they*, the singular first person against the plural and collective third person. In the modern philosophical tradition, the Cartesian cogito, followed by the Kantian transcendental Ego, maintained order between the *they*, putting them around the *I* who was like the Sun at the center of the Copernican system. But that idealistic solution, which very early obsessed the poet of "Whoroscope," is mystifying: Is it not the greatest lesson of modern sociology? Collective consciousness, i.e., the *they*, teaches me how, where, and when to say *I*. My own language could be the product of a mystified *I* and of mystifying *they*. The human linguistic condition is a sort of Manichean semantic mess, with the absolute impossibility of separating meanings from each others. *Un* ends with this agnostic recognition: I do not know where I am, but I will continue to say *I* and to place myself in front of all the *they*. Such is the *pronominal tragedy* of language, as the final expression of semantic dispersion and confusion. Doubt about the placeable reveals itself as doubt about the pronominal, which is the ultimate decision for nomination and the last hope for an assured reference — *my* reference to *myself*. The well-known last statement of *Un*, "I can't go on, I'll go on" is more than the linguistic fatality of having to go on within language and its codes; it is *the fatality of saying I without knowing what it means*. At certain moments, the scripter of *Un* wonders if the right pronoun would not be the impersonal deictic *that* (in French: *ça*) or *one* (in French: *on*). Without explaining why, Beckett does not explore this possibility. Maybe the answer should be sought thirty years later in the admirable poem entitled *Company*. Here the pronominal tragedy is relived, and the answer is — as the text proves by its almost total absence of *I* — a strict limitation of the discourse to the pronouns of second and third persons. "For the first personal and a fortiori plural pronoun had never any place in your vocabulary" (*Company*, pp. 86-87). The following text is a direct consequence of *Un* and its "ephectic" aporia (see *Un*, 4): "Since he cannot think he will give up trying. Is there anything to add to this esquisse? H is *Unnamability*. Even M must go. So W reminds himself of his creature as so far created. W? But W too is creature. Figment" (*Company*, p. 63; my emphasis).

Let us complete this analysis with a collage of *Un*'s comments on pronouns:

> But enough of this cursed first person [in French: "Cette putain de première personne"], it is really too red a herring, I'll get out of my depth if I am not careful. But, what then is the subject? Mahood? No, not yet. Worm? Even less. Bah, any old pronoun will do, provided one sees through it... [77]. I shall not say I again, ever again, it's too farcical. I shall put in its place, whenever I hear it, the third person, if I think of it... [94]. In the meantime no sense in bickering about pronouns and other parts of blather. The subject doesn't matter, there is none. Worm being in the singular, as it turned out, they are in the plural, to avoid confusion, confusion is better avoided, pending the great confounding... [102; notice the Manichean implications]. [Words] say they, speaking of them, to make me think it is I who am speaking. Or I say they, speaking of God knows what, to make me think it is not I who am speaking... [115]. He wants me to be he... then he says I, as if I were he, or in another, let us be just... [163]. He feels me in him, then he says I, as if I were he, or in another, let us be just, then he says Murphy, or Molloy, I forget, as if I were Malone... [163]. It's the fault of the pronouns, there is no name for me, no pronoun for me, all the trouble comes from that, that, it's a kind of pronoun too, it isn't that either, I'm not that either... [164].

Space is inconsistent. Subject, whatever the pronoun, is illusory: geometry and grammar founder. All that remains for the prisoner-scriptor is one last way-out, one last interrogation: *Where now?* It concerns obviously the problem of Time, but not of the reality of Time. Time is only approachable through its *linguistic expression*, i.e., through narration. The need of story, Beckett recognizes it, is as strong as the need of description. But what can be done when space is dissolved and the subject unreferrable—two sorts of unnamability? Time itself is a superposition of discrete events, a heap which puzzled the Greek

Sophists. In a very significant way, and following the Manichean denunciation of reality as confusion, Beckett rejects the clear-cut duality between time and eternity: the "now" of the three inaugurating questions is at the same time temporal and eternal; it is today surely, but also yesterday and tomorrow. Especially *I* does not refer to *hic et nunc*; another place, another time is always possible. Furthermore, because of the double impossibility of location and subjective enunciation, the third and ultimate impotence of language is experienced: the *unrelatable*. Far from announcing the era of the "new novel," Beckett, in his typical subdued manner, prophetizes the decline of the Narrative. It is evident that the relatable implies the assertive proposition, be it part of a description, of a story, or of a dialogue. However, to stop telling is not enough. Not enough either, to counterbalance patiently affirmations and negations, because that sort of balance dreamed of by the Sceptics does not break the syntactic structure of the proposition, and it continues to obey the principle of what logicians call "Truth-language."

That is why, in the first paragraph of *Un*, Beckett reviews the technique of Greek Scepticism: "How to proceed? By aporia pure and simple? Or by affirmations and negations invalidated as uttered, or sooner or later" (3)? Then he confesses the real difficulty: "I say aporia without knowing what it means" (4). He pursues: "Can one be ephectic otherwise than unawares" (4)? After the interrogation left without an answer, he mentions the play with the "yesses and noes" (4), and the paragraph ends in a state of pure confusion, simply overcome by the obligation to speak: "I shall never be silent. Never."

The question concerning the ephectics — those Sceptics who exercise by suspending their judgment — is central, and it gets a rhetorical, even grammatical, answer in the production of the text. Beckett finds out a technique of suspending one's judgment thanks to the *constant transfer of narrative assertion to the hypothesis or question-status*. That is why, from the first lines ("Unquestioning. I, say I. Unbelieving. Questions. Hypotheses, call them that") to the end of *Un*, the yesses and noes, counteracting their respective effects, *lose* their assertive power as well as their referential movement toward Truth or Reality, and they promote a paradoxical reference, which gives to *Un* its intense and tragic presence. The following quotes express this stylistic transference: "So they build up hypotheses that collapse on top of one another, it's human, a lobster couldn't do it" (119). "Suppositions all equally vain, it's enough to enounce them to regret having spoken, familiar tourment" (123). "Assume notably henceforward that the thing said and the thing heard have a common source, resisting for this purpose the temptation to call in question the possibility of assuming anything whatever" (144). "Am I to suppose that I am inhabited, I can't suppose anything, I have to go on..." (162). "that's all hypotheses... it's a question of going on, it goes on, hypotheses are like everything else, they help you on, as if there were need of help..." (165). The same phrase "that's all hypotheses" is repeated (167) and is connected with the act of naming: "I call that evening." Those remarks precede the extraordinary burlesque parody of a love story. Further on reappears "that's all hypotheses" (174). Beckett then adds: "Lies, these gleams too, they were to save me, they were to devour me, that came to nothing..."

We finally understand that the problems of space, subject, and time are one and the same, as simultaneous problems of description, subjectivation, and narration. They lead to the conversion and redirection of language into hypothetical zigzags. Because of their hypothetical nature, space, subject, and history cannot help the novelist in organizing his/her imaginary world and discourse. In consequence, the unnamable refers us to three basic limits: the unplaceable, the unpersonalizable, the unnarratable. Beckett tells us: Continue to use words at your own pleasure and fantasy, but do not pretend to build up with them harmonious worlds and histories for subjects and objects knowing what they are, where they stay, and when they come and go.

This is the secret meaning of the Beckettian phrase: "Imagination dead. Imagine." *Company* gives the conclusion, when *I* is replaced by a *one* who becomes a *you*. Such a narrative destruction begins with the following motif which plays the role of a musical and intellectual theme: "A voice comes to one in the dark, Imagine." And on page 75 the poet speaks of "the place to which imagination perhaps inadvisedly had consigned him." The last lines of *Company*, alloying pure poetry with pure criticism, are still answering the questions — the W-questions — of the *Unnamable*: "But with face upturned for good labour in vain at your fable. Till finally you hear how words are coming to an end. With every inane word a little nearer to the last. And how the fable too. The fable of one with you in the dark. The fable of one fabling of one with you in the dark. And how better in the end labour lost and silence. And you as you always were. Alone."

As a philosopher-reader and with the help of the Kantian theory of imagination, I propose to interpret Beckett's "fables" as *hypotheses of Imagination*, when Imagination realizes that it cannot achieve the idealist dream of reconstructing the world and the self in the same verbal effort, or it cannot apply to writing the vain principle of imitation which governs any sort of aesthetic realism. There is no literary virtue such as idealist or realist sincerity, or at least, these virtues belonged to a period of dogmatic narrative when the novelists ignored the dubious status of their ontological presuppositions. Now we should know that Space, Subjectivity, and Time are products of our linguistic imagination. They are but verbal hypotheses. As such, i.e., when they become aware of being imaginary forms, they can but undo themselves to escape from the ontological illusions occasioned by the natural, noncritical praxis of language. Beckett's works mark the successive phases of an infinite struggle within writing, not for Truth or Reality, but for its own and pure survival. Novels, plays, or poems stand between poetry and criticism:[7] deeply sceptic of their means and ends, they play a cat-and-mouse game between spontaneity and reflection, between poetry and philosophy. Fundamentally, Beckett is a poet, and who else could be the sincere writer? He would like to "express" and to "refer," but in a nonexpressive, nonreferential way, rediscovering the pictorial and musical powers of words as meanings. He uses philosophical techniques for literary purposes, beyond the fallacious pretense of finding truth or creating reality. He borrowed from philosophy its most radical problematics, but rejected any attempt to systematizing discourses. It would be absurd to look for a Beckettian theory of Space, Time, or Consciousness. For the poet

---

[7] In her recent study *Abysmal Games in the Novels of Samuel Beckett* (Chapel Hill: North Carolina Studies in the Romance Languages and Literatures, 1982), Angela Moorjani describes with lucidity and precision the "Beckettian assault on narrative procedures," which she interprets correctly as the "movement from direct to indirect quotation,... then from quotation to narration,... and from narration to glosses on narration... This movement also entails a progression from the mimetic to the abstract" (p. 15). I propose to call such a linguistic adventure "discours direct libre" as the intimate fusion of poetic and critical expressions, perception and reflection reunited by the liberated-liberating act of reference. Let us note also that the Beckettian tension between sense and reference offers a concrete solution to the famous Surrealist utopia looking for the point where the Conscious and the Unconscious, perception and imagination form a unique faculty of the mind, manifesting itself in a sort of sur-automatic writing, i.e., a spontaneous-reflective act of poetic creation.

those three words polarize linguistic extensions and restrictions. The Beckettian corpus tells us the humorous Odysseus of successive essays — failures to go more and more beyond the spatial-temporal-subjective order which gave to Western texts their grammatical and rational organizations. Beckett's exercises in impotence witness the will of reaching a stage which is not the "ineffable," the obscure night and luminous silence of the mystics, but pure poetry, when reference makes sense, originary rhythm, language returning to its "fundamental sounds," grammar and semantics subjected to the pitiless sincerity of philology.

Such is the linguistic lesson of *The Unnamable*, when and where the writer explores the virtualities of language for our century: the writer can no more assume the rights revendicated by the romanesque dream, even when that dream becomes an exercise in deconstructing its structures. Anti-novels, new novels, continue to rely on the objectivity of Space, the subjectivity of characters, and the causality of Time. Thus the Beckettian triple interrogation has no answer. The awareness of it is the proper life of *Un*, a text without beginning and end, starting and closing again and again, the only valid introduction, not to the "general grammar" thanks to which Port-Royalists and Encyclopedists hoped to justify our modernity, that is to say, our will to linguistic power and intoxication, but to the primitive energy of language. Nothing is more real than nothing: this metaphysical principle that Beckett liked to quote in *Murphy*, hides an aesthetic credo: the act of poetic faith in language is the only condition for feeling oneself real; the rest is vain literature and artificial paradise!

Let us give the last word to the linguist and ask him/her what to say about the Beckettian exercise in non-expressionism. In *Unspeakable Sentences*, at the end of a chapter entitled "Subjectivity and Sentences of Direct and Indirect Speech," Ann Banfield convincingly states: "Direct speech is at once expression and communication. On the other hand, thought, reported in the subordinate S of indirect speech, is always reduced to its content; it is not only not communication, it is also nonexpressive."[8] Linguists look for the characteristics of natural-normal language, especially when they follow the Chomskian belief in "universal grammar." To them *Un* may appear as a puzzling

[8] Ann Banfield, *Unspeakable Sentences: Narration and Representation in the Language of Fiction* (Boston: Routledge and Kegan Paul, 1982), p. 63.

challenge. Here is the most direct speech one can imagine whose objectives are the destruction of communicative and expressive codes. Actually Beckett does not obfuscate communication or annihilate expressive powers; nor does he fall into the sophistic trap of communicating noncommunication, nor of being so expressive that he demystifies expressive powers. He simply uses direct speech as if it were — not indirect speech, but what German criticism calls *Erlebte rede* and the French grammarians *discours indirect libre*. At the level of *Un*, Beckett's writing becomes "discours *direct* libre," i.e., language destructing bound variables and reducing grammatical deictics to anaphoric relations. Pronouns, as bound variables, are referred to an unnamable pronoun-source of all texts; spatial and temporal deictics (here and now) are subordinated to a "then" as the weakest possible liaison between linguistic systems and processes, so that ultimately the pitiless disorganization of the deictic codes produces an extraordinary effect of intense and conscious referentiality: in the linguistic field, nothing is more real and sincere than the unnamable in its own discourse, nothing is more communicative and expressive than the direct refusal to express and communicate; that is poetry for itself.

Existential Humanism and Literary Modes

EDITH KERN

The questions raised in Sartre's *L'Existentialisme est un Humanisme* and Heidegger's *Brief über den Humanismus* (*Letter on Humanism*) concerning Humanism, the answers given by both authors, and the manner in which their answers affected and determined literary forms and modes are perhaps even more challenging today than they were in the forties and fifties; it seems appropriate, therefore, to examine them once again with regard to their bearing on modern concerns.

Heidegger's *Letter on Humanism*[1] is an engrossing document, not only because it represents the philosopher's thought in a nutshell, but also because it takes issue with Sartre's *L'Existentialisme est un Humanisme*[2] and, thereby, continues an international dialogue the French philosopher had initiated with his frequent references to Heideggerian thought. By his response, Heidegger revived as it were the kind of international debate that had been possible in the Republic of Letters when its language had been Latin and scholars could disregard all national borders. The *Letter* achieved this effect, however, in an indirect way, for it was not addressed to Sartre himself but rather to Jean Beaufret who had asked Heidegger: "Comment redonner un sens au mot Humanisme?" (HH, 7). Nor am I aware of any evidence that Sartre entered into direct correspondence with Heidegger, correcting

---

[1] Martin Heidegger, *Über den Humanismus* (Frankfort A.M.: Klostermann, 1946); henceforth referred to as HH followed by page number(s).
[2] Jean-Paul Sartre, *L'Existentialisme est un Humanisme* (1946; rpt. Nagel, 1964); henceforth referred to as SH followed by page number(s).

240

what he might have considered a misinterpretation of his essay or accepting the criticism leveled against him. Yet Sartre's work—in terms of philosophy, literary criticism, and the existential forms into which he poured his fiction (or which he found appropriate for it)—continued to reflect an ongoing debate concerning our conception of man and *Humanitas* that is as intriguing as it is challenging.

What then is Heidegger's conception of Humanism as presented in his *Letter* to Jean Beaufret? It seems at times profound and at others hopelessly confusing. Though it always holds our attention, it is also mystical and mystifying. Without evoking religion per se, it seems to echo Pascalian sentiments as it envisions man as "thrown," thrust by Being into a universe without the loving protection and concern of a personal god. On reading Heidegger's insistence that man alone in the universe is entrusted with the witnessing of Being and that the care of language—like himself a part of Being—has been assigned to him by It, one is reminded of Chomsky's controversial conclusions concerning a "universal grammar" and our "innate equipment" for understanding it. Heidegger's conception of the individual, moreover, as being both unique and impersonal, subjective and objective in his relationship to the Truth of Being, evokes Mallarmé's letter to a friend, proclaiming his transcendence of any romantic subjectivity: "C'est t'apprendre que je suis maintenant impersonnel, et non plus Stéphane, que tu as connu, mais une aptitude qu'a l'univers spirituel à se voir et à se développer à travers ce que fut moi."[3] To understand Heidegger's method of asking questions and answering them, one should follow, I believe, the advice he himself gave in an essay entitled *Was ist das—die Philosophie?*[4] (*What Is That—Philosophy?*). He suggests there that we must not talk and ask *about* Philosophy; that we have to enter into it, dwell within it, and truly "philosophize" by moving within its realm. In this manner, he maintains, we are doing more than clearly envisioning a goal. We might even seem irrational, but, then, philosophy is not exclusively rational. It is in this spirit that his *Letter on Humanism* must be read and his conception of man's *Humanitas* may be understood.

Historically, Heidegger recapitulates, the terms *Humanism* and *Humanitas* offer no problem, since they are derivations from Latin *homo*.

[3] Cited in Edith Kern, *Sartre: A Collection of Critical Essays* (Englewood Cliffs, N.J.: Prentice-Hall, 1962), p. 6.
[4] Martin Heidegger, *Was ist das—die Philosophie?* (Pfullingen: Neske, 1956).

It was at the time of the Roman Republic that the Romans first spoke of *Humanitas* as the distinguishing mark of the *homo humanus*, the heir of Greek culture, erudition, and art, and the representative of Roman virtue. The *homo humanus* was contrasted with the *homo barbarus*, the non-Roman lacking such virtues. It was in this Roman sense that the word *Humanitas* was revived by the Italian Renaissance, in the fourteenth and fifteenth centuries, although *homo barbarus* now came to designate Gothic man, including medieval scholars and knights. Understood in this sense, *Humanitas* was again identified with the culture of the Ancients, now including that of Rome — a notion defied by the "Moderns" of the seventeenth century but revived with new vigor in the eighteenth century (HH, 10 ff.).

Since the meaning assigned to *Humanitas* is determined by the values assigned to human existence, Humanism does not always represent a return to the Ancients, however. To the Christian, to whom existence on earth is transitory, being human means to be concerned with the *salus aeterna*, the salvation of one's soul. To Marx, on the other hand, "natural man" is, above all, social man, a being whose essence evolves through his intercourse with others and who is defined by his work and his relationship to it. To Marx, it is the nature of man to be preoccupied with providing food and shelter, though Heidegger makes it quite clear that he considers Marx's historical materialism by no means materialistic. Sartre sees man's *Humanitas* in his responsibility for "making" his essence and, thereby, that of mankind, of which he is a part. While neither the Humanism of Marx and Sartre nor that of Heidegger is predicated on a revival of ancient culture per se, the work of each of these authors reflects an intimate knowledge and appreciation of the Ancients and in no way rejects the study of their lives and their literatures and philosophy. Heideggerian thought, in particular, returns to that of the pre-Socratics. Yet Sartre's Humanism stresses above all man's projecting himself into the future, and, while Marx's communism resembles that of the early Christians, it also envisions a future utopia. Heidegger, however, attempts to give a meaning to Humanism that — though embracing that of the Ancients — intends and presumes to be both older and newer because he believes it to be essential to mankind, even to prehistoric mankind.

If he criticizes Roman, Christian, and Sartrean Humanism alike, this is because they share a misconception of man proper to metaphysics, namely, that he is an *animal rationale* (HH, 12 ff.). Not only does Heidegger object to the duality evoked by this term, but also to man's comparison with an animal. To him, man is different from object, plant, or animal. Man is simply *Dasein* — a term that has suffered so much abuse that it must be dwelled on here by way of explanation.

The word *Dasein* originated, Heidegger informs us, in the eighteenth century, when German metaphysicians coined it to designate all *Gegenstände* (this word is a literal translation of "objects") in their reality, as opposed to their essence (HH, 15 ff.). When Heidegger maintains in his monumental work *Sein und Zeit* (*Being and Time*) that "the essence of *Dasein* lies in its existence," we may be struck by his odd phrasing, but he does not seem to us to contradict the eighteenth-century meaning of the word *Dasein*. But as his thinking progressed and with it his concern to express the unity of man with Being (as opposed to the duality suggested by *animal rationale* and *existentia* versus *essentia*), he came to alter the statement of *Being and Time* by replacing the word *existence* with *ec-sistence*. In this sense *Dasein* is clearly applicable only to man. For only man can ec-sist, that is, stand out, transcend himself. One might say that, in the sense in which "de-struction" is used by the German philosopher, he "de-structed" the eighteenth-century meaning of the word that had become a mere cliché, by dividing it into its grammatical components: *Da* (which might be translated as "here and now") and *Sein* (Being with a capital *B*). In this de-structured form, *Dasein* came to represent to Heidegger *only* the existence of man. The philosopher saw man as the "here and now" of Being, as that through which Being is localized and temporalized. For man's intelligence alone can shed light on *that which is*, and shedding light means to ec-sist, to be transcendent. Heidegger has also spoken of man as the "da" of Being, as the clearing wherein *that which is* comes to light and is differentiated. It is obvious, however, that to the German philosopher such transcendence has no religious significance and is neither a designation of any hereafter nor of anything supernatural. It is used, on the contrary, to indicate man's existence as Being-in-the-world.

Heidegger predicates man's transcendence, his ability to project himself outside himself without separating himself from Being, on his essential quality of caring. Indeed, by means of an ancient fable he tells, he suggests man's identification with "Care." In his *Letter on Humanism* he simply refers his correspondent Jean Beaufret to the passages in *Being and Time* that elaborate this notion, and it would be too cumbersome to reproduce his arguments here (HH, 19). But it is, I believe, indispensable to quote the fable of "Care" that he cites in Latin in *Being and Time*, although I shall do so using the English translation of John Macquarrie and Edward Robinson:

> Once when "Care" was crossing the river, she saw some clay; she thoughtfully took up a piece and began to shape it. While she was meditating on what she had made, Jupiter came by. "Care" asked him to give it spirit, and this he gladly granted. But when she wanted her name bestowed upon it, he forbade this, and demanded that it be given his name instead. While "Care" and Jupiter were disputing, Earth arose and desired that her own name be conferred on the creature, since she had furnished it with part of her body. They asked Saturn to be their arbiter, and he made the following decision, which seemed a just one: "Since you, Jupiter, have given its spirit, you shall receive that spirit at its death; and since you, Earth, have given its body, you shall receive its body. But since "Care" first shaped this creature, she shall possess it as long as it lives. And because there is now a dispute among you as to its name, let it be called *homo*, for it was made of *humus* (earth).[5]

Heidegger found embedded in this ancient fable *Dasein*'s interpretation of itself. As told by Higynus, the fable had been made known in German by Herder and was encountered by Goethe whom it so inspired that he made Faust's dramatic meeting with "Care" the crowning experience of his quest for the meaning of his existence. Only after being blinded by "Care," does Faust fully grasp what it means to be human.

In Sartre's novel *La Nausée*, nausea was to assume a similarly prodding role as that which Heidegger had assigned to "Care." Both nausea and "Care" represent forces that are part of man's ability to project and transcend himself and that lead him to "de-struct" as it were the surface grime of a world we know too intimately to be able to see it. What Roquentin in *La Nausée* sets out to do is precisely to *see*.[6] (It was only later that Sartre came to associate with man's ability to project himself also the anguish that is a result of his moral responsibility toward himself and others.) As Heidegger assures us, such "de-struction" is not negative (HH, 33). It rather enables man to *witness all that is*. It enabled Sartre's Roquentin to discern what he recognized as the existence of the *salauda*. Heideggerian man must be as close

[5] Martin Heidegger, *Being and Time*, tr. John Macquarrie and Edward Robinson (London: SCM Press, 1962), p. 242.
[6] Jean-Paul Sartre, *La Nausée* (Gallimard, 1938), p. 10.

as possible to Being and overcome the alienation imposed upon him by a technological age (the philosopher recognizes here his indebtedness to Marx's conception of history), in order to live up to the essence assigned to him by Being. He must open himself up to Being—something that poet and philosopher are best capable of doing.

Yet it is at this point that Heidegger's and Sartre's conceptions of man as the revealer of Truth differ. To Heidegger it is above all the poet and secondly the philosopher who are *engaged* in his rendering of Truth. To Sartre the prose writer is he who is *engaged*. While he assumes with Heidegger that we are "within" language, he thinks of it first and foremost as utilitarian and of the prose-writer as one who makes use of words.[7] Language is thus seen as a form of commmunication, and one that is at its best when it is forgotten, made invisible for the sake of the thought it has conveyed. To Heidegger language is more than rhetoric. It is part of the very ground of Being, and it is through being open to it that poet and thinker unveil the Truth of Being. The word *Dasein* revealed to him the very essence of *Humanitas*. Other words led him to different insights. In the *Letter on Humanism* he stresses, in particular, the word *Vermögen*, which in ordinary usage means "wealth" and, above all, "power" (HH, 7-8). But separated from its prefix *ver-*, the root *mögen* corresponds to English "may" with which it shares all its implications: permission, possibility, and even power in the verbal form of "might." In German, however, *mögen* has the additional meaning of "liking"—and Heidegger concludes, quite illogically though convincingly, that he who likes a person or a thing gains the power of understanding this person or thing in his or its essence. Liking, in his view, becomes the very essence of power, of a power, that is, which permits something to "essentiate" as we open ourselves up to it and let it come toward us. (The philosopher plays here on the German word *Herkunft*, which means "origin" but is composed of linguistic components meaning "coming hither.") Things can actually *be* only in this manner and because of the power of such liking. Only in this way do they reveal their relationship to Being. Such frequently tortured etymologizing that stumps the translator and is usually enjoyed by some of Heidegger's readers and found maddening by others, evokes the prose of James Joyce and the poetry of Mallarmé. Heidegger would have considered them revealers of Being, as it is Being that counts in his philosophy. Being

---

[7] Jean-Paul Sartre, *Qu'est-ce que la littérature?* (Gallimard, 1948), pp. 28 ff.

thrust man into his essence which is that of being Its guardian. Being assigned to him language and made him the custodian—not the manipulator—of language. It is obvious that to the German philosopher the meaning of Humanism is man's, *Dasein*'s, fulfillment of its essence as light and clearing of Being and as the guardian of Its language. Does this mean that Being supplies man with a universal grammar, as Chomsky maintained, with "conditions that a system must meet to qualify as a potential human language, conditions that are not accidentally true of the existing human languages, but that are rather rooted in the human 'language capacity,' and thus constitute the innate organization that determines what counts as linguistic experience and what knowledge of language arises on the basis of this experience"?[8] One is tempted to think so, while being puzzled as much by the "innate organization" as by the power of Being to assign such essences to man.

Should one conclude, then, that Heidegger's Being is a deity? One is easily led to do so, especially when he speaks of It in terms reminiscent of biblical references to God, such as "It is Itself." But fully anticipating such a reaction, the philosopher assures us that his notion of Being corresponds not at all to God or any other divinity but rather is as mysterious as the *es* in German *es gibt* (there is) or the *il* in the expression's French equivalent *il y a*, and the "it" in English "it rains" (HH, 22-23). Languages, indeed, acknowledge the mystery that permeates our lives, that of the It of Being to which we owe our essence of being human, i.e., of being the *Da* of *Sein* that permits us to annul the subject/object relationship of traditional metaphysics and to replace it with that openness to Being that lets objects "essentiate."

Nevertheless, Heidegger's emphasis on Being could not but lead him to object to Sartre's statement in *L'Existentialisme est un Humanisme*: "Précisément nous sommes sur un plan où il y a seulement des hommes." He reversed it to read: "Précisément nous sommes sur un plan où il y a principalement l'Etre" (HH, 22-23). For to him, both Sartre's *hommes* and his *plan* are ultimately Being-sent (I am patterning this term here after God-sent). While both philosophers, therefore, assign the highest value to *Humanitas*, Heidegger thinks of Humanism in a more mystical, poetic, and philosophical way. Ethics enters into his conception only to the extent that man can be human only if he lives up to the essence assigned to him by Being. Sartre, on the other hand, equates Humanism with existentialism because his existentialism

---

[8] Ved Mehta, "John Is Easy to Please," *The New Yorker*, May 8, 1971, pp. 44-87.

implies that neither God nor Being but man himself creates his essence, as he makes himself through action and choice. The French philosopher's view, being both practical and ethical, allows the individual—in terms of the Kantian Imperative—only such freedom of action as he would grant others. Man is considered to be not only free, but "condamné à être libre," which implies responsibility for his fellow men, and even if God did not exist (the reference is implicitly to Dostoevsky's *Brothers Karamasov*) everything would not be permitted. In *L'Existentialisme est un Humanisme* Sartre maintained—referring in particular to Heidegger's conception of "human reality"—that "l'existence précède l'essence" in man, i.e., "que l'homme existe d'abord, se rencontre, surgit dans le monde, et qu'il se définit après" (SH, 35-37). But Heidegger simply chides him for perpetuating the traditional metaphysical dichotomy between essence and existence and for merely reversing Plato. To Sartre, a moralist in the best French tradition, "être dans le monde" means "d'y être au travail, d'y être au milieu d'autres et d'y être mortel," in a manner that—though recognizing the Heideggerian conception of man as *Mitsein* (Being-with-others)— infuses the German philosopher's thought with an Ethics he did not intend it to have (SH, 68). For to him, Being-in-the-world was the very essence of man. Man was thought to be ethical if he lived up to this essence, that is, if he localized and temporalized Being and was open to its manifestations so as to be witness to them and It. Though both thinkers stress the notion of *engagement*, in particular with regard to man's ability and responsibility to reveal Truth, the term came to represent to Sartre more and more the individual's choice concerning the conduct of his life in a world he considered more and more in social and political terms.

Since language is so essential a part of each thinker's conception of Humanism, it is not surprising that literature also is assigned a crucial part in it. Heidegger thinks of poets and thinkers almost as priests in the service of Being from which they ec-sist, while being in Its proximity and, indeed, a part of It. His very use of Being-sent language, his dedication to the exploration of the Truth that it conceals within itself, are ample proof and illustration of this. To the youthful Sartre, as he tells us in his autobiography *Les Mots*, writing was likewise a sacred duty: "Je pensais me donner à la Littérature quand, en vérité, j'entrais dans les ordres. En moi la certitude du croyant le plus humble devint l'orgueilleuse évidence de ma prédestination... Tout chrétien n'est-il pas un élu?... l'Autre restait, l'Invisible, le Saint-Esprit, celui qui garantissait mon mandat et régentait ma vie par de grandes forces anonymes et sacrées... je tentai de dévoiler le silence de l'être par un bruissement contrarié de mots et, surtout, je confondis les choses avec leurs noms: c'est croire."[9] Only later did Sartre come to think of language and literature in more worldly terms. But whether by inclination or preoccupation with Kierkegaard as well as Heidegger, his early attitude toward literature resembled the "passionate inwardness" of the Danish philosopher and the almost divine service of the German thinker.[10] It is therefore not accidental that Simone de Beauvoir, the indefatigable and eminently intelligent participant in and chronicler of twentieth-century existentialism, referred to Kierkegaard's *Fear and Trembling* in an article entitled "Littérature et métaphysique" which was published in *Les Temps modernes* in 1946.[11] She called the work rightly a novel and concluded from it that fiction was better suited to convey existential notions than any philosophical essay. Although her own views are utilitarian rather than philosophical, they coincide inadvertently with those of the three existential thinkers mentioned. Heidegger's use of the fable of "Care" conveyed his notion of *Dasein* in vivid terms; Sartre's *La Nausée* contained the beginnings of his existential thinking, his plays dramatized much of what he had philosophized about the "Other"; and Kierkegaard's *Fear and Trembling* and *Either/Or* conveyed the existential dilemmas that concerned him in a beautifully poetic manner. As Simone de Beauvoir maintained, literature could portray existents *en situation* instead of merely talking about them. It showed Humanism in action as it were.

Yet there is more of a problem concealed in the very form of Kierkegaard's *Fear and Trembling*[12] than Beauvoir's utilitarian approach permits her to realize. Its unusual mode and narrational patterns and techniques reflect Kierkegaard's own *Christian Humanism*: his notion that "Truth is Subjectivity," that it can be attained only through the individual's passionate inwardness, through his God-relationship, and that such Truth precludes our knowledge of that of the Other. On the surface, *Fear and Trembling* seems to convey Kierkegaard's notion of the Knight of Faith by means of the biblical story of Abraham and

---

[9] Jean-Paul Sartre, *Les Mots* (Gallimard, 1965), pp. 208-09.

[10] Sören Kierkegaard, "Concluding Unscientific Postscript," in Robert Bretall, *A Kierkegaard Anthology* (New York: Modern Library, 1946), p. 214.

[11] Simone de Beauvoir, "Littérature et métaphysique," *Les Temps Modernes* (1946), pp. 1153-63.

[12] Sören Kierkegaard, *Fear and Trembling*, tr. Walter Lowrie (Garden City, N.Y.: Doubleday, 1954), *passim*.

Isaac. When Abraham, obeying the voice of God that bids him to sacrifice his only son, takes Isaac to Mount Moriah to make ready for the sacrifice, he follows his belief in defiance of all social law and rationality. Not only society but also his own wife and son would have condemned him, had they understood his seemingly unnatural intentions. But as Kierkegaard pursues the psychological and moral implications of this moving tale, he juxtaposes it with folktales that at first appear unrelated. The intricate narrative structure of the entire work becomes apparent only after we learn from Kierkegaard's Diaries that he saw himself in the figure of Abraham, as the Knight of Faith who had been willing to surrender what he loved most. For he had been engaged to Regina Olsen and had, in what he considered obedience to God, broken his engagement to her. Abraham, therefore, served him not only as the emblem for the Knight of Faith but as his own objective correlative. To him, however, Regina was not returned through divine grace. She married another. Yet, like Abraham, Kierkegaard was unable to explain his sacrifice to his contemporaries who believed him to have been trifling with the affections of the young woman and would not have understood that he was obeying a higher command, one that meant to set Regina free of her dependence on him. Once we understand, however, Abraham's function as an objective correlative to Kierkegaard's own existential and personal experience, we begin to understand also that the other tales told are but variations on the same theme of sacrificial love and its redemptive power.

There is, for instance, the tale of "Agnes and the Merman" (*ibid.*). Agnes is seduced by the Merman, a thoroughly evil creature, but it is her complete and innocent surrender to what she believes to be his true love that transforms his evil intentions. In the tale of "Tobias and Sarah" taken from the *Book of Tobit*, it is the young woman who represents the forces of evil in that any man who loves her is doomed to perish — until the redemptive power of Tobias's love for her breaks the demonic spell (*ibid.*). *Fear and Trembling* is punctuated, moreover, by a refrain, so poetic that it alone would justify the novel's subtitle "A Dialectic Lyric." It sings of the mother's love for her child and her apparent withdrawal of that love when she weans the child: "When the child has to be weaned the mother blackens her breast, but her eyes rest just as lovingly upon the child. The child believes it is the breast that has changed, but that the mother is unchanged. And why does she blacken her breast? Because, she says, it would be a shame

that it should seem delicious when the child must not get it" (*ibid.*).
Yet the mother's sacrifice seemed small to Kierkegaard as compared
to that of Abraham-Kierkegaard who had to blacken himself in order
to set Regina free.

We are mainly concerned, however, with what obligated
Kierkegaard to conceal this Abraham-Kierkegaard identity within the
intricate variations on its theme that *Fear and Trembling* represents.
This question becomes even more compelling when we realize that
Either/Or, published in the same year, namely 1843, is yet another
variation on that theme. The *Either* consists — as we are told by the
book's fictitious editor Victor Eremita — of a bundle of manuscripts
apparently written by author *A*, an aesthete; the *Or*, of letters written
to *A* by *B*, an ethical judge. The last part of *A*'s pile of manuscripts
is "The Diary of the Seducer" that *A* claims to have found, clearly
distancing himself from the Seducer Johannes (the Danish form of
Giovanni) and condemning, in fact, the conduct of this calculating,
manipulating mind that tries to turn life and human relationships into
art by molding the young woman in such a way that she will freely
surrender to him and by refining himself into the Don Juan myth.
Johannes is the direct counterpart to *B*, Judge Wilhelm who, in his
letters, praises the ethical bond of marriage and extolls the virtues
of his own wife.[13]

But if Kierkegaard plays with his readers intricate games of hide
and seek, he also hints at their solution. For his fictitious editor Victor submits that these two writers might well have been one and the
same person, each being the other's "possible," in the way in which
all fiction is merely conjecture and represents a subjunctive mode.
The implication is, of course, that they were also Kierkegaard's own
possibles as opposed to that truth that is subjectivity and that could
be known only to him and told only in an indicative mood and only
in the first person or through the mask of an objective correlative.
Kierkegaard's literary modes thus conform to his existential views,
as do Sartre's in *La Nausée*, where *editors* also claim to have *found* Roquentin's diary.[14] It is true — and Kierkegaard is fully aware of this —
that this is simply "a trick of the novelist," but it is equally true that
both he, and Sartre after him, used the trick to different purposes.

---

[13] Søren Kierkegaard, *Either/Or*, 2 vols., tr. D.F. and L.M. Swenson (Garden City,
N.Y.: Doubleday, 1959), *passim*.
[14] *La Nausée*, p. 7.

Both wanted to disguise the all-too-easy identification of author and protagonist that existential thought encourages the reader to make.[15] It was only years later in his autobiography that Sartre revealed that he thought of himself as Roquentin: "Je réussis à trente ans ce beau coup: d'écrire dans *La Nausée*... l'existence injustifiée, saumâtre de mes congénères et mettre la mienne hors de cause. *J'étais* Roquentin, je montrais en lui, sans complaisance, la trame de ma vie; en même temps j'étais *moi*, l'élu, annaliste des enfers, photomicroscope de verre et d'acier penché sur mes propres sirops protoplasmiques."[16] Indeed, what Sartre was to write in *Questions de méthode* concerning Flaubert's relationship to Madame Bovary cannot but shed light on the manner in which he viewed his own relationship to Roquentin.[17] Sartre took Flaubert's statement "Madame Bovary, c'est moi" as proof that the author objectified himself in Emma, a woman of whom Baudelaire had said that she possessed the madness and willpower of a man. Though the philosopher-critic considered Flaubert by no means an "inverti," he believed that the novelist could make her his objective correlative only because, in existential terms, she belonged to the "champ de ses possibles," was within the range of his possibles (*ibid.*, p. 196). It is interesting, however, that Flaubert — though writing at about the same time as Kierkegaard — did not expect his readers to detect any identity between him and Madame Bovary and felt no need to use "the trick of the novelist" in order to conceal it. He was simply innocent of existential preoccupations. The notions concerning the Self and the Other that fundamentally determined Kierkegaardian literary modes as well as those of the young Sartre were happily ignored by him, as he opted for an omniscient narrator and an even more omniscient author.

It is not accidental but existentially conditioned, however, that all of Kierkegaard's fictitious editors and pseudonymous authors write in the first person or that Sartre's Roqentin is essentially — not accidentally — alone. It equally conforms to their existential tenets that they have chosen the open-ended form of the diary for their protagonists rather than modes that permit a narrator to look back upon his life and its events and see them fall into a systematic pattern. For Kierkegaard had maintained that human existence is a perpetual

[15] *Either/Or*, I, 9.
[16] *Les Mots*, pp. 209-10.
[17] Jean-Paul Sartre, *Questions de méthode* (Gallimard, 1960), *passim*.

becoming and could be defined only after one's death. And Sartre had held with equal conviction that man, as long as he lived, was in the process of defining himself through his actions. Even as late as 1960 he was to advise anthropologists that "l'homme se définit par son projet. Cet être matériel dépasse perpétuellement la condition qui lui est faite; il dévoile et détermine sa situation en la transcendant pour s'objectiver par le travail, l'action ou le geste" (*ibid.*, p. 209).

The existential notion of the Other that proved so restrictive to Kierkegaardian modes of writing and Sartre's *La Nausée* was to be expanded by the French author in Heideggerian terms, as we shall see, and it is important to evaluate that *rapprochement* in its humanistic implications. Kierkegaard had written in his *Concluding Unscientific Postscript*:

> With respect to every reality external to myself, I can get hold of it only through thinking it. In order to get hold of it really, I should have to be able to make myself into the other, the acting individual, and make the foreign reality my own reality, which is impossible. For if I make the foreign reality my own, this does not mean that I become the other through knowing his reality, but it means that I acquire a new reality, which belongs to me as opposed to him... When I think about something that another has done, and so conceive a reality, I lift this given reality out of the real and set it over into the possible; for a *conceived reality* is a possibility, and is higher than reality from the standpoint of thought, but not from the standpoint of reality. This also implies that there is no immediate relationship, ethically, between subject and subject. When I understand another person, his reality is for me a possibility.[18]

This relegation of the Other to the realm of conjecture is reflected equally strongly in the literature of Kierkegaard and in Sartre's *La Nausée*. Roquentin experiences Others merely as incomprehensible entities that he enoounters in restaurants and libraries. They express themselves seemingly in clichés and utter platitudes, incapable of any true dialogue. Even he and Anny have remained puzzling to each other, although they have known each other for a long time. While, in Kierkegaardian terms, they had danced a dance meant for two, each dancer had followed only his own inner melody.

In *L'Etre et le néant*, however, Sartre was to develop the notion of the Other and subsequently came to develop new fictional patterns

[18] *Kierkegaard Anthology*, pp. 226-27.

apt to be expressive of it.[19] Philosophically, he proved the existence of the Other through a second *cogito*, surging up within the Self as it becomes conscious—through the Other's Look—of being also defined by a power outside itself. The Other's Look may deprive the Self wholly of its essential freedom—that of making itself and seeing itself as the center of its world—unless the Self reasserts its authenticity in defiance of the Other's fixating judgment. As is well known, such notions were ingeniously dramatized by Sartre in his *Huis-clos*, but, in his *Les Chemins de la liberté*, they led him to invent new narrative techniques and patterns. Rejecting traditional depiction of his fictional characters, he had those who were inauthentic define themselves as whatever Others chose to see them. They discovered themselves exclusively in the eyes of the Other. Thus Daniel writes to his friend Mathieu:

> Je n'ai jamais eu ce que je suis... Mes vices, mes vertus, j'ai le nez dessus, je ne puis les voir, ni prendre assez de recul pour me considérer d'ensemble. Et puis j'ai je ne sais quel sentiment d'être une matière molle et mouvante où les mots s'enlisent; à peine ai-je tenté de me nommer, que déjà celui qui est nommé s'est confondu avec celui qui nomme et tout est remis en question... Un instant, en ce soir de juin où il m'a plu de me confesser à toi, j'ai cru me toucher dans tes yeux effarés. Tu me voyais; dans tes yeux j'étais solide et prévisible; mes actes et mes humeurs n'étaient plus que les conséquences d'une essence fixe. Cette essence c'est par moi que tu la connaissais, je te l'avais décrite avec mes mots, je t'avais révélé des faits que tu ignorais et qui t'avaient permis de l'entrevoir. Pourtant c'est toi qui la voyais et moi je te voyais seulement la voir... J'ai compris alors qu'on ne pouvait s'atteindre que par le jugement d'un autre, par la haine d'un autre. Par l'amour d'un autre aussi, peut-être.[20]

If the Other's Look deprives those who are inauthentic almost completely of their freedom to change, Sartre was to assign to it, later yet, a more positive role within the normal course of human interchange. In his *Questions de méthode* he came to formulate a Heideggerian dialectic in which the individual engages with the Other in order to make himself. As Sartre describes there Flaubert's emergence as an author—and that of *Madame Bovary* in particular—he seems to evoke Heideggerian notions of man's Being-in-the-world, a world wherein *Dasein* (the individual's subjective/objective existence) is juxtaposed with *Mitsein* (Being with Others):

[19] Jean-Paul Sartre, *L'Etre et le néant* (Gallimard, 1943), pp. 275-364.
[20] Jean-Paul Sartre, *Le Sursis* (Gallimard, 1945), pp. 466-67.

Cette relation immédiate, par-delà les éléments donnés et constitués, avec l'autre que soi, cette perpétuelle production de soi-même par le travail et la *praxis*, c'est notre structure propre: pas plus qu'une volonté, elle n'est un besoin ou une passion, mais nos besoins comme nos passions ou comme la plus abstraite de nos pensées participent de cette structure: ils sont toujours *en dehors d'eux-mêmes vers*... C'est ce que nous nommons l'existence et par là, nous n'entendons pas une substance stable qui se repose en elle-même mais un déséquilibre perpétuel... Comme cet élan vers l'objectivation prend des formes diverses selon les individus, comme il nous projette à travers un champ de possibilités dont nous réalisons certaines à l'exclusion des autres, nous le nommons aussi choix ou liberté.[21]

If this dialectical process represents the very core of Sartre s "méthode progressive-régressive," it must clearly be recognized as Heidegger's conception of man as *Dasein*, as the "here and now" of Being, as Being-in-the-world, localizing and temporalizing It.

Heidegger's notions of time so integral to his conception of *Dasein* and, thereby, of his conception of Humanism, had preoccupied Sartre as early as 1939, as evidenced by his essay of that year, "A propos de *Le Bruit et la fureur*: La Temporalité chez Faulkner."[22] His voice assumed Heideggerian overtones when he stated there that "consciousness can exist within time" only on condition that it becomes time as the result of the very movement by which it becomes consciousness. "It must become 'temporalized.'" He granted that the time of a nail, a clod of earth, or even an atom might be that of a perpetual present but proclaimed that man, not being a thinking nail, could not be plunged into time as if it were a bath of sulphuric acid. He not only agreed with both Kierkegaard and Heidegger that man can no longer be evaluated at each moment and defined as the sum total of what he has, but he also concurred with the German philosopher's assumption that human consciousness implies projection — or that *Dasein*, by its very nature, ec-sists — because it is determined by what Heidegger called "the silent force of the possible," that is, by the future rather than the past. Such notions of the nature of man, of his *Humanitas*, as temporalized Being-in-the-world, led Sartre to criticize Faulkner's technique of dwelling in an "unspeakable present, leaking at every seam," invaded suddenly by the past, and filled with

---

[21] *Questions de méthode*, pp. 209-10.
[22] Jean-Paul Sartre, "A propos de *Le Bruit et la fureur*: La Temporalité chez Faulkner," *La Nouvelle Revue Française* (June 1939), pp. 1057-61.

"monstrous and discontinuous obsessions" and "intermittances of the heart." Sartre's critical vocabulary betrays, of course, the similarities he detected between Faulkner's handling of time and that of Proust, whom he equally condemned, although he was fully aware of the fact that, to the characters of Faulkner's fictional world, the past is merely an unbearable burden, whereas to Proust's Marcel recapturing it means salvation. Both authors failed in his view in that they saw man merely as the sum total of what he has, rather than as "the totality of what he does not yet have" but might have with all that such a vision of *Humanitas* implies in terms of attenuating the present and its formless brutality. While Sartre's *La Nausée* had, in many ways paid homage to Proust's *A la recherche du temps perdu*, it had already both mocked and challenged its conception of the past, of music (Roquentin listened to an American popular song rather than great music), and even to some extent of art as the salvation of man. Both Anny and Roquentin came to declare the past as dead and surviving only in words or pictures that falsely glorified it.

But Sartre's conception of man as Being-in-the-world, as projecting himself into the future and, at the same time, temporalizing Being, determined yet more decisively the narrative modes of his tetralogy *Les Chemins de la liberté*. Unlike Roquentin, though like him fundamentally alone, each character in this tetralogy is presented as Being-in-the-world and as a temporalizer of Being. An entire chorus of voices, moreover, serves as background to the novels' main characters, and political history intrudes in the form of simulated meetings held by actual historical world leaders, that the reader is privileged to eavesdrop on. In this fusion of fiction and the lived reality of actual nations, the characters created by the author are as it were engaged in a dialectic in the process of which they define themselves and challenge the reader to do likewise. We are reminded of Sartre's statement in *Questions de méthode*: "Dans cet univers vivant, l'homme occupe pour nous une place privilégiée. D'abord parce qu'il peut être historique, c'est-à-dire se définir sans cesse par sa propre praxis à travers les changements subis ou provoqués et leur intériorisation, puis le dépassement même des relations intériorisées."[23] To evoke the mood of a world wherein the existents of the novels reside in perpetual progression and regression, the author packed innumerable facts and characters not only into each chapter or paragraph, but even into a single sentence. He did so in

[23] *Questions de méthode*, pp. 231-32.

particular in the third volume of the tetralogy, *Le Sursis*. For instance, in a sentence beginning with the personal pronoun *elle* and clearly referring to the nurse of one of the many characters, the same pronoun serves toward the sentence's middle to designate a totally different woman, located miles away and engaged in different activities. A *non* ending one statement may, as if in dreamlike echoing association, begin another, made elsewhere and in a different context. In this volume— unlike those preceding it—the world is no longer observed through a first-person consciousness concealed under a third-person narration but rather by an impersonal human consciousness spreading itself over the entire universe.[24]

Nowhere do we feel the impact of *Humanitas* as *Dasein* more strongly, however, than in an episode of *Le Sursis*, reminiscent of Flaubert's scene at the Comices in *Madame Bovary*. In this scene, Rodolphe seduces with his words of love an eager and romantic Emma, though romance seems to be belied by the very background noise of the public speakers and the milling crowd. As romantic and political "high-mindedness" grotesquely mingle, they seem to mock each other's vulgarity, while Flaubert "like God in creation" remains invisible and amuses himself at the expense of rural pomposity and lack of morality. The corresponding scene in Sartre's *Le Sursis* is one wherein Ivich and Mathieu find refuge in his Paris apartment and, almost inadvertently, make love to each other. At the same time, the great national powers—invisible and inaudible to the lovers—meet to decide whether to declare war on Hitler or to appease him, and thereby willy-nilly affect the lives of the lovers. It is the all-knowing author who intrudes to put on record that Chamberlain and Daladier have decided to annul the existence of Czechoslovakia and have let it become a part of Hitler's Reich. Ivich and Mathieu are unaware of the decision and its simultaneity with their love-making.[25] But the author, seeing them as Being-in-the-world and in dialectical relationship with Others with whom they share it, cannot separate them from such events in the manner in which he could isolate Roquentin. This view forced him likewise to abandon the I-Roquentin relationship of *La Nausée* and to replace it with an orchestration of consciousnesses, a multidimensionality that not only corresponded to his more Heideggerian notion of *Humanitas* as

[24] Edith Kern, *Existential Thought and Fictional Technique: Kierkegaard, Sartre, Beckett* (New Haven: Yale University Press, 1970), pp. 145-55.
[25] *Le Sursis*, pp. 494-501.

Being-in-the-world, but also to his subjective/objective interpretation of *Dasein*. As Sartre put it in *Qu'est-ce que la littérature?*, speaking of the authors of his time: "A notre certitude intérieure d'être 'dévoilants' s'adjoint celle d'être inessentiels par rapport à la chose dévoilée."[26] In the course of his quest for literary modes apt to be expressive of existentialism as humanism, Sartre's Kierkegaardian stress on subjectivity had come to transform itself into such relatively subservient anonymity.

Sartre's definition of Existentialist Humanism in *L'Existentialisme est un Humanisme* shows the author's involvement with Heideggerian thought:

> Il n'y a pas d'autre univers qu'un univers humain, l'univers de la subjectivité humaine. Cette liaison de la transcendance, comme constitutive de l'homme — non pas au sens où Dieu est transcendant, mais au sens de dépassement — et de la subjectivité, au sens où l'homme n'est pas enfermé en lui-même mais présent toujours dans un univers humain, c'est ce que nous nommons l'humanisme existentialiste. (SH, 93)

One realizes at the same time that this definition falls short of Heidegger's notion that man is Being-sent and, while ec-sisting and temporalizing It and shedding the light of his intelligence upon It, remains a part of It, guarding It as well as the Being-sent language. Heideggerian Humanism seems as valid today on the level of thought as that of Sartre is in social-ethical terms. For Heidegger's conception of *Dasein* — going beyond that of Sartre — seems to imply that, at a given time, all men share and, indeed, might temporalize and reveal Being-sent structures of thought, regardless of the specific disciplines to which they adhere. If Heidegger objects to technology, he does so because of its single-mindedness and its obliviousness of the fact that all thought of our time springs from what he calls the ground of Being. He believes that our artificial division of knowledge into social and natural sciences, on the one hand, and literature and philosophy, on the other, is due to this narrowness of thought. If we can ignore the sometimes annoying preciousness of his language, his notion of Humanism might well usher in a new era, one in which we heed these common structures of thought that all humankind and all disciplines share because they represent the very ground of Being.

[26] *Qu'est-ce que la littérature?*, p. 50.

Oracular Lives: Sartre and the Twentieth Century

PETER CAWS

In literary more than in philosophical studies, perhaps (but in philosophical studies too to some extent) we are accustomed to thinking of history as if it divided itself up as the centuries of our numbering system suggest it should. The numbering system is, of course, arbitrary, and nothing requires that events should adapt themselves to it — although some cultural feedback no doubt takes place, a subjective sense of the new, for example, in January, or at the beginning of a decade (or a millennium). Our century is the last of the second thousand years of the Christian era (another arbitrary determination) and it occupies an ambiguous position: ordinally new, cardinally old. Also it is a century almost filled by the life of Jean-Paul Sartre (1905-1980) and more so even by that of Henri Peyre (born 1901). It seems appropriate in this context to consider the relation of lives and epochs.

The question is interesting in connection with Sartre (with whom I shall mainly be concerned in what follows) not only because he bears a particular relation to our own epoch, or at any rate to part of it, but also because he himself, in his later work, develops definite views as to the way in which lives define and bear witness to epochs, views which form part of the theory of history with which his major philosophical work closes. The question of closure in Sartre's philosophical career — marked as it was by so many conspicuous cases of incompleteness — is one that I have dealt with elsewhere,[1] but it

---

[1] Peter Caws, "*L'Idiot* Savant," in proceedings of the Sartre colloquium, Cerisy-la-Salle, 1979 (forthcoming).

is worth mentioning at the start that if closure is to be found it is at the very end of the published corpus, in volume 3 of *L'Idiot de la famille*, where the view customarily attributed to the later Sartre, i.e., that found in the *Critique of Dialectical Reason*, is abandoned in favor of a more modest and realistic one.

The extravagant view of the *Critique*, briefly put, is that history is a double and simultaneous dialectic in being and in knowing, and that at any point a complete and lucid totalization is possible as a basis for political action. There is only one history, and it is essentially intelligible. The modest view in the *Idiot* is that history is multiple and recursive, that the history of one epoch is as much as we can grasp at one time, and that this history depends on the availability of an "oracular life" which "follows the same curve" as the epoch and as it were embodies it.[2] Sartre explains his use of the term "epoch" as follows: "I give this name to every historical temporalization to the extent that it produces its own frontiers" (*IF*, 440); according to this view the twentieth century would not count as an epoch, but then neither would the July Monarchy, strictly speaking (since its beginning and end were contingent), although that is the period Sartre chooses as a test case.

The relation of an oracular life to an epoch, however defined, is clearly a special case of the more general relation of any individual to history, Sartre's view of which does change radically from the earlier to the later works. The young Sartre was not particularly interested in history, since for him everything began with the project of the existential subject. We are thrown into the world and face the future, whether we like it or not; our past does not constrain us, except in the sense that it contributes to the facticity of our situation — we are responsible for it, but then we are responsible for the whole world — and the same is true of history in general. Sartre is scornful of Freud because of his preoccupation with the subject's history, to such an extent that for psychoanalysis the future does not exist.[3] The individual is absolutely free and defiantly central in his own world.

This heroic position did not survive the pressures of Sartre's own history, particularly his politicization by the events of the Second World War. Without retracing all the intermediate steps we find, on shifting attention to the *Critique*, a subject almost wholly determined by

---

[2] Jean-Paul Sartre, *L'Idiot de la famille*, III (Gallimard, 1971-1972), 440 (hereafter abbreviated *IF* followed by page number[s]).

[3] Jean-Paul Sartre, *Being and Nothingness*, tr. Hazel Barnes (New York: Philosophical Library, 1956), p. 453.

society and family, whose freedom is reduced to "the small movement which makes of a totally conditioned social being someone who does not render back completely what his conditioning has given him";[4] no longer the center of the world, the individual—even Sartre himself, or to put it more strongly, *especially* Sartre himself (and thus by generalization especially each one of us)—is "n'importe qui" ("just anyone"), an interchangeable and nonprivileged member of a society whose history, in its dialectical unfolding, poses a problem to his understanding as well as to his action. (Strictly speaking, the centrality of the subject is not lost but is reduced to the equivalence of multiple centers.) Universal liberty has given way to nearly universal slavery, under the pressure of scarcity; the individual can hardly make his epoch, but under suitable circumstances he may still bear witness to it.

Let me first, then, set out in greater detail the relation between the individual and his epoch in the late Sartre, and then consider Sartre's own relation to our epoch. The case in which the former relation is worked out is of course that of Gustave Flaubert, and the method of its working out is announced by Sartre as early as *Questions de méthode* as the "progressive-regressive method."[5] The double movement of the method is required in order to get from history to the individual and then back again; from the family and the social and political conditions of the day one zeroes in, as it were, on the situation uniquely occupied by the individual in question, and then from his subjectivity in that situation one projects, in principle, the actions that constituted his contribution to the historical totalization of his age. The hinge between the two phases of the method is the interior subjectivity of the individual in question, and that this should be passed through rather than jumped over is crucial, even though Sartre, as Simone de Beauvoir reports, "had a horror of the inner life."[6] For him the subject is authentic enough, but it is momentary, and its role is summed up as the interiorization of exteriority and the re-exteriorization of interiority—a dynamic process in the course of which whatever insertion of freedom into determination human action can

[4] Jean-Paul Sartre, *Between Existentialism and Marxism*, tr. John Mathews (New York: Pantheon, 1974), p. 35.
[5] Jean-Paul Sartre, *Search for a Method*, tr. Hazel Barnes (New York: Knopf, 1963), pp. 85 ff.
[6] Simone de Beauvoir, *La Force de l'âge* (Gallimard, 1960), p. 194.

achieve has to be effected. It should be noted that while the free subject does not "give back the totality of what it has received from its
conditioning" it is not as a matter of practice *necessary* for the subject
to realize its freedom, and in the *Critique* Sartre envisages a situation
in which individuals serially related to others may remain exterior
to the whole group activity on which history rests and thus have no
interaction with it at all:

> There is no guarantee that a given bureaucrat or clerk will one day,
> by integration into a group, cease to be an Other both for himself and
> for Others. At this moment, manipulated by things (his *office*, as a col-
> lective, his boss as an Other), he is for other men a factor of alterity,
> of passivity and of counter-finality, as if he were a thing (a Spanish ducat)
> circulating through men's hands. There is no guarantee that, in itself
> and for him, this situation contains the seed of a contradiction.[7]

If *everyone* were like this (and that cannot be excluded if it is possible
for anyone) then history would become a purely causal matter and
could be treated positivistically rather than dialectically, but Sartre
does not consider this possibility.

In the *Critique* the dialectic of history is worked out for groups up
to the level of social classes such as the bourgeoisie and the proletariat.
But history proper, for the Marxist, is the dialectical struggle *between*
these classes, and the problem that arises is that, each having its collective awareness (in the restricted sense Sartre allows this term, i.e.,
as distributed over the group, so that each individual is the group
concentrated into one, or is one with the power of the group—a
somewhat optimistic view of the way classes actually work) and its
collective project (in a similar sense), neither at the same time can
realize this project because of the countervailing force of the other.
The project of the proletariat is the overthrow of the bourgeoisie, but
if this is to be done *intelligently* the project of the bourgeoisie has to
be understood from the inside; history cannot be a mere clash of forces
if it is also to be dialectically intelligible—it must be the history of
some single subject, mankind perhaps. As long, therefore, as there
are two subjects of history, mutually blind to one another's interiority, the intelligibility of the result cannot be guaranteed. The *Critique*
fails completely to resolve this problem. One of the whimsical forms
in which Sartre acknowledges this failure is a footnote to an account

[7] Jean-Paul Sartre, *Critique of Dialectical Reason*, tr. Alan Sheridan-Smith (London:
NLB, 1976), p. 324 (hereafter abbreviated *CDR* followed by page number[s]).

of the group activity of a football team, in which the cooperation of the members of the group and the totalization of their collective moves is being discussed; in the note Sartre says: "In fact, in a football match, everything is complicated by the presence of the opposite team" (*CDR*, 473). In another note he admits that actual cases are more complicated than his method allows for, and adds: "But what is important to us here is the abstract and formal clarity of the schemata. One can encounter the complexity of the real for oneself and at leisure" (*CDR*, 460). The *Critique* ends with a promise to confront the reality of History in the next volume, and yet its project too is to be "still formal" (*CDR*, 813).

It is the absence of a suitable subject for history as a whole that leads Sartre, in the *Idiot*, to reverse the terms of the equation: history is possible just to the extent that a subject can be found for it. This is the point of entry of the doctrine of oracular lives, which he calls "diachronically significant" (*IF*, 442). These are lives that span an epoch and express it; the epoch contains, admittedly, nothing but lives, but it does not sum itself up in just any life. Sartre compares the *effort* of one of these significative lives — which are not to be confused with historically active or decisive lives — to that of an actor in a play:

> It is sometimes said of an actor that he "has one or two acts, etc., in him," by which is understood that he can *hold* the exhausting tension of a role for twenty or forty minutes and that after that time he gives out. In a similar way we must recognize that an individual, as a function of the society in which he lives, of the mode of production, of the technical knowledge available at the time, of the structure of the family, of antecedent circumstances, of the historic future which reveals itself as his destiny, but also of the singularity of his own previous history and of his biological characteristics, inherited or acquired, has twenty, forty, or sixty years "in him." And it has already been understood that it is not a question here of the "life expectancy" that statistics discovers for the newborn of a given period, although this constitutes the framework in which programming has to be determined, but rather of the concrete duration of human existence as this is delimited, if not by death, at all events by the deterioration of the life remaining. (*IF*, 442)

For the subject of this existence it is a matter of being acted upon by social and familial influences, etc., and of living them *consciously* in order to contribute, to the historical development, not acts, but significations; his life is therefore *retotalizing*, that is to say, capable of reintegrating the dispersed elements of historical becoming and making them coherent again. It is true that if one could really totalize *any* life one would validate it in the same way: "every real life," says Sartre in a note, "—however *insignificant*—is significative insofar as it is totalized" (*IF*, 443). This safeguards egalitarian principle. But such totalization is historian's work and cannot be done for every life. The minds that count are the ones who can effect their own validation.

Now the writer is above all the producer of signification; his sensibility permits him to follow a program of life in which the social developments of the epoch find their reflection. For Sartre, then, Flaubert did not *subsequently become* one of the chief witnesses to the middle of the nineteenth century, he *was at the time* linked to contemporary history, rather like a speedometer to a car. The image is too mechanical:

> It goes without saying that the slowing-down of social exchange or of global temporalization does not necessarily result immediately in the brakes being applied to individual temporalization, any more than a general acceleration translates itself into a singular one. It is the general shape of the curve that counts. (*IF*, 441-42)

But what does it mean exactly to express an epoch by "following the same curve"? I cite at length, in order to give full weight to Sartre's claim, the passage in which he develops this idea:

> Thus the diachronic finitude of an individual is particularized by the finitude of the social projects which envelop him and give him—by enlarging or shrinking the field of his possibilities, hence of his choices— his destiny as a *finite* man and his particular alienations. In this sense a life like that of Gustave and an epoch such as that of Louis-Philippe can enter into reciprocal relations on a *real* basis: it is enough if the same factors condition the one and the other and that these factors totalize them and are retotalized by them in such a way that they present the same curve, that is the same profile of temporalization. It is necessary also, of course, that the one and the other, starting from the same "antecedent circumstances," should be oriented towards the same goal, facing the same obstacles, with the same intentions.
>
> From this perspective we can perfectly well understand the effect of acceleration that transforms life into an oracle, that is into a diachronic shortcut with respect to the general evolution of the society... The two finitudes make one because the smaller is a moment in the larger and the density of the individual, in the case of a *real* identity, is none other than that of the epoch. (*IF*, 440)

This is plainly too good to be true. Flaubert, one feels, would have been extremely surprised to learn it. If we *now* think of him as a witness to his epoch, as a typical or paradigm case, that certainly requires an explanation, and such an explanation would no doubt have two principal elements, one of which would show how Flaubert was able to live the events of his time as he lived them, and the other of which would show how he was able to write what he wrote and why we still read him. In this connection the light that the *Idiot* throws on his life is invaluable. But if Flaubert appears as the best historian of 1848 (the *Sentimental Education* being his only contribution to history in any strict sense), it is only because the enthusiasms and confusions of the moment offered him the background, for which he had been looking for some time, against which he could display the contingent evolution of his anti-hero — a background sufficiently agitated to push the unhappy Frederic in a suitable number of different directions — and because he painted this background with pitiless accuracy; and if we still read him it is because his project was among other things a *style* ("as rhythmic as verse, as precise as the language of the sciences"),[8] and that he realized this better than almost any writer before or since. At all events it does not seem to be a matter of some privileged relation with the epoch in the *a priori* and indeed almost metaphysical sense that Sartre seems to imply. As to *Madame Bovary*, the situation is even clearer: it is at least in part *because* of Flaubert that we judge his epoch as marked to such an extent by the sentimentality of the popular novel, a genre then spreading through Europe.

Flaubert's life certainly presents some exceptional features, which account for his having been able to observe from close up the profound changes that were taking place around him. He was able, for example, to be a spectator of the confrontation between the scientific spirit and religious belief; he lived, through his father, the interior reality of the bourgeoisie, through his elder brother a psychoanalytic crisis *avant la lettre*, and through his friends the literary life of Paris in the nineteenth century. He is therefore one of our most valuable sources for the understanding of that century; one might say that he is its historian *to the extent that history is possible*. Here, in fact, is one of my principal differences with Sartre: he seems to believe, even if

---

[8] Gustave Flaubert, "Letter to Louise Colet," *Oeuvres complètes*, XIII (Club de l'Honnête Homme, 1971), 186.

it requires for its expression an oracular life, that there does nevertheless exist something objective that might be called "the history of the epoch," but I believe that there can only be "the history of Flaubert," or of someone else, using this expression in the sense of "the history of the Venerable Bede" rather than in the sense of "the history of Mr. Polly," and that epochs are *always* creations *ex post facto*, susceptible to revision in the light of new factual discoveries but also in the light of new possibilities of interpretation, new sensibilities, new forms of awareness. One thing is sure: Sartre did not choose Flaubert for attention because he was the oracle of his epoch, but because he was Flaubert. To understand Flaubert it is necessary to understand the epoch, but Flaubert himself helps to define it for us. Something of what transpired in it transpired also, to a certain extent, in him. But the microcosm/macrocosm relation is much less intimate and much harder to determine than Sartre seems to think.

Even under this muted conception of the oracular life, however, it is possible to ask whether, with respect to our own epoch, Sartre's life was one, or if not what was his relation to our time. I move therefore to the second and concluding part of this paper: what is the "curve" of the twentieth century, the "profile of its temporalization"? Of course it is not over yet, although that does not in itself prevent Sartre, according to his own theory, from being its oracle, since he also says that an epoch "can complete itself in an individual well before coming to an end socially" (*IF*, 443); as our recent contemporary, the effect of his work may continue to grow with time, and I have had occasion to remark elsewhere that "it may well be that the moment of the greatest historical relevance of the *Critique of Dialectical Reason* is yet to come."[9] It is therefore perhaps too early to broach the question of the relation between Sartre and the twentieth century in a global sense. But within the century there is of course one epoch, brief but intense, with which the name of Sartre is intimately linked in the popular imagination, namely the postwar period of the forties, the epoch of Saint-Germain-des-Prés and existentialism and the nightclubs of the Latin Quarter, of Juliette Greco and Boris Vian, of the successes of *Existentialism is a Humanism* and *What Is Literature?* and *No Exit* and, above all, *Nausea* (even though the latter had been first

[9] Peter Caws, *Sartre* (London: Routledge and Kegan Paul, 1979), p. 4.

published before the war). (I have often wondered, given the reputation of existentialism as a visceral philosophy, what image we would have of this period of intellectual history if Gallimard in 1938 had accepted Sartre's title *Melancholia*.) Now it is easy enough to see what it was in Sartre's position that was appealing at a time when France, and indeed civilization in general, was emerging from a long ordeal which had led to the collapse of its most stable institutions: the affirmation of individual existence against absurdity; the acceptance of the responsibility of each for all, which amounts to the acceptability of all to each, even under the form of a refusal; the relief of discovering that writing is also doing, when action in the normal sense had been overtaken by the monstrosity of real events. At the time, there is no doubt, Sartre expressed something that summed up the sentiments of a generation, and it is legitimate to ask (as he asked for Flaubert) what it was in his formation that prepared him for this role of witness to his epoch.

I shall not attempt a complete account here, but will content myself with drawing attention to the most striking feature of the case, namely the absence (in sharp contrast to Flaubert) of a father. It would be an extremely interesting exercise to bring together the biographies of great men without fathers; an analogous case, not unconnected with that of Sartre because of the conjunction of their two lives at the time of Vietnam, would be that of Bertrand Russell, another philosopher whose unbreakable certitude may perhaps be traced to the same lack. For the son, the existence of the father is like the existence of God, the impossible in-itself-for-itself: in-itself because the father is a distinct being, who has the objectivity of things in the world, for-itself because the son is precisely his father's project, which may well be lived as such by the son in spite of himself. The absence of a father, on the other hand, may imply the absence of God—or it may imply, in special cases, a privileged relation with Him, as for example in the case of Isaac Newton. Frank Manuel has shown how Newton, born after the death of his father (which, according to Lincolnshire folklore, was taken to confer supernatural powers) and, furthermore, on Christmas Day, and prematurely at that, as if this meaningful date had been predetermined, considered himself in some sense the Son of God: this status gave him in his own eyes a kind of familial authority as the discoverer of the mathematical secrets of Creation.[10] Sartre's case was the opposite; the nonexistence of a human

---

[10] Frank Manuel, *Portrait of Isaac Newton* (Washington: New Republic Books, 1979).

father meant, in the end, the nonexistence of God, or as Sartre himself put it, the complete absence of a super-Ego. At the same time, he manifested a strange preoccupation with God, like the atheist in *The Words*, "a God-obsessed crank who saw His absence everywhere and who could not open his mouth without uttering His name; in short, a gentleman who had religious convictions."[11] It was perhaps only for someone so convinced of the importance of the question that God would have deigned to reveal, as He did to Sartre one morning in 1917, His own disappearance (*TW*, 157). It is not without interest to note that this revelation of nonexistence took place at La Rochelle, where the family had settled after the remarriage of Sartre's mother — under the influence, therefore, of a false father who had at all costs to be denied.

Now at the moment of the Liberation, France also wished to disavow a father — or at least a leader who looked like one — who had betrayed it, and it is easy to see how someone who had never felt the least trace of respect for paternal authority might have appeared as a public example of the free man, of the already-liberated man. It was in effect a time of liberation not only from the Germans but also from all traditions of political and social organization. Everything had to be reinvented: hence the necessity of "project" and "commitment," and hence also an exceptional chance actually to realize new projects, which diminished progressively as order and the lines of social determination reestablished themselves. This situation is reminiscent in another way of that of the child, or rather of the adolescent, whose future is open, for whom adventure is still possible. And in this way also Sartre was the man of the hour — and remained it, perhaps, to a greater degree than in the former case, since he seems to have managed to preserve his youth throughout his life. It is remarkable that someone of Sartre's generation should have been so strong a focus of identity for the revolutionaries of 1968, for example; clearly, chronological age had nothing to do with it. That was another point, perhaps, at which his "curve" rejoined that of the epoch, and indeed where politically committed writing is concerned he may come to be seen as having followed it more closely in the interim than many people supposed. In an essay published in 1968, Henri Peyre says of Sartre that "his position in the middle of our century is only comparable to that of

---

[11] Jean-Paul Sartre, *The Words*, tr. Bernard Frechtman (Greenwich, Conn: Fawcett Premier Books, n.d.; New York: George Braziller, 1964), p. 62 (hereafter abbreviated *TW* followed by page number[s]).

Diderot two hundred years ago; his literary kingship today is not unlike that of Voltaire in his day."[12]

Nevertheless, the century seems to have got away from Sartre, if I may so put it; it has not learned his lesson, and towards the end of his life, in his acknowledged relation to the young Maos—whom he supported even though he disagreed with them, for the simple reason that they were violently opposed to the established regime— there is evidence that a kind of despair had set in. The fatality of cold-war interpretations of history (as opposed to the causality of genuine historical projects—this is a contrast of attitude to which Sartre drew attention in the early days after World War II) turns the political world into a sort of Juggernaut against the relentless workings of which the opposition of even the most committed revolutionaries is ineffectual. The enterprise of opposition is worth it, but the rewards are minimal: "For the Maos,... whenever revolutionary violence is engendered among the masses, it is immediately and profoundly moral because the workers, heretofore objects of capitalist authoritarianism, become, even if only for a moment, the subjects of their own history."[13] This "even if only for a moment" has in context a certain pathos: we ride the "curve" of the epoch, but only for a short distance, after which it veers off again into alienation. Yet even here it may be that we are misled into thinking that the epoch is to be defined *politically*. Sartre's very sympathy with other people who have to struggle to be even momentarily the subjects of their own history may be the clue to a relationship with the epoch that will outlast any merely political iden-tification. What is remarkable about this sympathy is its depth and genuineness. It is not so much that Sartre put himself into the situa-tion of the oppressed workers as that he recognized himself in his situa-tion as strictly equivalent to them in theirs; he lived a kind of radical egalitarianism on the subjective level that represents a major advance over the theoretical egalitarianism on the objective level that we have inherited, in principle, from the Enlightenment. He really came to see himself as "n'importe qui," and his assessment of himself at the end of *The Words*—"a whole man, composed of all men and as good as all of them and no better than any" (*TW*, 160)—seems to have been absolutely sincere. Let me in conclusion reexamine Sartre's place in our epoch in this light.

[12]　Henri Peyre, *Jean-Paul Sartre* (New York: Columbia University Press, 1968), p. 3.

[13]　Jean-Paul Sartre, "Les Maos en France," in *Situations X* (Gallimard, 1976), p. 45.

It is worth recalling that according to his own account Sartre was brought up as a nineteenth-century man (*TW*, 40). While he was involved through his insistent criticism in the main episodes of postwar history (Algeria, Vietnam, and so on) there is nevertheless a sense in which his point of view, in spite of himself perhaps, was ahistorical. The idea of the primacy of history, in fact, seems to have been borrowed by him, almost piously, from Marx. In the *Critique*, as we have seen, he hardly gets to history properly speaking, but he starts from an analysis of phenomena (the practico-intert, worked matter, scarcity, seriality, etc.) that are more fundamental than history, whose nature and consequences he was able to explain independently of the vicissitudes of what we normally mean by history. Whether he had the forties or the whole century "in him," to use his own expression, is not of great moment, since their history will certainly be recounted by others. But that he should have seen, and above all *lived*, the status of the subject as "just anyone," the centrality of *each* human being as the "universal singular," that is something we should cling to in his work at all costs. Perhaps all the rest, from the *Imagination* to the *Idiot*, was required to validate this single truth. It gives us the possibility, and the hope, of finally vanquishing history with its singularities and its inequalities, of realizing an "end of history" not from without, as the last stage of a dialectical struggle, but from within, as a free project of equals, conscious at once of their uniqueness and their community. If from the writings of Sartre we could extract nothing more than just this realization, the twentieth century would truly become his epoch.

Contributors

GEORGES MAY, who succeeded Henri Peyre as Sterling professor of French at Yale University, is the author of several books dealing primarily with French literature of the seventeenth and eighteenth centuries. He is currently working on a study of Antoine Galland's *Mille et une nuits*.

ROBERT GREER COHN is professor of French at Stanford University and the author of *L'Oeuvre de Mallarmé: "Un Coup de dés," Toward the Poems of Mallarmé, Mallarmé: "Igitur," Mallarmé's Masterwork: New Findings, The Poetry of Rimbaud, The Writer's Way in France, Modes of Art*, vol. I of *A Critical Work*. He is now finishing the second volume, *Ways of Art (in France)*.

HANNA CHARNEY is professor of French and comparative literature at Hunter College and the CUNY Graduate Center. Author of *Le Scepticisme de Valéry* and of *The Detective Novel of Manners: Hedonism, Morality, and the Life of Reason*, she has also written on Musil and Valéry, Mann and Valéry, Balzac and James, Flaubert and Sartre, on Butor, on the relations between film and the novel, and on problems of narrative structure.

†JEAN HYTIER was professor of French at Columbia University. Director of Letters in the first de Gaulle government and former French delegate to UNESCO, he was awarded the Académie Française prize for his *La Poétique de Paul Valéry*. Other notable achievements include editions of Pascal and Valéry, books on Iran and Gobineau, on Gide, on the techniques of modern French verse, and on the aesthetics and theory of literature.

MICHELINE TISON-BRAUN is professor emeritus of French literature at CUNY. Born in France, she has studied the intellectual background of contemporary literature, and is the author of *La Crise de l'humanisme, Poétique du paysage, L'Introuvable Origine*, and of several monographs on French writers, including Tzara, Sarraute, and Malraux.

JEANINE PLOTTEL is professor of French at Hunter College and the CUNY Graduate Center where she is director of the Twentieth-Century Conference. Editor of the *New York Literary Forum*, she has written extensively on

270

nineteenth- and twentieth-century French literature, including a book on Paul Valéry and numerous articles on surrealism, Raymond Roussel, psychoanalysis, semiotics, and poetics, as well as autobiography.

VICTOR BROMBERT is Henry Putnam University professor of Romance and comparative literatures at Princeton University. His book, *The Romantic Prison*, won the Harry Levin Prize in comparative literature (1979). He has recently completed a study of the novels of Victor Hugo.

BETTINA L. KNAPP is professor of French and comparative literature at Hunter College and the CUNY Graduate Center, and a lecturere at the C.G. Jung Foundation in New York. She is the author of *Theatre and Alchemy*, *Archetype, Dance, and the Writer*, and monographs on Jouvet, Artaud, Nerval, Maeterlinck, Céline, Claudel, and Anais Nin.

JOHN W. KNELLER, University professor of humanities and arts at Hunter College and the CUNY Graduate Center, is president-emeritus of Brooklyn College. Author or coauthor of books and articles on nineteenth-century French literature, he has served as editor-in-chief of the *French Review* and as associate editor of *Yale French Studies*.

ÉLÉONORE M. ZIMMERMANN is professor of French and comparative literature at SUNY Stony Brook. Author of *Magies de Verlaine* and *La Liberté et le destin dans le théâtre de Racine*, she has written numerous articles on seventeenth-century theater and nineteenth-century poetry, and is presently working on a study of Baudelaire.

ANNA BALAKIAN is professor of French literature and chairman of the department of comparative literature at New York University. Her writings include *Literary Origins of Surrealism*, *Surrealism: The Road to the Absolute*, *The Symbolist Movement: A Critical Appraisal*, and *André Breton, Magus of Surrealism*, and papers on Mallarmé, Breton, Eluard, Char, and on comparative literature, as well as the recent collaborative edition of *The Symbolist Movement in the Literature of European Languages*.

JAMES LAWLER, professor of French at the University of Chicago, specializes in modern French poetry. Currently working on a study dealing with aspects of the prose poem and on the poetry of Paul Claudel, he is the author of works on Paul Valéry (including *The Poet as Analyst*), of *The Language of French Symbolism*, and of *René Char: The Myth and the Poem*.

MARY ANN CAWS is Distinguished professor of French and comparative literature at Hunter College and the CUNY Graduate Center, where she directs the French Ph.D. program, and was President of the Modern Language Association for 1983. She has translated and edited Breton, Char, Reverdy, Tzara, Mallarmé and St. John Perse, and is most recently the author of *The Eye in the Text: Essays on Perception, Mannerist to Modern*, *The Metapoetics of the Passage: Architextures in Surrealism and After*, and *Reading Frames in Modern Fiction*.

J.H. MATTHEWS, professor of French at Syracuse University, and editor of *Symposium*, has published twenty-one books, many of them on surrealism. His most recent publications are *Surrealism, Insanity, and Poetry* and *Eight Painters: The Surrealist Context.*

DIANA FESTA-McCORMICK is professor of French at Brooklyn College and the CUNY Graduate Center. She has published numerous articles on nineteenth- and twentieth-century writers, two books on Balzac (Prix Guizot 1973), and *The City as Catalyst.* A volume on Proust is forthcoming.

ROBERT W. GREENE, professor of French at SUNY Albany, is the author of *The Poetic Theory of Pierre Reverdy, Six French Poets of Our Time: A Critical and Historical Study*, and of numerous articles on twentieth-century French poetry and fiction.

MICHEL BEAUJOUR is professor of French, associate chairman of the department of French and Italian, and associate director of the Institute of French Studies at New York University. He has written extensively on French culture, on Renaissance literature, and on surrealism. His latest book is *Miroirs d'encre: Rhétorique de l'autoportrait.*

NEAL OXENHANDLER, professor of French and comparative literature at Dartmouth College, is currently working on a project dealing with the issue of affectivity in literature. Author of *Scandal and Parade*, he has taught and published in the field of modern literature and theory, including works on film.

EDOUARD MOROT-SIR is W.R. Kenan, Jr. professor emeritus at the University of North Carolina at Chapel Hill, and has served as French Cultural Attaché to the United States. His publications are in the areas of epistemology, the theory of literature, the history of ideas, and the history of literature. Among his publications are *La Pensée négative, La Pensée française d'aujourd'hui*, and *La Métaphysique de Pascal.* He is coeditor of *Littérature Française* and coauthor of *Du Surréalisme à l'empire de la critique.*

EDITH KERN is Doris Silbert emeritus professor in the humanities at Smith College, and a member of the Council of Scholars of the Library of Congress. She is the editor of *Jean-Paul Sartre* (Twentieth-Century Views), author of *Existential Thought and Fictional Technique: Kierkegaard, Sartre, Beckett*, and most recently of *The Absolute Comic.*

PETER CAWS is University professor of philosophy at George Washington University. Author of *The Philosophy of Science: A Systematic Account, Science and the Theory of Value, Sartre (The Arguments of the Philosophers)*, he is the editor of several works, including collections on American and French philosophy.

Books by Henri Peyre

Louis Menard, 1822-1901. Yale University Press, 1932.

Bibliographie critique de l'hellénisme en France, 1843-1870. Yale University Press, 1932.

Three Classic French Plays. (Editor with Joseph Seronde). Heath, 1935.

Shelley et la France. Paul Barbey, 1935.

Nine Classic French Plays by Corneille, Molière, Racine. (Editor with Joseph Seronde). Heath, 1936.

Seventeenth-Century French Prose and Poetry. (Editor with E.M. Grant). Heath, 1937.

Hommes et oeuvres du 20e siècle. R. Correa, 1938.

L'Influence des littératures antiques sur la littérature française moderne. Yale University Press, 1941.

Le Classicisme français. Editions de la Maison Française, 1942.

Essays in Honor of Albert Feuillerat. (Editor). Yale University Press, 1943.

Problèmes français de demain: Réflexions à propos d'un livre récent. Moretus, 1943.

Writers and Their Critics: A Study of Misunderstanding. Cornell University Press, 1944. Revised edition published as *The Failures of Criticism*, 1967.

Les Générations littéraires. Boivin, 1948.

Pensées de Baudelaire: Recueillies et classées. (Editor). J. Corti, 1951.

Connaissance de Baudelaire. J. Corti, 1951.

The Cultural Migration. (With other authors). University of Pennsylvania Press, 1953.

The Contemporary French Novel. Oxford University Press, 1955. Revised edition published as *French Novelists of Today*, 1967.

Observations on Life, Literature and Learning in America. (Essays). Southern Illinois Press, 1961.

Baudelaire: A Collection of Critical Essays. (Editor). Prentice-Hall, 1962.

Literature and Sincerity. Yale University Press, 1963.

Contemporary French Literature. (Editor). Harper, 1964.

Splendors of Christendom. Time-Life Books, 1964.

Qu'est-ce que le classicisme? Nizet, 1965.

The Literature of France. Prentice-Hall, 1965.

Essais de méthode, de critique et d'histoire. (Gustave Lanson, editor). Hachette, 1965.

The Literature of France. Vol. I. Prentice-Hall, 1966.

Historical and Critical Essays. University of Nebraska Press, 1968.

Jean-Paul Sartre. Columbia University Press, 1968.

Fiction in Several Languages. (Editor). Houghton, 1968.

Qu'est-ce que le romantisme? Presses Universitaires de France, 1972.

Qu'est-ce que le symbolisme? Presses Universitaires de France, 1976.

STANFORD FRENCH AND ITALIAN STUDIES

Editor: Alphonse Juilland